THE LEXINGTON SCHOOL FOR THE DEAF
EDUCATION SERIES
BOOK VII

Vocabulary Norms for Deaf Children

by

Toby Silverman-Dresner, Ph.D.

and

George R. Guilfoyle, Ph.D.

LEXINGTON SCHOOL FOR THE DEAF

This research was supported by the Office of Education, Department of Health, Education and Welfare, Grant Number: OEG 0-8-000419-1792, Project Number: 7-0419.

The Alexander Graham Bell Association for the Deaf
Washington, D.C.

The Authors

Toby Silverman-Dresner, Ph.D., and George Guilfoyle, Ph.D.

Dr. Silverman-Dresner is a Research Associate in the Research Department of the Lexington School for the Deaf. She obtained a B.A. in Psychology from Brooklyn College, City University of New York, an M.A. in Special Education from Teachers College, Columbia University, and a Ph.D. in Educational Psychology from New York University. Dr. Silverman-Dresner is a certified teacher of the deaf. Her current research activities are in the area of infant cognitive development.

Dr. Guilfoyle holds the title of Research Associate in the Research Department of the Lexington School for the Deaf. He obtained a B.A. in Psychology from The City College, City University of New York, and a Ph.D. in Educational Psychology from New York University. Dr. Guilfoyle is the author, along with Dr. Alan Lerman, of the recently published study: "Pre-Vocational Behavior in Deaf Adolescents." He is currently engaged in curriculum development for the deaf child.

Acknowledgments

The authors wish to express their sincere appreciation for the more than generous cooperation and assistance given our research staff members by the faculties and students of the many schools which participated in this project. Space does not allow us to mention individuals. We would be remiss, however, in not identifying the participating schools. In alphabetical order, they are:

Alabama School for the Deaf, Talladega
Alexander Graham Bell School for the Deaf, Cleveland, Ohio
American School for the Deaf, West Hartford, Connecticut
Archbishop Ryan Memorial Institute for the Deaf, Philadelphia, Pennsylvania
Arizona State School for the Deaf and Blind, Tucson
Arkansas School for the Deaf. Little Rock
Austine School for the Deaf, Brattleboro, Vermont
Beverly School for the Deaf, Beverly, Massachusetts
Boston School for the Deaf, Randolph, Massachusetts
Bruce Street School, Newark, New Jersey
California School for the Deaf, Berkeley
California School for the Deaf, Riverside
Central Institute for the Deaf, St. Louis, Missouri
Chinchuba Institute for the Deaf, Marrero, Louisiana
Clarke School for the Deaf, Northampton, Massachusetts
Colorado School for the Deaf and Blind, Colorado Springs
Crotched Mountain School for the Deaf, Greenfield, New Hampshire
De Paul Institute, Pittsburgh, Pennsylvania
Eastern North Carolina School for the Deaf, Wilson
Edna E. Davis School for the Deaf, Spokane, Washington
Elim Christian School, Palos Heights, Illinois
Florida State School for the Deaf and Blind, St. Augustine
Gallaudet School for the Deaf, St. Louis, Missouri
Georgia School for the Deaf, Cave Springs
Governor Baxter State School for the Deaf, Falmouth, Maine
Hawaii School for the Deaf and the Blind, Honolulu
Horace Mann School for the Deaf, Roxbury, Massachusetts
Hosford Day School, Portland, Oregon
Idaho State School for the Deaf and Blind, Gooding
Illinois School for the Deaf, Jacksonville
Indiana School for the Deaf, Indianapolis
Institute of Logopedics, Wichita, Kansas
Iowa School for the Deaf, Council Bluffs
Kansas School for the Deaf, Olathe
Kendall School for the Deaf, Washington, D. C.
Kentucky School for the Deaf, Danville
Lexington Deaf Oral School, Lexington, Kentucky
Lexington School for the Deaf, New York, New York
Louisiana State School for the Deaf, Baton Rouge
Margaret S. Sterck School for the Hearing Impaired, Newark, Delaware
Marie H. Katzenbach School for the Deaf, West Trenton, New Jersey
Marlton Elementary School, Los Angeles, California
Maryland School for the Deaf, Frederick
Michigan School for the Deaf, Flint
Mill Neck Manor, Lutheran School for the Deaf, Mill Neck, New York

Minnesota School for the Deaf, Faribault
Mississippi School for the Deaf, Jackson (N. Green Capers Avenue)
Mississippi School for the Deaf, Jackson
Missouri School for the Deaf, Fulton
Montana School for the Deaf and Blind, Great Falls
Mystic Oral School for the Deaf, Mystic, Connecticut
Nebraska School for the Deaf, Omaha
New Mexico School for the Deaf, Santa Fe
New York State School for the Deaf, Rome
North Carolina School for the Deaf, Morganton
North Dakota School for the Deaf, Devils Lake
Ohio School for the Deaf, Columbus
Oklahoma School for the Deaf, Sulphur
Oregon State School for the Deaf, Salem
Pennsylvania School for the Deaf, Philadelphia
Pilot School for the Deaf, Dallas, Texas
Rhode Island School for the Deaf, Providence
Rochester School for the Deaf, Rochester, New York
St. Francis de Sales School for the Deaf, Brooklyn, New York
St. John's School for the Deaf, Milwaukee, Wisconsin
St. Joseph's Classes for Children with Hearing Impairment, Lake Ronkonkoma, New York
St. Joseph Institute for the Deaf, University City, Missouri
St. Joseph's School for the Deaf, New York, New York
St. Mary's School for the Deaf, Buffalo, New York
St. Rita School for the Deaf, Evandale-Cincinnati, Ohio
School for the Deaf, Junior High School 47-M, New York, New York
School of Listening Eyes, Wichita Falls, Texas
South Carolina School for the Deaf and the Blind, Spartanburg
South Dakota School for the Deaf, Sioux Falls
State School for the Deaf, Baton Rouge, Louisiana
Suffolk School for Deaf Children (Holy Cross Lutheran Church), Commack, New York
Tennessee School for the Deaf, Knoxville
Texas School for the Deaf, Austin
Tucker-Maxon Oral School, Portland, Oregon
Utah Schools for the Deaf and the Blind, Ogden
Virginia School at Hampton, Hampton
Virginia School for the Deaf and the Blind, Staunton
Washington State School for the Deaf, Vancouver
Western Pennsylvania School for the Deaf, Pittsburgh
West Virginia School for the Deaf and Blind, Romney
Wisconsin School for the Deaf, Delavan
W. Roby Allen School, Faribault, Minnesota
Wyoming School for the Deaf, Casper
Yeshiva Institute for the Hard of Hearing and Deaf, Brooklyn, New York

THE LEXINGTON SCHOOL FOR THE DEAF
EDUCATION SERIES

Developed at The Lexington School
26-27 75th Street
Jackson Heights, Queens
New York, N. Y. 11370

Foreword

Vocabulary Norms for Deaf Children by Drs. Silverman-Dresner and Guilfoyle is the most important reference book to be published for teachers of the deaf during the past 25 years. The authors have come to grips with one of the most important aspects of the reading problem by creating what should become the main source book for teachers, researchers, and test construction specialists in controlling the vocabulary level of reading materials to be used by deaf students. Educators of the deaf will now know at what age the majority of deaf students really comprehend specific words by definition, by part of speech, and by topical classification. Thus, classroom quizzes, standardized test questions, and reading achievement studies can be controlled accurately enough so that answers given by deaf students cannot be ascribed to an imprecise knowledge of the vocabulary chosen by the tester. This is not to say that the teaching of language to the deaf child will become any easier for teachers, but that the provision of this basic list should assist all of us involved in the field with a baseline from which to start most of our efforts.

I direct the attention of the researcher to the national character of this study. The authors could have undertaken a far easier, and presumably as valid, study by the use of a small random sample of schools for the deaf. However, they wisely assumed the burden of including every school in the United States willing to participate. It is a tribute to the schools listed in the acknowledgment section of this book that they aided in such a momentous effort.

As Executive Director of the Lexington School, I take pride in presenting this major reference work to our professional field. I look forward to its immediate use and to its eventual revision and improvement, and am personally gratified to know that such fundamental undertakings can be accomplished in an atmosphere of helpfulness, cooperation, and mutual concern for deaf children by educators of the deaf from a variety of school programs which represent every known methodology in the United States.

Leo E. Connor, Ed. D.
Executive Director
Lexington School for the Deaf

Preface

The data used in *Vocabulary Norms for Deaf Children* are derived from an earlier study: *The Deaf Child's Knowledge of Words* (Final Report, Project No. 7-0419, Grant No. OEG 0-8-000419-1792, Office of Education, Bureau of Research). It differs from this report, however, in several significant respects: (1) It includes only words "known" by deaf children; (2) The definition of knowing a word has been changed; i.e., a word is here considered to be known if at least 62.5% (or 50% when corrected for guessing) of the original sample correctly responded to it, in contrast to a value of 67% used in the earlier report; (3) Unlike the earlier report, all percentages reported have been corrected for guessing; (4) Several additional analyses of the results appear in the current report; (5) The bulk of the current report is given over to four different ways of presenting the words known by deaf students.

T.S.D. & G.R.G.

Contents

Objects

Animals

Concepts

Events

Groups

Physical States

Time

Figures and Tables

I
The Creation of a 7300-Word Pool

NEED FOR ASSESSING THE WORD KNOWLEDGE
OF THE DEAF CHILD

The major source of visual information for the deaf child is in the form of printed materials, such as textbooks, children's magazines, and children's newspapers. Consequently, skill in reading is far more crucial for him than for his hearing peer who has access to auditory as well as visual sources of information. Yet the deaf child is far below the hearing child in reading comprehension (Furth, 1966). Two factors — the unusual educational importance of printed material for the deaf child, and his poor comprehension of it — make it imperative that the process of reading among deaf children be better understood.

One of the variables involved in reading comprehension is vocabulary level (Seashore & Eckerson, 1940). There is, however, little systematic information on the reading vocabulary of the deaf child. This in itself is a sufficiently compelling reason for making a survey of this kind. But there is a more important reason: virtually all of the reading material used in schools and classes for the deaf has been written for the normally hearing child. Such materials are based upon presumed age-graded vocabulary lists obtained from hearing children. The educator of the deaf who uses this standard reading material finds it necessary to continually simplify the vocabulary of these texts. If, for example, she wishes to teach a fourth grade history unit on the founding of the country, she must first rewrite a large portion of the text, as well as teach a number of new words (e.g., "taxation without representation"). The task of continually editing such material places an unnecessary burden upon these teachers. A more efficient solution would be to construct reading materials based upon the actual reading vocabulary knowledge of the deaf child.

In order to obtain an estimate of this knowledge, a large sample, or pool, of words is necessary. One could, of course, generate a word sample, for example, by taking words from a standard dictionary, in some random fashion, or by listing all of the words used in a selected number of graded readers. Procedures such as these are both costly and time consuming. A more reasonable approach is to use words drawn from one or more of the principal sources of vocabulary lists for hearing children. There are three such sources: (1) *Dale 3000 Word List* (Dale & Chall, 1948), (2) *Children's Knowledge of Words* (Dale & Eichholz, 1960), and (3) *The Teacher's Word Book of 30,000 Words* (Thorndike & Lorge, 1949). Of these, only the first two are appropriate. *The Teacher's Word Book*, which lists words according to their frequency of occurrence in various types of reading material, was not used for two reasons. First, the only useful list (the "J count") was not restricted enough for our purposes. It had been compiled by counting words from a sample of books recommended for children from grades three to eight. Secondly, the count itself is somewhat out of date, inasmuch as the original lists were compiled in 1931.

The Dale-Chall list, on the other hand, was created by presenting lists of words to a sample of fourth grade children who were asked to check off the words that they "knew." Vocabulary tests were then constructed from a pool of these words and subsequently given to children at various grade levels. The level of each word was then defined to be the grade at which 67% of its members chose the correct definition. A more comprehensive list of over 17,000 words was later compiled (Dale & Eichholz, 1960). These lists constituted the initial word pool used in the present study.

INITIAL WORD POOL

The Dale-Chall list, involving grades one, two, and three, in conjunction with the Fourth and Sixth Grade Lists from the *Children's Knowledge of Words* (Dale & Eichholz, 1960) provided an initial pool of 14,852 words. Of these, certain words were automatically screened out. They included virtually all of the following word classes:

(1) hyphenated words (e.g., passer-by, pell-mell)

(2) interjections (e.g., ah, oh)

(3) contractions (e.g., let's, can't)

(4) sound words (e.g., moo, baa)

(5) certain word variants (e.g., "do" was kept, while "did" was not)

(6) brand names (e.g., Kodak, Kleenex)

In addition, several words appeared on more than one list. To which list a particular word was assigned depended upon which grade produced at least 61% correct identifications, this being one standard deviation below the cutoff value of 67%.

CONSTRUCTION OF DEFINITIONS

Definitions were written for the remaining words. Four dictionaries were used. The primary source was the *Thorndike-Barnhart Beginning Dictionary* (Thorndike & Barnhart, 1962), since it was the lowest grade level dictionary available at the time. The remaining sources in order of importance were the *Rodale Synonym Finder* (Rodale, 1961), the *Webster's Seventh New Collegiate Dictionary* (1964), and *Roget's International Thesaurus* (3rd edition, 1962). Thus, for each word a number of possible definitions were available. Several criteria were used in deciding upon the best one. The best definition was one:

(1) that best preserved the definition used by Dale and his associates.

(2) that contained words either at the same or at a lower grade level than that of the stimulus word. For example, "obtain" is listed as a sixth-grade word; its best definition is "get" which is on the Dale-Chall F list, that is, the list appropriate for the first, second, and third grade children.

(3) that was as short as possible. For example, "owner" is used as the best definition of "landlord" in lieu of the longer one: "person who owns buildings or land that he rents to another." Where a long definition was unavoidable, extraneous words were eliminated. Thus, the definition of "knapsack" as "a leather or canvas bag for clothes, equipment, etc... carried on the back" was shortened to "bag carried on the back."

(4) that was general rather than specific. For example, rather than defining "rat" as "small animal," the more general definition of "animal" was used.

Words which did not meet the above criteria were eliminated. In the case of the Dale-Chall F words, for which no definitions were provided, the most frequently occurring synonym appearing in *The Synonym Finder* was chosen. In some cases, however, the most frequent synonym was not one that could be expected to be known by a deaf child. In those cases an alternate synonym was selected. For example, the most frequent synonyms for "last" which appear on the Dale-Chall list, are "model, shape, pattern, form, etc. ." However, three educational psychologists agreed that this meaning would probably be less familiar to a child in one of the first three grades than would the alternate meaning, "in the rear, in back of," which was used instead.

CONSTRUCTION OF DECOYS

The remaining words with their definitions were alphabetized and arranged into nine books of letters (e.g., Book One contained all words beginning with the letters "a" and "b"). Since the test format was of the multiple choice type, it was necessary that each word be provided with three decoys (incorrect definitions) in addition to its definition. Beginning with the letter "a" in Book One, each word received decoys from the definitions of words in two of the remaining eight books. The definitions were randomly selected alternately from each of the two books. For example, all decoys for words in Book One were obtained from definitions of words in Books Three and Seven; all decoys for Book Two came from definitions appearing in Books One and Four, and so on. The decoys so selected were retained only if they met the following criteria:

(1) All decoys had to be on the same or at a lower grade level than that of the stimulus word.

(2) All decoys had to contain approximately the same number of words (plus or minus one word) as the correct definition.

(3) In those cases where part of the stimulus word appeared in the correct definition (e.g., *bar*tender), at least one of the three decoys had to contain the same part. In some cases this meant inventing a decoy by adding a suffix such as "ing" or "ed" to the root word. (This procedure has been used by Dale and his associates.)

(4) Where the stimulus word contained suffixes such as "ly" or "ed," or prefixes such as "mis" or "pre," at least one decoy

preserved this form.

(5) Where the correct definition began with the same letter as the stimulus word, at least one decoy began with this letter.

CONSTRUCTION OF TEST FORMS

The final pool of 7300 words (actually 7290 words, 10 words being repeated to bring the total to 7300), together with their definitions and decoys (the position of the correct definition was varied randomly), was fed into a computer programmed to generate 73 sets of 100 randomly selected items each. These sets of items were then converted into 73 typewritten "tests." Each test consisted of a cover page and 10 test pages. The cover page consisted of a set of simplified instructions, a code designating the particular set of 100 items (i.e., A,B,...Z,AA,BB,...UUU), and a place for indicating the child's age and sex.

ADMINISTRATION OF TEST FORMS

Letters requesting cooperation in the study were mailed to all schools for the deaf in the United States listed in the Directory of the *American Annals of the Deaf* for the years 1966 and 1967. Of these, 89 schools actually participated in the survey.

Packages of test forms, together with teacher instruction sheets, were mailed to each school prior to the day of testing. On the appointed day a tester from the Lexington School appeared, met with the teachers and staff, distributed the test forms, and explained the procedures for instructing and proctoring the students. The tester also spent time answering questions from the teachers, and during the course of the day, moved throughout the school giving assistance to the teachers when it was needed.

The actual testing was done by the classroom teacher, who instructed her pupils and proctored their responses. All children responded to two forms (i.e., 200 words) and were given a break between forms. Care was taken to ensure against the possibility of a child receiving two copies of the same form. In addition, tests were packed and distributed in such a way that few if any of the same forms were administered to a particular age group in a particular school, depending upon the size of the school population.

At the conclusion of the testing day, all tests were returned, repacked, and mailed back to the Research Department of the Lexington School for the Deaf, where they were transmitted to a computer center for scoring and analysis.

II
The Results of the Testing Program

PRELIMINARY PROCESSING OF RESULTS

All tests were searched for identification data (age and sex). Those tests on which an age was not indicated were automatically discarded. Approximately 2500 tests were lost because of this. Tests which failed to include sex identification were included for use in the word analysis, however, as no distinction was made between boys and girls. The remaining 26,414 tests were scored by machine, and the percentage of correct responses (uncorrected for guessing) to each word was obtained and arranged alphabetically by two-year age groups. The results reported are from the responses given by children 8 through 17 years of age.

CHARACTERISTICS OF THE TEST FORMS

As noted earlier, the final pool of 7300 words of varying levels of difficulty was divided into 73 sets of 100 words each. These sets were created by a computer programmed to assign words randomly to each set. This produced 73 sets of words whose overall level of difficulty was assumed to be approximately equal, differences in level of difficulty presumably being a matter of chance.

The most direct way of testing this assumption is to look at the average number of correct responses to each of the 73 forms. Are these averages roughly similar, or do they vary a great deal? Referring to Figure 1, it can be seen that these averages do not appear to vary much. The mean of the distribution is 38.9 correct responses (uncorrected for guessing). Since plus or minus two standard deviations (SDs) from the mean account for approximately 98% of the cases involved, with an SD of 1.6, the range of average scores encompassed is from 35.7 to 42.1 correct responses, a span of only 6.4 points. This homogeneity extends to the variability of individual test forms. Looking at Figure 2, it can be seen that the SDs

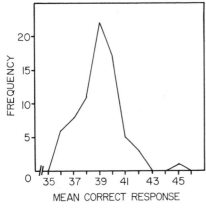

Fig. 1. Distribution of mean correct responses to 73 vocabulary test forms by samples of deaf boys and girls (8 - 17 years).

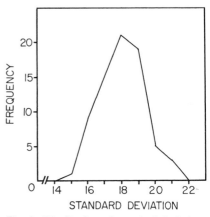

Fig. 2. Distribution of standard deviations associated with mean correct responses to all forms by 73 samples of deaf boys and girls (8 - 17 years).

associated with each individual mean number of correct responses are very similar; i.e., with a mean of 18.0 and an SD of 1.25, 98% of the cases range from 15.5 to 20.5, a span of only five SD units.

Granted that the 73 test forms are roughly equal both in average level of difficulty and in individual variability, it was also assumed that all forms would be used approximately the same number of times. Nevertheless, Figure 3, which shows the distribution of sample sizes associated with the 73 test forms, is slightly negatively skewed, there being a larger number of samples above the mean of 362 than below it (SD = 30.5). One explanation of this is that errors made in packing the tests origi-

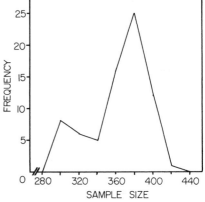

Fig. 3. Distribution of samples of varying size of deaf boys and girls taking all 73 vocabulary test forms.

nally resulted in certain test forms being used less frequently than others. It is also possible that a certain proportion of the 2500 tests discarded because they lacked complete identification data came from one or two particular forms. Unfortunately, the form codes of those discarded tests were never recorded, so that a precise determination cannot be made. It is unlikely, however, that this variability in sample sizes had any appreciable effect upon the average level of difficulty of the forms themselves.

SEX DIFFERENCES

When girls of all ages are compared to boys, on all 73 forms, the results indicate that: (1) the samples of boys taking all forms (see Figure 4) were on the average larger than those of the girls (the mean sample size for boys was 193, that of the girls was 163), and (2) the mean of the average number of correct responses (shown in Figure 5) to all forms was higher for girls than for boys; i.e., the girls, on the average, scored higher than the boys on all forms. For the girls, the mean number of correct responses was 41.1. For the boys, it was 37.5.

Since we are dealing essentially with the population of residential deaf students in the United States between the ages of 8 and 17 years, tests of significance between the means just mentioned are superfluous. Nevertheless, for those who may insist that what we are dealing with are simply very large samples, the "t" value associated with the differences between the means shown in Figure 5 was found to be 11.19. With 144 degrees of freedom, the probability that such a difference is the result of chance alone is much less than one time in a hundred.[1]

AGE DIFFERENCES

When the data are rearranged into five age groups (boys and girls combined) one finds an almost perfect linear relationship (shown in Figure 6) between mean correct response to all forms and age in years (for the years encompassed in this study). Beginning with the first age group (8-9 years), the mean correct response for each age group is: 27.1, 31.5, 39.0, 47.1, and 54.1. And like the sex differences observed, these age differences are, in all likelihood, true population parameters.

---

[1]With df = 150, $P(t \geq 2.609) \leq .01$

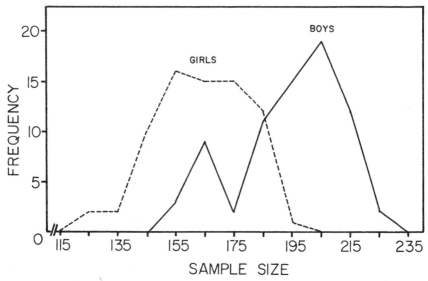

Fig. 4. Distribution of samples of deaf boys and girls (8 - 17 years) taking all 73 vocabulary test forms.

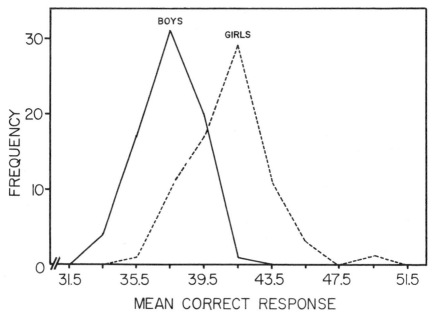

Fig. 5. Mean number of correct responses of deaf boys and girls (8 - 17 years) to 73 vocabulary test forms.

SYNTACTICAL DIFFERENCES

In breaking down the word pool by part of speech, the following word classes were used: nouns (N), verbs (V), adjectives (J), adverbs (D), function words and noun-related words. These last two classes are composites of several more traditional grammatical classifications. Function words, which in general have little lexical meaning, include prepositions (P), conjunctions (C) and interjections (I), while noun-related words include pronouns (R), noun determiners (ND) (i.e., a, an, every, no, the) and function nouns (FN) (i.e., all, another, any, both, each, either, enough, few, hers, his, many, more, most, much, neither, several, some). The percentages of these parts of speech in the pool are

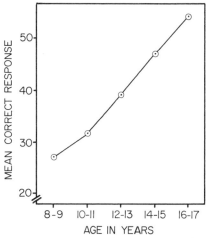

Fig. 6. Changes with age in mean correct responses of deaf boys and girls to 73 vocabulary test forms.

Table 1

Comparison of percentages of parts of speech in a 7300 word pool with those obtained by random sampling

PARTS OF SPEECH	7300 Word Sample	Random Samples[1]	
		27 pages at 100 page intervals	One word every other page
Nouns	58.1%	70.0%	68.0%
Verbs	20.4	11.0	10.0
Adjectives	17.3	16.0	19.0
Adverbs	2.5	2.0	3.0
Function Words	0.9	1.0	0.0
Noun Related Words	0.8	0.0	0.0
TOTALS	100.0	100.0	100.0

[1]Adapted from Table 11 of Seashore and Eckerson, op.cit.

compared in Table 1 to those obtained through random sampling. With the exception of verbs, which seem to be overrepresented in the present pool, the distribution of the six word classes is quite similar to what one would expect from a standard dictionary. Whether this distribution is similar to what we would find for spoken English is, of course, another question.

Table 2

Number of correct identifications[1] of three classes of function words by samples of deaf children in five age groups

AGE (in yrs)	Function Words			Total F-Words
	Preposition	Conjunction	Interjection	
8 - 9	00	00	00	00
10 - 11	00	00	00	00
12 - 13	03	00	00	03
14 - 15	10	04	01	15
16 - 17	21	07	02	30
Total in Sample	47	13	02	62

[1]corrected for guessing.

Tables 2 and 3 show the patterns of correct identification with age, of both function and noun-related words. When a word is said to be correctly identified (i.e., "known") it means, in this study at least, that no less than 62.5% (or 50% when corrected for guessing) of the sample of children responding to the word have circled the correct answer. In general, these tables show an almost geometrical increase with age. By the time deaf children reach 16-17 years of age, approximately 48% of the function words and 71% of the noun-related words appearing in this word pool are correctly identified. A similar pattern of gains can be seen in Figure 7, for the six major word classes, and in Figure 8, for all of the classes combined.

Notice that in both cases the frequency of correct identifications is plotted in log units. In general, the overall pattern of acquisition is one in which the relative gains are greatest during the earlier years.

Table 3

Number of correct identifications[1] of noun related words by
samples of deaf children in five age groups

AGE (in yrs)	Noun Related Words			
	Pronouns	Noun De-terminers	Function Nouns	Total
8 - 9	01	00	00	01
10 - 11	03	01	00	04
12 - 13	10	02	04	16
14 - 15	24	03	09	36
16 - 17	27	04	11	42
Total in Sample	27	05	17	59

[1]corrected for guessing.

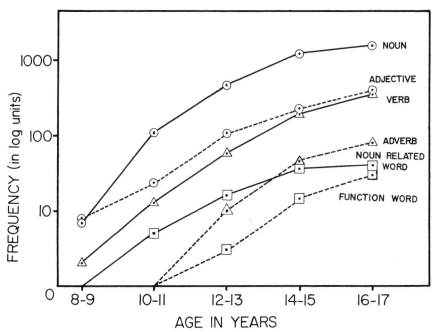

Fig. 7. Changes with age in log number of correct responses of deaf boys and girls to six word classes.

Put another way, the number of total words "known" at each age group beginning with the youngest are: 18, 157, 660, 1560 and 2545. The increase from 18 (at 8-9 years) to 157 (at 10-11 years) is approximately ninefold; the increase from 157 to 660 is roughly fourfold; that from 660 to 1560, slightly more than double, and that from 1560 to 2545 slightly less than double.

COMPARISONS WITH OTHER POPULATIONS

Our results suggest that, in general, deaf girls have larger vocabularies than do boys. This agrees with results reported on language studies involving hearing children (McCarthy, 1946). Similarly, there is an increase in written vocabulary size with age. This increase appears to be somewhat different from that obtained with hearing children. McCarthy (1946) cites a study by Smith (1941) who attempted to establish norms for hearing children using the Seashore-Eckerson vocabulary test. For grade one (6 years old), the

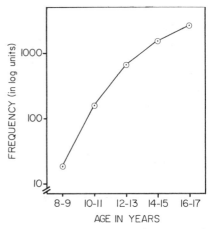

Fig. 8. Number of words (in log units) correctly identified by deaf boys and girls in five age groups.

average vocabulary was estimated to be 23,700 words, and at grade 12 (18 years old), 80,000 words. This is approximately a four-fold increase in vocabulary size, and it is likely that this increase is linear, in contrast to the curvilinear increase among deaf children. However, because in one case we are dealing with *estimated* vocabulary size, it is difficult to draw any conclusions from this comparison.

IMPLICATIONS FOR FUTURE RESEARCH

The fact that the number of words known in common by deaf children increases steadily with age despite the fact that the bulk of these children never achieve a reading competence beyond an elementary level suggests that the breakdown of the reading process is more likely attributable to grammatical problems than to vocabulary deficiencies. Exactly what these grammatical problems are and how best they can be overcome is crucial to the solution of the problem of the deaf reader. What is needed is an investigation similar to the present one but smaller in scope (i.e., employing stratified random sampling) in which the deaf child's knowledge of various syntactic structures is explored, keeping the factor of vocabulary constant. The results of such a study, like those of the present one, can be applied immediately by the instructor of the deaf, not only in dealing with specific grammatical problems, but in preparing special reading materials.

SUMMARY

In an attempt to assess the reading vocabulary knowledge of the deaf child, an initial vocabulary pool of 14,852 words was reduced to 7300 words. These words were fed into a computer which produced 73 sets of 100 randomly selected words each. The sets were then converted into 73 vocabulary "tests" and administered to 13,207 deaf students between the ages of 8 and 17 years, from 89 schools for the deaf in the United States. Analysis of the results indicates that, in general, deaf girls know more words than do deaf boys, and that older children know more words in common than do younger ones. Four lists of words known in common by better than 62.5% of samples of children in five age groups have been compiled for the use of the teacher of the deaf, and for research personnel.

III
The Construction of the Word Lists

The words in the vocabulary lists should be used primarily for rewriting existing reading material and for constructing new materials. The words should not be regarded as goals to be attained, since the lists are simply a description of what words are *known in common* by samples of deaf children of various ages. Neither an individual child's performance nor the performance of an entire class or school should be compared to the percentages reported here, as school, regional, and individual differences are bound to exist. In the final analysis the individual teacher must decide which words to teach, depending upon the children's ages and the subject matter.

WORDS BY AGE AND PERCENT CORRECT

The first list (Chapter IV) presents all words known by each of the five age groups (8-9, 10-11, 12-13, 14-15, 16-17 year olds) together with the percentages (corrected for guessing) of the original samples correctly identifying them. Thus, the first entry for the 8-9 year olds is "bad 56.8." This means that 56.8% of a sample of 8-9 year olds correctly identified the word "bad." From this list, one can get an immediate idea of the words known at any age level. In general, the lists are cumulative. That is to say, the words known by 8-9 year olds are known by the older age groups. There are, however, a few inversions. For example, "activity" is known at the 14-15 year old level, but not at the 16-17 year old level.

The percentages reported for these words are based upon different sized samples. To get an estimate of the average sample size per word, sample sizes for the first 100 words appearing in the original 7300-word list were used to derive mean sample sizes for each two-year age group and for all ages combined. The means and standard deviations for each age level are given below:

Age (in years)	Mean Sample Size	Standard Deviation
8-9	64.6	9.2
10-11	78.1	10.8
12-13	72.7	8.6
14-15	72.4	8.1
16-17	60.9	6.8
All ages	69.7	10.7

It should be noted that the mean sample size for all 73 forms (see Figure 3) is 362. If we assume an approximately equal number of students at each age level, we arrive at an average sample size per age level of 362/5 or 72.4, which is quite close to that obtained for the first 100 words, 69.7.

WORDS BY PART OF SPEECH AND EARLIEST AGE KNOWN

The second list (Chapter V) presents the words according to the following parts of speech: noun (N), noun determiner (ND), pronoun (R), function noun (FN), adjective (J), verb (V), adverb (D), preposition (P), conjunction (C) and interjection (I). Classifying by part of speech was relatively straightforward. Problems arose only when a word could belong to several classes. In those cases, a fixed procedure was used. If the word had a synonym definition it was grouped according to the word class of the synonym. For example, the word "half" can be a noun, an adjective, or an adverb. It is listed as an adverb because its definition, "partly," is an adverb. However, when both the word and its definition could belong to more than one class, or where the part of speech could not be gleaned from a multi-word definition, the word was assigned to a class by random procedures. In addition, the earliest age at which each word is known is presented with the part of speech.

WORDS BY TOPICAL CLASSIFICATION, PART OF SPEECH AND EARLIEST AGE KNOWN

In an attempt to organize the words for easier use in writing and rewriting materials for the classroom, each word was typed on a card, together with its definition, and the cards were sorted into various piles. The resulting major classifications are shown in Figure 9. The

WORD POOL			
ACTIONS	ATTRIBUTES	OBJECTS	UNCLASSIFIED
Affect	Activity	People	Noun Related Words
Bathe	Brightness	Plants	
.	.	Animals	Function Words
.	.	Concepts	
.	.	Institutions	Conjunctions
.	.	Products	Interjections
Touch & Smell	Wetness	Structures	Prepositions

Fig. 9. Distribution of 2545 words by major topical classes.

words are arranged into four broad classes: actions, attributes, objects and unclassified words. Actions are primarily verbs, attributes are primarily adjectives and adverbs, and objects are primarily nouns. All nouns, verbs, and adjectives, and most adverbs were placed into at least one of these classes. The remaining words, including function words and noun-related words, were left unclassified (UNCL).

Each word class has a title and a number ranging from 01 to 92. Words falling into a particular class are listed in alphabetical order with part of speech, earliest age at which known, and any other classes to which the word may belong. For example, "surprise V 16: 22" which appears under **01 ACTIONS, Affect** also appears under **22 ATTRIBUTES, Certainty**. A complete list of the titles is given below:

ACTIONS

01 Affect	06 Give & Take	11 Move	16 Stop & Start
02 Bathe	07 Grow	12 Perceive	17 Think
03 Change	08 Hit	13 Preserve	18 Touch & Smell
04 Communicate	09 Join	14 Remember	19 Use
05 Damage	10 Judge	15 Shine	

ATTRIBUTES

20 Activity	27 Distance	34 Notoriety	41 Strength
21 Brightness	28 Evaluation	35 Numerosity	42 Temperature
22 Certainty	29 Flavor	36 Position	43 Temporality
23 Clarity	30 General	37 Primacy	44 Texture
24 Color	31 Hardness	38 Shape	45 Weight
25 Danger	32 Humanness	39 Similarity	46 Wetness
26 Direction	33 Loudness	40 Size	

OBJECTS

Animals

47 Air	49 General	52 Products
48 Enclosures	50 Insects	53 Water
	51 Land	

Concepts

54 Closure	56 Groups	58 Physical	59 Time
55 Events	a. General	States	a. Days
a. General	b. Social	a. Change	b. General
b. Social	57 Numbers	b. General	c. Hours
c. Travel		c. Light	d. Months
		d. Sound	e. Seasons

Institutions

60 The Arts	62 Education (cont)	67 Science (cont)
a. Entertainment	d. Reading Matter	d. Geography
b. Fantasy	e. Roles (See Roles,	e. History
c. Graphics	Education)	f. Linguistics
61 Business	f. Writing	g. Mathematics
a. Finance	63 Government	h. Meteorology
b. Money	64 Law	i. Mineralogy
c. Sales	65 Medicine	j. Oceanography
d. Work	66 Religion	68 Sports
62 Education	67 Science	a. Actions
a. Courses	a. Agriculture	b. Athletes
b. General	b. Anatomy	c. Games & Toys
c. Locations	c. Forestry	d. Recreation
		69 Warfare

People

70 Behavior
    a. Assistance
    b. Awards
    c. Errors
    d. Intentions

71 Roles
    a. Age
    b. Education
    c. Family
    d. General
    e. Occupation
    f. Sex

72 States
    a. Emotional
    b. General
    c. Identity
    d. Physical

Plants

73 Flowers
74 Fruits & Berries

75 General
76 Nuts & Grains
77 Products

78 Trees
79 Vegetables

Products

80 Clothing
81 Containers
82 Food
    a. Beverages
    b. Cooking
    c. Eating
    d. General
    e. Meals
    f. Meats
    g. Sweets

83 Instruments and
    Measures
84 Machines and Tools
85 Misc. Objects
86 Personal Effects
87 Textiles
88 Transportation
    a. Mode
    b. Operation

Structures

89 Buildings
90 Houses
    a. Applicances
    b. Furniture
    c. Parts
    d. Supplies
    e. Wares
    f. Washing
91 Locations
92 Thoroughfares

WORDS BY DEFINITION AND TOPICAL CLASSIFICATION

The last list presents all of the words in alphabetical order, together with their definitions and decoys, in their original order. This list enables the teacher to discover whether a particular word is known by at least one age group. In addition, each word is followed by a topical classification number, enabling the teacher to discover conceptually similar words. For example, the word "accidental" is followed by "(22)." Referring to the third list (Chapter VI) the teacher will discover that category 22 is labeled **ATTRIBUTES, Certainty,** and contains such related words as "possible," "unlikely," "nearly," etc.

In the event that a teacher wishes to test her pupils on particular words, it must be clearly understood that for every pupil, there is a one-in-four probability that the child will guess the correct answer. This, of course, was not a problem in the study itself, since we were dealing with *groups* of students, and could therefore *correct for guessing*. One cannot do this for a single pupil's response to a single item. Under the circumstances it makes little sense to test for a word using a single test item. However, if one uses two test items to test for knowledge of a particular word, one can almost completely eliminate the guessing factor. What is required is a pair of items testing the same word. One gives a pupil credit for "knowing" the word only if he responds correctly to both items. For example, in the case where the definition is a single word (e.g., war: trace, savings, house, *fight*), one can create an alternate item simply by exchanging the original word with its definition; i.e., fight: trace, *war*, house, savings. Notice that the order of decoys and definitions has also been changed. Now, for each item the probability of guessing both correctly is $1/4 \times 1/4 = 1/16$ or 0.0625. Thus, if a pupil gets both items correct, you are almost certain (you will be wrong only 6.25 times in a hundred) that he "knows" the word in question. If he gets either one wrong, of course, he is not credited with "knowing" the word.

In the case where the definition is more than one word, the simplest solution is to create a simply worded fill-in sentence; e.g., "A thick book is _____: a baby, not thin, engine, rest." The scoring procedure is the same. However, it is advisable to present alternate items on a separate occasion. With these restrictions in mind, if the teacher still wishes to test her pupils on specific words, the following procedure is recommended:

(1) Make up an instruction sheet similar to the one shown in Figure 10. Use a similar format for presenting the vocabulary items, at a rate of six to eight items per page.

(2) Make up a poster, or use the blackboard, to present the first two items on the instruction sheet.

(3) Distribute the test booklets.

(4) Say: WRITE YOUR NAMES (and whatever other information is desired) AND LOOK UP AT ME.

(5) Say: READ THE WORD WITH THE LINE UNDER IT . . . (point) . . . THICK. READ THE ANSWERS . . . NOT THIN, A BABY, REST, ENGINE. Ask: WHAT WORD MEANS THE SAME AS THICK? Get responses from the pupils. Say: DRAW A CIRCLE . . . (illustrate) . . . AROUND THE WORDS "NOT THIN."

Have the pupils circle *Not Thin* even though it is already circled.

(6) Do the second example with the class in the same way.

(7) When completed, say: NOW DO THE OTHER TWO BY YOURSELF.

(8) Check all papers to see that everyone understands what they must do. If there are any errors, repeat the instructions.

(9) When you are certain that all pupils understand the instructions, proceed with the testing. There should be no time limit.

NAME _____
Read the underlined word. Read all the answers 1,2,3,4. Circle the answer that means the same as the underlined word.

thick	war
1. not thin *(circled)*	1. trace
2. a baby	2. savings
3. rest	3. house
4. engine	4. fight *(circled)*
carry	dad
1. rock	1. all
2. fold	2. new
3. egg	3. father
4. take	4. poem

Fig. 10. Suggested format for vocabulary test instructions.

IV
Words by Age and Percent Correct

Words known by each age group are presented sequentially, beginning with the youngest age group: 8-9, 10-11, 12-13, 14-15, 16-17 years. Following each word is the percentage (corrected for guessing) of the original sample of students who correctly identified the word. There are several cases where a word has two definitions. Both variations are accompanied, in most cases, by a synonym. These synonyms are not necessarily the original definitions which may have run to several words, and which appear on a different list. They do, however, preserve the original meaning.

AGE 8-9

bad 56.8
blue 76.3
brown 59.4
bunny 50.8
cap 54.6
clock 50.0

fifteen 51.0
gray 55.6
green 54.5
look 58.5
mailbox 54.9
mommy 57.3

red 64.6
sad 52.5
see 50.8
she 56.6
wind 50.8
yellow 51.3

AGE 10-11

afraid 50.6
airplane 69.7
apple 51.8

bad 75.0
balloon 58.1
banana 62.4
bank (for money) 53.7
baseball 66.2
basketball 61.2

bear 54.1
beautiful 51.0
bird 57.1
black 54.5
blouse 54.1
blue 61.3
boat 54.5
boot 53.2
bread 55.6
brown 71.8

brownie 65.0
bunny 68.1

camel 55.0
cap 55.6
cat 50.0
cheese 50.5
cherry 53.4
child 50.2
classroom 54.4

clock 66.6
clothe 51.8
color 60.4
comb 54.2
cook 59.8
cow 56.1
cracker 55.0
cream 63.2

daddy 57.1
December 61.4
dentist 60 2
desk 55.0
doll 57.8
door 54.4
drawing 66.2
duck 51.8

eagle 51.7
eat 54.4
eight 54.2
eighteen 55.0
elephant 72.0

farmer 50.6
February 60.9
fifteen 51.7
five 52.4
football 56.8
fox 64.4
Friday 61.2
fun 64.0

garden 50.5
grandparent 58.0
gray 65.7
green 83.6

hop 60.1
horse 54.4
hospital 75.0
hot 55.6
house 65.4

January 64.8
jelly 57.1
jellyfish 52.4
juice 52.6
July 61.3

kite 52.0
kitten 65.2

lamb 59.7
large 53.2
light 55.0
look 70.1

mail 68.4
mailbox 70.0
mama 60.5
me 62.5
milk 64.2
Monday 66.1
monkey 60.0
moose 50.6
mouse 50.0

no 50.6
noon 53.4
November 54.4
nurse 50.5
nursery 50.9

orange 60.0
owl 56.2

page 54.4
pancake 59.7
pear 58.0
pet 51.4
picture 53.6
pig 57.8
playground 50.6
plaything 67.7
policeman 56.0
pony 64.5

pool (of water) 52.4
potato 74.6
pray 64.6
puppy 60.9
purple 66.1

rabbit 51.0
railway 50.5
rain 52.5
red 61.3
roadway 51.3
robin 66.1

sad 60.1
salad 50.0
schoolmaster 52.2
sea 57.8
see 78.0
seventh 54.0
she 67.0
shoe 63.3
six 50.0
sixth 60.4
skirt 62.5
sleepy 52.6
slow 54.9
snowy 57.8
soup 62.1
store 54.1
strawberry 54.1
Sunday 58.1
sunflower 52.1
swim 70.0

teacher 54.0
thin 50.1
Tuesday 66.6
twenty 61.3
two 56.6

unhappy 58.6
us 62.9

walk 56.8
warm 51.3
wash 69.0
watch 57.4
Wednesday 56.9

weekend 67.2
white 71.4
wind 63.3
woodland 56.9
woodwork 57.8

woody 53.2
write 60.0
yellow 60.9
zebra 50.4

AGE 12-13

address 60.6
after 63.8
airplane 73.7
airport 64.9
alligator 59.2
America 75.6
American 57.4
angry 50.9
ant 69.8
apple 85.7
April 71.8
arithmetic 64.4
arm 63.4
army 65.0
ask 74.1
aunt 71.3
autograph 50.5
awful 57.4

babe 51.3
baby 52.6
bacon 56.1
bad 79.2
bag 54.4
bake 62.9
baker 54.4
bakery 66.6
ball 67.8
balloon 61.6
banana 71.4
bank (for money) 77.2
bank (of a river) 54.1
banker 54.1
barber 59.4

barn 63.4
baseball 78.6
basketball 76.8
bath 54.9
bathroom 66.6
bean 72.4
bear 80.9
beautiful 80.6
bedroom 78.9
beef 66.1
beefsteak 51.7
beer 79.0
belt 61.4
berry 59.8
best 70.8
better 57.1
Bible 58.6
big 68.4
bigger 67.2
billion 54.9
bird 75.4
birthday 63.3
black 76.4
blackberry 61.6
blacksmith 57.8
bleed 50.0
bloodshot 52.1
blow 53.6
blue 85.6
blueberry 61.0
bluebird 51.0
bluejay 69.4
boat 71.4
boating 56.6

body 52.8
book 66.2
bookrack 50.0
boot 67.8
bottle 66.4
bowl 52.0
bowling 64.2
box 59.7
boy 58.4
bread 63.8
bright 51.8
brightness 58.0
bring 70.1
broom 61.3
brown 89.7
brownie 60.9
buckskin 55.6
building 67.0
bull 52.0
bunny 91.0
burn 57.6
busy 65.3

cabbage 67.0
cabin 57.6
calf 70.1
camel 58.6
camera 57.3
camp 59.4
candy 51.6
cap 80.9
captain 51.7
card 68.0
carrot 64.9

cat 56.2
catfish 65.0
cattle 65.6
cavern 53.2
celery 54.5
cent 53.2
cheese 76.6
cherry 77.2
chicken 76.6
child 72.9
chipmunk 56.1
chocolate 70.1
church 75.4
circle 51.6
circus 58.9
city 50.5
classroom 68.8
clear 70.1
climb 51.2
clock 80.0
clothe 68.9
clothes 50.5
cloud 63.2
clown 65.3
coat 77.2
cocoa 61.8
coconut 54.4
coffee 77.4
coin 56.1
cold 59.2
college 59.3
color 80.4
colored 67.6
comb 74.6
combat 59.6
cook 82.2
cookie 87.7
cost 50.2
cousin 59.2
cow 83.7
cracker 51.7
crayfish 61.0
crayon 63.8

cream 62.5
crow (bird) 58.0
cup 61.8
curl 57.4
cute 66.6

daddy 74.9
dance 69.0
dark 67.7
darkness 57.6
daughter 53.6
day 71.8
daylight 62.5
dead 57.0
deaf 61.6
December 79.4
deer 69.4
dentist 63.8
desk 81.2
dictionary 52.1
die 68.4
dime 73.7
dinner 58.9
dirt 58.0
dirty 51.8
dish 60.4
dog 78.1
doll 75.6
dollar 71.6
donkey 74.6
door 55.6
doorway 59.4
downstairs 54.4
draw 80.2
drawing 76.2
dress 76.5
driver 50.6
driveway 67.2
dry 67.6
duck 77.2

ear 58.9
earth 53.7

easy 57.3
eat 76.8
eight 76.4
eighteen 63.2
eighth 53.6
electrical 57.4
elephant 71.8
eleven 66.2
every 56.1
everybody 55.6
everything 61.2
everywhere 60.1
eye 61.6

face 65.2
false 58.6
family 68.8
fan 63.6
far 67.2
faraway 58.5
farmer 73.6
fat 50.5
father 69.7
fatherly 52.8
February 83.0
field 53.6
fifteen 79.4
fifth 70.6
fifty 67.4
fight 51.4
finger 69.4
fire 62.6
fireproof 52.1
fish 72.0
five 54.8
flash 61.6
flashlight 61.7
flower 57.3
fly 59.6
food 75.4
foot 61.4
football 77.2
footwear 59.6

forehead 50.9
forest 52.0
forty 54.8
four 69.4
fourteen 72.6
fourth 66.2
fox 76.2
freezer 55.6
Friday 80.2
friendly 54.5
frighten 50.9
frog 80.9
full 57.8
fun 77.7
fur 57.4

game 52.5
garage 52.6
garden 72.9
gate 50.9
gift 51.8
giraffe 59.4
girl 69.4
girlish 57.8
glove 51.0
glue 57.6
go 67.2
goat 61.4
godmother 58.9
goldfish 54.9
golf 57.8
goose (bird) 56.1
grade 65.3
grandfather 70.5
grandpa 53.8
grandparent 75.7
grape 70.8
grapefruit 74.6
grass 52.5
gray 81.4
green 86.6
greenhouse 62.6
grocery 52.8

grow 55.0
gymnasium 57.6

hair 67.3
hairdresser 54.4
ham 64.9
hamburger 62.4
hammer 52.1
handsome 56.2
hardy 52.5
hat 66.6
hay 50.0
hear 58.6
hearer 50.5
hearing 71.8
heart 59.6
hen 60.5
henhouse 69.7
her 61.2
hers 51.2
highway 62.9
his 53.2
home 65.7
homesick 50.2
hop 71.3
horse 73.6
hospital 71.0
hot 73.7
house 65.3
housekeeping 54.4
housetop 59.6
hundred 69.7
hungry 61.4

iced 56.1
icy 50.0
ill 50.5
illness 54.0
in 50.2
indoor 61.8
indoors 62.2
insect 51.2

jacket 61.8
January 80.4
jelly 78.2
jellyfish 64.9
jet 52.0
job 61.8
joke 54.4
joking 51.0
juice 73.3
July 88.2
June 80.9

kangaroo 68.8
keep 53.4
kitchen 59.6
kite 70.8
kitten 70.5
kitty 67.8
know 56.2

lake 59.6
lamb 65.0
lamp 71.8
large 54.2
last 70.4
laugh 56.1
law 53.4
lazy 57.4
lemon 62.2
lemonade 52.4
letter 65.0
library 80.0
light 66.2
lightning 51.0
lion 74.4
listen 63.2
little 70.9
locker 62.4
log 56.1
long 56.9
look 76.4
lookout 50.5
lot 55.6

lovely 56.1
lover 61.6
low 63.6

mad 56.6
mail 72.9
mailbox 81.2
mailman 65.3
mama 58.4
mammal 51.8
many 64.0
March 70.1
mathematical 55.6
May 69.7
me 77.2
meal (repast) 52.8
meat 74.0
merry 54.4
milk 91.8
milky 72.9
million 61.6
minute 72.9
mirror 53.7
Miss 74.9
mitten 50.2
mommy 64.9
Monday 89.4
monkey 77.7
month 57.4
morning 67.2
motorcar 54.5
mountain 60.0
mouse 61.8
movie 68.6
muddy 53.4
muskrat 53.6

name 50.5
nation 51.3
neither 52.1
nest 83.0
newborn 52.9
nice 61.6

nickel 61.2
night 59.4
nine 70.5
nineteen 52.6
ninety 56.6
no 69.7
noise 51.8
noisy 66.6
noon 69.3
nose 62.8
not 54.1
November 90.1
nurse 50.2

oaken 59.4
oatmeal 65.0
ocean 56.6
October 72.9
office 56.1
old 56.1
onion 64.9
orange 75.4
outrun 52.6
over 57.6
overlook 61.4
overshoe 53.6
owl 73.3

page 62.5
paint 70.1
pan 64.5
pancake 77.2
parade 56.9
parent 62.6
parrot 53.2
party 65.0
pay 71.3
pea 50.2
peach 61.4
peanut 65.7
pear 67.7
pencil 67.7
penny 67.2

people 59.8
pet 66.2
phone 63.6
picture 67.2
pig 83.8
pill 56.1
pineapple 57.8
pink 73.3
plane 58.6
play 86.5
playful 53.7
playground 53.6
plaything 64.9
plum 52.0
pocket 61.0
policeman 71.0
pond 57.4
pony 72.5
pool (water) 63.2
popcorn 51.7
pork 57.7
postman 78.1
potato 89.8
pray 72.9
puppy 71.8
purple 89.8
push 61.4

queen 69.8
question 55.0

rabbit 69.0
race 68.4
racer 64.6
railroad 68.9
railway 67.2
rain 69.7
rainbow 57.6
rainy 51.0
ranch 50.0
rancher 51.7
rat 67.6
real 50.6

red 85.6
rest 58.9
rice 52.4
rich 54.8
river 52.6
road 57.4
roadway 65.6
robin 87.8
rooster 54.5
root 60.0
rose 69.7
round 61.7
rug 55.6

sad 78.0
sailboat 73.3
sailor 57.3
sale 50.9
sandwich 63.8
schoolboy 65.4
schoolhouse 57.8
sea 68.1
seal 67.8
second 60.6
see 80.6
seed 56.1
September 83.0
seven 81.6
seventh 65.3
sewing 58.0
shadow 54.8
shampoo 52.8
she 76.1
sheep 77.4
shine 65.6
ship 70.8
shoe 75.3
short 61.3
shower (bathe) 53.6
silly 53.6
sing 54.9
sister 60.0
six 76.6

sixth 63.8
skate 50.5
ski 56.6
skirt 69.4
skunk 67.2
sky 62.1
sleepy 57.8
slow 71.3
small 68.6
smoke 53.6
snail 57.6
snow 64.5
snowy 77.4
soft 51.3
soldier 57.3
someone 54.8
son 53.2
song 64.5
sorry 70.1
soup 63.6
south 59.0
spider 59.6
spoon 55.6
sport 57.4
spring 66.6
springtime 55.6
squirrel 77.0
stepfather 52.6
stick 59.7
stone 57.0
store 66.1
storm 54.4
strawberry 71.8
street 57.6
strong 51.4
study 57.7
suit 54.2
summer 70.4
Sunday 59.6
sunflower 66.1
sunny 54.2
sunshine 51.7
sweetheart 55.6

swim 79.3

table 62.4
tablecloth 65.6
talk 54.4
tea 73.3
teacher 85.2
teaspoon 55.6
telephone 63.3
tell 63.2
ten 63.0
their 58.1
thin 68.0
thousand 59.6
three 65.3
thumb 72.9
thundercloud 54.9
Thursday 75.4
tiger 85.8
today 78.1
toe 64.9
tomorrow 66.1
towel 62.8
toy 78.1
train 63.4
tree 64.9
truck 51.7
true 55.6
Tuesday 91.8
turkey 64.6
turtle 67.7
twelve 54.8
twenty 67.2
twin 67.7
two 78.6
type 51.7

uncle 65.0
underground 53.3
unhappy 65.3
upside 55.6
upstairs 54.4
us 61.8

valentine 50.9
vegetable 62.9
very 77.7
visit 77.7

wait 62.9
wake 56.1
wakeful 51.7
walk 76.2
walker 58.0
wall 52.5
warm 77.7
wash 79.6
washing 59.0
washroom 60.0
watch 71.6
waterway 50.0
weak 55.6
Wednesday 84.8

week 69.7
weekend 79.7
weekly 52.5
weighty 61.6
when 50.6
where 76.9
white 71.7
who 51.8
whose 54.9
wildcat 60.6
wind 74.9
window 56.2
windy 51.2
wing 64.5
winter 56.6
witch 65.6
wolf 63.4
woman 65.3
woodcutter 68.9

wooded 61.8
woodland 74.2
woodpecker 61.2
woodwork 59.6
woody 75.7
wool 53.7
workroom 60.9
worm 55.6
write 77.2
wrong 51.4

yard 52.1
year 86.0
yellow 86.8
yesterday 74.9
young 52.9

zebra 73.3
zoo 71.8

AGE 14-15

a 64.0
above 54.9
act 60.4
activity 52.1
actor 58.4
add 53.3
address 77.7
adult 67.8
afar 52.1
afire 57.7
afraid 72.1
after 80.1
again 54.1
aged 71.7
ago 54.2
agree 50.5
aid 54.2
air 61.6
aircraft 70.5
airplane 85.8

airport 71.4
airy 52.9
alligator 58.5
allowable 56.2
almost 54.9
aloud 64.5
alphabet 60.4
alphabetical 61.6
amaze 54.9
amen 52.2
America 78.8
American 78.4
and 56.1
angel 52.9
angry 61.8
animal 65.0
answer 67.0
ant 81.4
anybody 51.4
anyone 54.2

anywhere 56.2
apartment 60.4
ape 56.2
apple 80.2
April 81.2
apron 55.6
arithmetic 70.4
arm 79.4
army 71.8
artist 51.2
ask 78.8
asleep 63.4
athletic 51.7
aunt 77.4
author 50.9
auto 57.8
autograph 69.6
avenue 50.5
awake 56.2
award 61.0

away 63.6
awful 70.0
awhile 51.0
ax 85.8

babe 54.9
baby 79.2
bacon 68.6
bad 98.0
bag 73.0
baggage 57.7
bake 76.6
baker 86.2
bakery 77.4
ball 72.1
balloon 70.5
banana 81.4
bank (for money) 79.0
bank (of a river) 72.6
bankbook 59.3
banker 62.2
baptism 58.8
barber 77.2
barn 74.0
baseball 82.8
basement 67.0
basketball 100.0
bat 63.6
bath 82.1
bathe 62.5
bathroom 74.2
battery 75.2
bay 63.3
bean 76.5
bear 91.2
beard 51.0
beat 61.0
beautiful 81.8
beautify 59.6
beaver 68.9
become 55.6
bedroom 90.5
bee 76.1

beef 75.6
beefsteak 83.0
beer 79.4
beet 59.7
beetle 71.7
before 55.6
begin 58.5
beginner 62.5
believe 64.9
bell 82.6
belt 63.4
bench 50.2
berry 74.4
best 88.9
better 56.1
Bible 69.0
big 82.8
bigger 81.8
bigness 58.2
billion 70.1
bird 74.1
birthday 80.9
birthplace 57.7
black 91.6
blackberry 77.7
blackbird 60.8
blackness 59.8
blacksmith 67.6
blanket 50.0
bleed 51.4
bless 54.2
blind 70.1
blindfold 61.8
blizzard 52.8
blond 50.6
bloodshot 63.6
bloom 50.9
blossom 57.8
blouse 78.4
blow 54.6
blue 89.8
blueberry 75.7
bluebird 54.2

bluejay 75.6
board 61.2
boardinghouse 59.6
boat 67.8
boating 67.2
bobcat 78.9
body 73.3
boil 65.7
bomb 55.0
book 87.3
bookrack 72.2
bookseller 55.6
bookshelf 52.9
boot 75.4
boss 62.4
both 62.1
bottle 78.9
bottom 60.4
bouquet 50.2
bowl 81.2
bowling 73.3
box 52.6
boy 76.0
brake 58.4
branch 55.6
bread 86.8
breakfast 66.6
breath 64.9
breathe 64.8
breathless 78.4
breeze 50.2
breezy 57.4
brick 65.4
bridge 70.0
bright 75.0
brighten 62.4
brightness 60.1
bring 58.2
broom 79.7
brotherly 66.1
brown 91.7
brownie 76.5
buckshot 50.6

buckskin 57.6
bud 52.9
bug 95.0
build 64.6
building 69.3
bull 65.6
bunny 79.7
burn 66.6
bus 65.7
bushy 64.0
busily 60.0
business 50.2
busy 88.9
butter 65.0
butterfly 71.8
buy 67.0
buyer 56.6

cab 57.8
cabbage 88.9
cabin 58.4
cafe 59.7
calendar 60.5
calf 76.1
call 51.0
calm 50.9
camel 78.4
camera 80.2
camp 79.7
campus 63.6
canal 52.9
candle 62.2
candlestick 57.8
candy 75.0
canoe 61.8
cap 84.2
capital (gov't) 51.4
capital (chief) 54.1
captain 52.4
car 87.8
card 57.1
cardboard 70.8
cargo 59.6

carrot 74.1
cash 70.4
cashier 53.8
cat 80.1
catch 69.4
catfish 77.7
cattle 64.4
caution 52.8
cavern 62.1
celery 68.8
cent 82.1
center 50.2
cereal 54.2
chair 56.2
champion 51.0
championship 54.4
change (modify) 64.0
change (money) 68.9
chapter 55.6
cheese 76.1
cherry 92.4
chest 53.2
chew 53.8
chickadee 57.6
chicken 84.2
child 73.6
chipmunk 53.8
chocolate 78.4
church 75.2
churchman 70.0
churchyard 53.2
cigar 57.6
cigarette 61.8
circle 72.9
circus 73.3
city 66.6
civil 52.9
class 75.2
classmate 58.4
classroom 87.8
cleanse 51.8
clear 66.2
climb 59.6

clock 82.4
closet 66.1
cloth 61.6
clothe 84.1
clothes 71.7
cloud 79.0
cloudburst 50.9
cloudless 57.4
cloudy 58.1
clown 82.5
club 64.4
coat 84.8
cocoa 76.5
coffee 86.5
coin 71.7
cold 69.3
collar 54.5
college 73.7
collie 57.6
color 78.0
colored 74.4
colorful 72.2
colt 60.4
comb 77.2
combat 70.8
come 69.0
comeback 52.1
comfortable 60.0
comma 63.2
community 54.1
congress 53.6
cook 94.9
cookie 85.4
copper 66.6
corn 60.1
correct 71.8
cost 67.7
costume 57.7
cottonwood 65.2
count 53.3
country 64.0
courthouse 52.1
cousin 63.6

cow 91.8
cowboy 60.0
cowhide 50.2
crab 54.9
cracker 56.8
cranberry 57.6
crawl 58.2
crayfish 77.4
crayon 64.1
crazy 70.0
cream 91.3
creamy 56.2
crossword 62.4
crow (bird) 79.4
crush 50.0
cub 54.1
cuckoo 50.8
cup 75.0
curl 69.7
cut 50.6
cute 65.3
cutworm 54.9

daddy 87.3
daily 50.0
dam 51.4
damage 56.2
dampen 52.2
dance 77.7
dancer 64.9
dangerous 51.7
dark 62.5
darkness 64.8
darling 52.6
daughter 77.4
day 75.2
daydream 57.6
daylight 70.1
dead 69.0
deadly 58.6
deaf 68.8
deafen 65.3
deafness 71.6

dear 57.8
death 50.6
December 93.7
deer 74.9
degree 70.0
dentist 81.2
desk 90.1
dictionary 62.8
die 94.2
diet 56.1
different 52.8
dig 54.9
dime 75.7
diner (place) 50.9
dinner 74.6
dirt 77.7
dirty 75.7
disappointment 53.4
dish 82.4
dividend 51.0
dog 86.6
doll 87.8
dollar 84.8
donkey 67.2
door 76.8
doorway 60.5
dormitory 60.1
doubtless 51.3
doughnut 75.0
dove 51.0
downfall 75.6
downstairs 64.9
dozen 56.2
dragonfly 62.1
draw 84.4
drawing 82.9
dream 73.7
dress 86.1
dressmaker 71.2
drip 56.8
drive 62.4
driver 72.2
driveway 68.9

drown 55.6
drummer 56.8
drunkard 67.7
drunkenness 51.3
dry 80.0
duck 71.4
dunce 54.9

each 58.9
eagle 82.4
ear 79.4
early 52.2
earth 67.0
earthquake 61.8
earthworm 56.1
east 64.8
easy 76.4
eat 92.4
eight 88.6
eighth 77.2
eighty 56.1
elbow 66.1
electric 83.4
electrical 77.0
electrician 51.0
elephant 90.0
elevator 69.7
eleven 80.6
end 81.4
engine 54.9
engineer 51.3
English 72.6
enjoyment 60.9
enlarge 55.6
enthusiastic 53.2
evening 65.8
evergreen 59.4
evermore 56.1
every 70.4
everybody 64.8
everyone 58.4
everything 67.4
everywhere 70.1

evil 62.1
exit 57.4
eye 75.2
eyebrow 65.3
eyesight 53.2

face 84.8
faith 59.6
fall 61.2
false 74.1
family 81.7
fan 64.0
far 81.6
faraway 77.7
farm 67.6
farmer 68.6
farmhouse 62.6
fast 64.9
fat 72.9
father 74.8
fatherly 64.9
favorite 59.6
February 85.3
feed 69.7
feel 59.7
female 78.1
few 75.2
field 65.8
fifteen 88.1
fifth 83.3
fifty 77.7
fight 79.8
fighter 62.1
finger 65.2
finish (stop) 65.6
finish (surface) 53.2
fire 85.8
fireproof 70.5
firewood 54.9
fireworks 53.2
fish 68.6
five 89.8
flash 64.8

flashlight 60.1
flat 51.0
flea 59.6
flood 68.1
floor 66.6
flour 55.6
flower 63.7
fluid 50.0
fly 65.0
fog 71.4
food 92.2
foolish 56.1
foolishness 54.1
foot 70.9
football 84.8
footwear 77.2
forehead 68.0
foreleg 50.6
forepaw 55.6
forest 74.6
forget 58.8
fork 53.8
forty 67.7
four 90.4
fourteen 76.8
fourth 78.8
fox 82.6
freeze 74.1
freezer 69.4
Friday 87.8
friend 60.1
friendly 62.5
frighten 63.8
frog 83.3
frost 57.7
frosty 64.2
frozen 69.2
fruit 68.4
fudge 51.4
fuel 61.0
full 61.8
fun 87.4
funeral 60.5

fur 75.6
furnishings 68.5

gallon 63.2
game 74.1
garage 65.7
garden 82.1
gardener 61.8
gardenia 52.1
gas 58.9
gate 79.2
gentleness 61.2
geography 56.2
giant 73.7
gift 73.3
gingerbread 62.1
giraffe 71.3
girl 88.4
girlish 68.6
give 58.4
glad 72.9
globe 50.5
glove 90.6
glue 66.6
go 76.4
goat 77.7
godmother 69.2
golden 58.8
goldfish 69.2
golf 80.9
good 62.1
goose (bird) 69.8
government 60.8
governor 66.1
grade 75.7
graduate 76.6
grandchild 71.7
grandfather 78.4
grandpa 60.5
grandparent 89.2
grape 77.7
grapefruit 77.2
grass 69.2

grasshopper 63.0
grassy 69.7
grave 53.6
gravity 50.9
gray 90.2
grayheaded 57.7
green 88.6
greenhouse 76.5
greeting 62.4
grocer 58.6
grocery 60.2
ground 59.7
group 56.2
grow 74.9
gulf 55.0
gunner 69.8
gymnasium 66.6
gymnastics 59.4

hair 56.2
hairdresser 62.5
hairy 52.4
ham 89.3
hamburger 80.5
hammer 82.4
hand 71.2
handbag 63.2
handkerchief 54.2
handle 62.9
handsome 68.1
hangman 50.2
happily 64.5
happiness 50.4
happy 53.6
hard 78.8
hardy 70.4
harmful 55.6
hat 70.9
hate 57.0
hateful 50.6
hawk 50.2
hay 70.4
hayfield 52.9

haystack 51.2
he 70.0
head 69.7
headache 68.4
headlight 57.7
headwater 60.0
health 50.2
hear 74.2
hearer 65.3
hearing 73.3
heart 73.0
heater 69.0
heaven 54.2
heavy 83.6
heel 59.4
height 54.9
hen 65.8
henhouse 63.8
her 77.2
here 69.7
hero 53.3
hers 73.7
high 70.1
highland 63.6
highroad 71.2
highway 68.6
him 50.6
hippopotamus 61.4
his 53.2
historian 51.3
hog 55.6
hole 57.1
holiday 60.5
home 81.7
homelike 62.1
homemaker 64.9
homesick 79.7
honesty 61.0
hoopskirt 57.7
hop 75.3
hope 64.0
horse 72.0
horsehair 50.0

horseman 62.1
horseshoe 56.2
hospital 88.2
hot 79.7
hotel 57.1
hour 77.9
hourly 60.0
house 86.9
household 69.7
housekeeper 63.8
housekeeping 72.6
housetop 62.2
housewife 68.8
human 55.6
hummingbird 66.6
hundred 75.0
hungry 75.0
hunter 64.4
huntsman 72.9
hurriedly 57.8
hurry 84.5
husband 73.7

I 62.4
icebox 55.6
iced 68.4.
icy 83.0
idea 55.6
ill 68.4
illness 74.1
imaginable 60.2
improvement 64.2
in 67.0
inch 56.2
index 60.5
indoor 75.6
indoors 83.7

industrious 53.0
infection 64.9
inn 62.6
insect 60.8
into 77.0

iron 51.3
isle 53.2
it 64.2

jacket 85.0
jacks 65.1
January 87.4
jar 56.9
jay 52.1
jelly 68.1
jellyfish 70.8
jet 79.7
jeweler 63.0
jigsaw 56.2
job 89.0
joke 70.1
joker 57.7
joyful 63.3
juice 91.7
July 88.0
jump 54.2
June 93.3
junior 63.6

kangaroo 76.5
keep 57.4
keeper 51.4
key 64.2
kid 72.4
kind 51.3
kindness 60.4
kiss 78.4
kitchen 74.4
kite 67.0
kitten 78.4
kitty 63.7
knife 70.5
knot 50.9
know 53.0
knowledge 59.0

lady 70.0
ladybug 58.4

lake 79.3
lamb 71.2
lamp 80.9
land 69.7
language 54.1
large 71.8
last 73.7
late 60.1
laugh 77.2
laughter 51.3
laundry 62.9
law 75.4
lazy 70.5
lead 58.2
learn 68.2
leather 76.6
leave 65.8
lemon 78.4
lemonade 78.4
length 50.2
letter 66.6
lettuce 53.8
liberty 62.2
library 86.0
lie 58.9
life 64.9
light 81.6
lighten 61.0
lightning 75.3
like 52.4
lime (fruit) 63.0
lion 96.2
lip 52.5
list 58.5
listen 61.8
little 76.8
live 63.8
lizard 66.2
locker 68.8
log 75.7
long 76.4
longitude 54.2
look 95.7

lookout 52.8
lose 64.8
loser 64.8
lot 62.2
loud 60.4
loveliness 50.0
lovely 71.3
lover 56.2
low 74.8
lukewarm 60.6
lumber 51.4
lumberman 51.4
lunch 74.2
lung 57.8

machine 50.0
mad 65.0
madman 57.8
mail 92.4
mailbox 94.1
mailman 73.7
male 65.0
mama 71.6
mammal 62.1
man 71.8
manager 64.8
manly 52.6
many 75.4
map 75.6
maple 62.2
march 54.2
March 73.0
mark 69.9
marriage 70.9
mask 50.9
mathematical 64.9
mathematics 65.7
May 80.2
maybe 56.8
me 83.0
meal (repast) 73.6
mean 51.3
measure 53.6

meat 74.9
medicine 63.6
meet 50.6
melon 73.3
merry 52.2
middle 51.3
milk 78.1
milky 78.4
mill 52.4
million 58.4
miner 60.0
minute 57.1
mirror 78.4
Miss 73.7
mistake 59.6
mistaken 53.6
misunderstand 57.4
mitten 59.6
moist 50.0
mommy 76.1
Monday 90.5
money 77.0
monkey 85.0
month 77.4
moose 70.5
morning 72.6
most 58.4
moth 55.6
mother 74.6
motherly 59.2
motor (drive) 66.1
motorcar 69.3
mountain 83.0
mouse 76.5
mouth 50.0
move 71.3
movie 80.1
muddy 55.6
music 56.2
mustard 61.7
mystery 71.6

nail 58.9

name 60.0
nameless 53.2
nation 64.9
near 51.4
nearby 54.0
nearly 56.1
neck 70.5
needle 55.0
Negro 63.6
neighbor 61.6
neither 52.9
nest 89.4
never 51.4
nevermore 60.6
nice 64.8
nickel 62.1
niece 56.1
night 83.6
nightcap 50.6
nightfall 69.0
nine 76.6
nineteen 71.4
ninety 70.0
no 72.1
nobody 53.2
noise 61.3
noisy 73.3
noon 80.2
north 60.4
nose 71.2
not 65.2
note 56.8
November 86.8
now 50.9
nurse 83.8
nursery 60.6
nut 50.4

oak 65.0
oatmeal 71.3
obey 66.6
ocean 67.2
October 89.7

octopus 61.0
office 90.8
officer 53.0
often 60.4
old 71.6
on 81.2
once 62.4
onion 78.6
only 54.2
open 58.6
opposite 50.0
orange 85.4
order (arrange) 62.1
ought 64.4
our 60.4
ourselves 62.5
out 71.3
outer 51.0
oven 54.2
over 59.3
overboard 56.1
overcoat 67.6
overhead 60.6
overjoy 59.0
overlook 56.2
overpower 52.6
overshoe 63.6
overspread 53.7
owl 90.9
own 64.9
oyster 54.4

page 84.4
pail 64.0
paint 79.2
painting 80.1
pajamas 69.6
pal 53.8
pan 67.0
pancake 77.2
papa 65.7
parade 61.0
paragraph 50.4

parent 75.7
parrot 56.2
part 61.8
party 80.2
pass 50.8
past 50.4
paste 71.8
paw 58.2
pay 81.6
payment 62.2
pea 76.4
peace 55.0
peach 73.3
peanut 76.6
pear 86.0
pecan 57.8
pencil 70.8
penny 87.8
people 74.1
period 61.6
person 84.9
pet 82.4
phone 67.2
phonograph 57.7
photo 52.9
physical 57.8
pick 50.9
pickle 50.8
picnic 58.6
picture 86.8
piece 56.9
pig 77.0
pill 60.4
pillow 56.1
pin 60.4
pine 57.8
pineapple 60.5
pink 79.4
plane 78.8
plant 53.2
planter 51.2
plastic 52.1
plate (dish) 75.4

play 90.6
playful 57.1
playground 72.1
playmate 51.4
plaything 84.1
please 50.9
pleasurable 87.8
pledge 50.2
plum 67.0
pocket 73.3
pocketbook 68.1
point 54.9
poisonous 52.2
polar 51.4
policeman 84.2
polish 53.6
pond 71.7
pony 77.2
pool (water) 83.6
poorhouse 71.3
pork 71.7
possible 50.9
postage 55.6
postcard 60.0
postman 84.4
postmaster 53.4
postscript 62.4
potato 97.4
pound 56.6
pour 51.4
powerful 65.6
pray 81.3
preserve 55.0
president 51.4
prince 53.6
princely 50.9
princess 52.4
print 53.4
problem 59.7
proud 57.7
pumpkin 68.2
puppy 80.5
purple 90.0

purse 55.6
push 66.6
pussy 54.2

queen 76.4
question 75.4
quick 67.4
quickly 63.8
quickness 52.9
quiet 58.1
quit 58.8

rabbit 91.8
raccoon 77.4
race 87.4
racer 58.2
railroad 90.8
railway 70.1
rain 82.9
rainbow 65.8
rainy 75.3
raise 58.6
raisin 59.2
rancher 54.4
rapidly 50.2
raspberry 66.1
rat 81.7
read 70.1
real 50.6
red 94.9
regular 51.7
rent 66.6
report 58.2
reporter 51.2
rest 73.3
return 62.1
review 60.6
rib 57.8
rice 65.8
rich 67.0
ride 56.6
rider 53.2
right 60.0

ring 65.7
river 68.8
road 72.5
roadway 74.8
roar 53.6
robin 87.4
roof 68.9
roofing 65.0
roommate 57.8
rooster 77.0
root 62.4
rose 84.4
rough 52.4
round 67.2
route 71.2
rub 50.0
rug 68.2
rush 50.0

sad 87.3
saddle 50.0
sailboat 85.8
sailor 74.9
salad 64.1
sale 70.8
salesman 65.7
salewsoman 72.2
sand 71.8
sandwich 80.0
Saturday 56.2
sausage 51.4
save 54.9
saver 57.8
saw 60.4
say 56.1
scale 56.1
schoolboy 69.6
schoolhouse 78.1
schoolmaster 53.4
schoolroom 63.7
scientist 67.2
scissors 53.2
score 69.6

scrapbook 53.2
scream 52.0
sea 88.6
seal 78.1
seaman 56.5
seaplane 57.1
seashore 59.4
seaside 60.1
season 53.7
second 80.0
see 94.1
seed 74.1
seedling 57.4
seesaw 56.2
sell 53.8
seller 52.2
sentence 70.8
September 88.6
seriousness 51.3
settler 50.2
seven 79.4
seventh 72.6
seventy 76.4
sew 65.8
sewing 70.9
sex 61.2
shadow 61.2
shake 50.8
shampoo 61.0
sharp 50.5
she 91.6
sheep 81.4
sheet 53.3
shellfish 60.0
shepherd 51.0
sheriff 50.2
shine 77.3
shiny 66.6
ship 87.0
shipyard 50.5
shoe 87.7
shoemaker 81.3
shop 75.0

shopkeeper 51.0
shopper 56.1
shopping 59.2
short 78.0
shout 55.0
shovel 79.1
show 58.2
shower (rain) 62.5
shower (bathe) 64.8
shrimp 57.8
shut 65.6
sick 72.9
sicken 58.4
sickness 51.7
signal 59.4
silk 53.3
silkworm 61.6
silly 62.5
silver 62.5
silverware 54.1
sin 58.2
sing 72.9
sink 55.0
sister 72.9
sit 58.4
six 80.6
sixpence 52.8
sixteen 53.2
sixth 85.4
ski 56.1
skin 55.6
skinny 51.3
skip 65.0
skirt 88.6
skunk 83.6
sky 61.6
sleep 58.9
sleepless 56.2
sleepwalker 54.1
sleepy 68.1
sleigh 57.6
slip 51.0
slipper 54.5

slop 51.4
slow 88.2
small 72.9
smile 54.0
smoke 65.6
smokestack 51.3
snail 68.8
snow 73.7
snowbank 54.9
snowflake 60.0
snowy 86.6
soak 64.8
soapsuds 64.1
soft 56.2
soldier 88.1
some 61.6
someday 50.0
soneone 54.4
somewhere 57.7
son 72.1
song 77.2
songster 50.9
soon 63.3
sore 52.2
sorrowful 65.2
sorry 65.7
sound 75.6
soup 73.7
south 86.5
speak 52.2
speaker 56.1
speech 71.6
spell 67.4
spend 83.0
spendthrift 54.9
spoon 76.0
sport 80.9
spotlight 62.2
spray 56.6
spring 75.8
springtime 73.3
spy 60.1
squeeze 53.6

squirrel 76.8
start 61.3
starve 55.6
stay 55.0
steak 68.2
steamship 55.0
steer 53.4
step 71.7
stepfather 63.8
stepmother 63.3
stew 54.4
stick 73.7
stiff 60.0
stilts 60.2
stocking 62.8
stomach 63.8
stone 70.1
stop 64.5
store 86.0
storm 70.9
stormy 58.5
stove 76.0
strawberry 84.1
stream 64.1
street 84.4
stroke 51.4
student 63.6
studio 52.6
study 75.7
subtract 57.7
subtraction 61.2
suit 60.6
summer 73.7
sun 55.6
Sunday 83.3
sundown 54.2
sunflower 75.4
sunlight 69.7
sunny 70.0
sunshine 77.2
sunshiny 60.0
supermarket 58.4
supervisor 61.8

supper 68.2
swamp 58.1
sweater 82.8
sweep 74.8
sweeper 60.2
sweetheart 71.4
swim 80.1
syrup 58.1

table 70.8
tablecloth 64.8
tablespoon 68.6
tableware 69.3
tag 50.5
take 58.4
talk 62.1
talker 56.9
tall 64.1
tan 71.4
tape 56.1
tasty 51.8
tax 61.6
taxation 54.9
taxi 64.8
tea 90.9
teacher 86.6
team 54.8
teaspoon 82.4
teens 67.2
telephone 85.4
tell 69.6
temptation 50.9
ten 82.6
tennis 59.6
tent 58.1
thank 50.2
thankless 54.2
their 53.8
there 60.6
thermometer 62.2
thin 81.2
think 51.4
thinker 61.0

third 74.0
thirst 56.1
thirsty 64.2
thirty 65.3
thought 64.2
thoughtful 65.3
thousand 70.9
three 79.6
throat 62.4
thumb 84.9
thunderbolt 50.0
thundercloud 52.8
thunderous 55.6
Thursday 88.0
ticket 67.7
tiger 79.2
tight 50.2
tiny 69.0
title (name) 64.8
toast 74.1
toaster 57.7
tobacco 60.0
today 73.3
toe 69.2
toilet 51.7
tomato 50.4
tomorrow 89.8
ton 53.4
tongue 50.6
tonight 51.3
too 51.0
toothache 74.1
tornado 60.1
touch 67.6
towel 74.2
toy 83.3
track 57.8
tractor 66.2
trade 54.4
trailer 61.4
train 83.3
trash 70.1
traveler 57.7

tree 68.1
trip 52.4
troop 68.5
trouble 64.9
truck 65.7
true 56.1
truthful 54.4
try 50.2
tub 50.9
Tuesday 78.1
turkey 72.1
turn 70.9
turtle 79.7
twelve 81.8
twenty 78.0
twin 72.9
two 91.6
type 62.5
typewriter 70.1

ugly 50.5
umbrella 69.4
uncle 72.6
unclean 70.8
uncover 50.9
under 66.6
underground 73.7
undone 59.2
undress 70.5
unfailing 54.0
unfair 55.6
unfriendly 68.6
unhappiness 56.2
unhappy 74.1
unhealthy 53.4
unhurt 64.0
unkind 55.6
unlearned 62.8
unlock 68.8
unlovely 51.4
unlucky 57.1
unnamed 66.6
unpack 53.2

unsuccessful 50.0
untaught 50.6
until 54.2
untrue 54.1
unwilling 60.8
up 57.4
upper 58.4
upside 57.7
upstairs 56.1
us 80.0
use 61.4
useful 62.1

valentine 69.7
vegetable 85.0
very 87.4
victorious 50.2
village 64.4
violet 50.2
visit 77.3
visitor 53.4
vitamin 60.4
vocabulary 55.6
voice 52.2
voiceless 60.9
vote 67.2
voter 71.0

wait 73.7
wake 73.3
wakeful 59.6
walk 88.9
walker 75.8
wall 59.2
want 68.0
warehouse 52.2
warm 82.4
warmth 61.6
warning 50.9
wash 89.4
washbowl 59.0
washer 58.4
washing 63.8

washroom 63.2
watch 84.2
watchtower 55.6
waterfall 59.6
waterway 88.2
wave 53.6
way 52.2
wayside 50.2
we 64.9
weak 76.5
wear 60.0
web 52.1
Wednesday 91.7
weed 50.0
weedy 51.4
week 90.9
weekend 85.4
weekly 57.6
weigh 74.5
weight 69.7
weighty 60.4
western 57.8
wet 81.8
whale 73.3
wheat 56.6
wheel 65.3
when 60.1
whenever 52.0
where 58.8
whereabouts 59.2
wherever 59.2

whirlpool 72.9
whirlwind 76.6
white 80.1
who 72.6
whoever 64.9
whom 58.5
whose 70.1
why 65.4
wildcat 66.1
wind 98.0
windmill 63.8
window 62.5
windy 64.2
wing 63.7
wink 61.8
winner 69.3
winter 71.7
wire 64.0
wish 58.9
witch 62.2
witchcraft 50.0
without 55.6
wolf 67.8
woman 87.0
womanhood 51.0
womanly 60.4
wood 59.3
woodchuck 51.0
woodcraft 50.0
woodcutter 89.7
wooded 71.2

woodland 78.1
woodpecker 80.6
woodsman 59.6
woodwork 62.5
woody 70.8
wool 54.2
workman 61.2
workroom 79.7
world 72.9
worm 62.5
worry 58.6
worthless 51.0
wrap 51.2
wrestler 62.4
write 91.7
wrong 71.6

yard 63.6
year 92.4
yearly 61.8
yellow 88.6
yesterday 84.9
you 58.4
young 69.3
youngster 55.6
youth 66.6

zebra 67.4
zero 60.6
zoo 86.6

AGE 16-17

a 59.2
abbreviation 68.8
about 54.6
above 61.6
accidental 62.5
account 50.0
ache 52.2
acorn 51.0
acre 57.6

act 97.4
actor 65.0
add 69.6
addition 55.6
additional 57.8
address 87.6
adopt 56.4
adult 71.7
adventure 54.8

afar 54.6
afire 72.1
afraid 81.2
after 79.6
again 64.1
age 62.2
aged 57.4
ago 68.4
agree 57.0

agreement 69.0
aid 70.1
air 84.9
aircraft 75.0
airplane 95.7
airport 74.6
airway 50.6
airy 57.8
alarm 53.2
alcohol 63.0
alike 54.0
alive 59.6
alligator 63.8
almost 72.8
aloud 66.6
alphabet 69.0
alphabetical 76.6
amaze 69.2
amen 62.2
America 96.0
American 92.8
amount 51.8
an 54.0
and 74.1
angel 69.6
angry 71.0
animal 76.1
another 65.7
answer 72.5
ant 89.8
anybody 74.6
anyhow 65.0
anywhere 69.2
apartment 67.3
ape 65.2
apple 93.8
approval 56.2
April 95.4
arctic 58.1
arithmetic 79.4
arm 83.0
army 84.0
arrangement 60.8

arrive 53.6
arrow 71.6
art 58.6
artist 70.1
ask 84.6
asleep 79.3
aspirin 72.8
assuredly 53.7
astronomy 65.6
athletic 56.2
athletics 51.4
atlas 51.8
atmosphere 60.5
attendance 51.3
aunt 92.5
author 50.0
auto 64.8
autograph 63.6
autumn 57.1
avenue 63.8
awake 82.4
award 63.4
away 80.2
awful 67.7
awhile 56.4
ax 90.6

baboon 56.8
baby 86.2
babyhood 54.8
back 72.4
bacon 80.6
bacteria 53.0
bad 92.5
bag 74.6
baggage 70.4
bake 79.8
baker 83.8
bakery 87.4
balance 58.8
bald 53.2
ball 83.6
ballet 60.5

balloon 83.0
ballroom 53.4
banana 91.0
bank (for money) 92.4
bank (of a river) 80.9
bankbook 64.9
banker 70.4
baptism 62.4
barber 70.6
barn 83.0
barometer 54.2
base 52.4
baseball 83.6
basement 67.2
basketball 96.1
bat 57.8
bath 76.6
bathe 76.8
bathroom 77.3
batter 51.3
battery 75.2
battlefield 53.2
bay 79.0
beach 59.7
beak 56.4
bean 78.1
bear 90.4
beard 55.6
beat 54.4
beaten 57.1
beautiful 90.1
beautify 51.7
beauty 67.2
beaver 70.4
because 74.6
become 70.1
bed 56.2
bedclothes 51.4
bedroom 93.0
bee 86.0
beef 98.0
beefsteak 85.8
beehive 59.2

beer 91.0
beet 72.2
beetle 65.6
begin 62.1
beginner 76.5
begone 50.9
behave 55.6
behind 51.3
believe 71.2
bell 87.2
below 54.8
belt 81.6
berry 87.3
beside 55.6
best 81.7
better 88.9
beyond 50.9
bib 54.0
Bible 82.1
big 88.4
bigger 89.4
bigness 58.0
bill 65.6
billboard 51.8
billion 74.6
biography 53.2
bird 95.2
birthday 83.8
birthplace 76.1
bite 62.2
black 87.8
blackberry 94.0
blackbird 62.5
blackness 69.8
blacksmith 86.2
blade 55.6
blank 55.6
blanket 74.8
bleed 65.0
bless 63.8
blessing 75.2
blind 81.3
blindfold 74.6

blindness 74.4
blizzard 59.6
blockhouse 50.2
blond 65.0
bloodhound 54.6
bloodshot 66.6
bloom 54.6
blossom 76.1
blouse 75.4
blow 69.8
blowout 58.5
blue 91.8
blueberry 91.2
bluebird 68.9
bluejay 84.2
board 51.0
boardinghouse 57.4
boat 91.0
boating 89.0
bobcat 86.9
body 71.6
boil 54.8
bomb 67.2
bomber 50.9
bonfire 62.6
book 94.9
bookkeeper 71.0
bookrack 89.0
bookseller 78.5
bookshelf 56.2
boot 88.6
boss 71.8
both 79.6
bother 84.6
bottle 87.4
bottom 74.4
boundary 66.6
bowl 74.2
bowling 84.6
box 59.7
boxer 57.1
boy 94.2
boyish 65.0

brain 66.6
brake 58.9
branch 63.2
bravery 54.8
bread 92.1
breakable 69.2
breakfast 84.8
breast 50.2
breath 68.0
breathe 72.6
breathless 70.1
breeze 55.6
breezy 57.8
brick 82.5
bride 53.6
bridegroom 51.7
bridge 76.1
bright 85.7
brighten 67.2
brightness 80.2
brilliance 54.0
bring 61.2
broke 66.0
brook 51.3
broom 74.5
broomstick 67.8
brotherly 72.6
brown 98.1
brownie 86.1
brush 79.0
bucket 56.8
buckshot 52.6
buckskin 72.5
buffalo 64.0
bug 76.6
bugle 56.4
build 66.6
builder 55.6
building 86.4
bull 71.0
bullet 60.2
bulletin 72.8
bum 60.5

bump 55.6
bumper 63.4
bundle 51.7
bunny 93.3
burn 94.9
burro 52.6
bus 79.6
bushy 54.6
busily 53.6
business 70.9
busy 87.2
butter 85.4
butterfly 78.9
buy 78.1
buyer 61.6
by 59.2

cab 80.1
cabbage 89.0
cabin 74.8
cactus 52.2
cafe 67.2
cage 63.4
calendar 65.0
calf 81.6
call 73.0
calm 66.0
camel 86.1
camera 79.4
camp 86.2
campus 72.5
cancer 58.1
candle 55.6
candy 86.5
cane 55.6
canoe 70.4
canyon 60.9
cap 92.2
capital (gov't) 70.4
capital (chief) 53.6
captain 72.9
car 88.2
card 67.2

cardboard 65.8
cardinal 56.2
care 57.7
career 62.8
careless 50.2
cargo 80.4
carpenter 50.9
carrot 86.0
cart 55.6
cartoon 61.8
cartoonist 62.1
case 55.6
cash 78.1
cashier 65.6
castle 60.0
cat 96.0
catch 79.7
catcher 67.2
catfish 80.2
cattle 70.0
cauliflower 58.5
cause 56.2
caution 55.6
cavern 76.6
celery 76.8
cemetery 54.2
cent 74.6
center 57.7
century 53.6
cereal 63.2
ceremony 56.2
chair 58.8
champion 72.8
championship 73.3
change (modify) 78.1
change (money) 74.6
chapter 53.4
charming 56.4
chase 54.1
cheap 60.1
check 57.7
checkers 56.2
cheek 57.7

cheerful 58.2
cheese 92.9
chemistry 66.6
cherry 95.4
chest 68.4
chew 68.9
chick 62.5
chickadee 66.6
chicken 82.6
chieftain 50.2
child 80.6
chin 56.9
chip 60.5
chipmunk 77.7
chocolate 84.1
choir 52.2
choose 67.8
chop 52.2
chorus 51.0
church 90.8
churchman 74.2
churchyard 65.0
cigar 66.6
cigarette 74.6
cinnamon 62.2
circle 74.9
circulation 57.7
circulatory 50.0
circus 86.8
city 84.8
civics 51.7
civil 51.8
class 81.8
classmate 71.6
classroom 97.4
clean 51.8
cleanse 58.1
clear 82.4
clerk 51.4
climb 64.8
clippers 54.6
clock 86.6
clockwise 53.8

closet 65.3
cloth 80.6
clothe 98.1
clothes 80.9
cloud 84.5
cloudburst 72.9
cloudless 56.1
cloudy 65.6
clown 92.4
club 68.2
clubhouse 54.2
coachman 64.6
coal 66.6
coast 65.8
coastal 54.1
coat 88.4
cocoa 83.3
coconut 79.3
coffee 91.8
coin 83.3
cold 63.8
collar 67.2
collection 55.6
college 79.6
collie 61.0
colony 58.5
color 88.2
colored 61.6
colorful 68.1
colt 82.4
column 53.3
comb 68.4
combat 76.1
come 66.6
comeback 64.4
comfortable 63.3
commandment 54.0
commission 56.4
commissioner 68.2
communism 61.8
community 72.6
company 84.4
compass 65.0

complain 62.8
complete 60.0
condemnation 54.0
congress 74.2
constitution 53.0
constitutional 50.0
contact 56.2
contentment 51.7
cook 82.2
cookie 95.2
cooler 52.4
cooperation 59.4
copper 59.4
corn 68.5
corner 61.3
cornstarch 59.4
correct 79.0
cost 66.6
cottonwood 83.0
count 64.9
country 76.1
courthouse 77.7
cousin 86.9
cow 92.5
cowboy 51.7
crab 69.2
cracker 72.1
cradle 58.5
craft 61.8
craftsman 63.2
cram 52.6
cranberry 54.9
crawl 53.2
crayfish 86.8
crayon 75.6
crazy 79.0
cream 87.2
creamy 71.8
credit 64.6
crop 56.2
crossroads 66.6
crossword 63.3
crow (bird) 83.0

crow (boast) 63.2
crowd 54.6
crown 63.3
cry 64.8
cub 65.2
cuckoo 62.4
cup 82.8
cupful 53.2
curl 70.5
curve 54.9
customer 69.0
cut 65.6
cute 78.1
cutter 52.2
cutworm 51.0

daddy 86.4
daily 67.4
daisy 59.7
dam 72.5
damage 55.6
dampen 72.2
dance 86.2
dancer 51.7
danger 62.2
dangerous 69.3
dark 82.4
darken 51.0
darkness 72.2
darling 51.7
date 54.9
daughter 76.4
day 78.8
daydream 61.8
daylight 81.3
dead 75.4
deaden 59.2
deaf 89.4
deafen 74.6
deafness 76.4
deal 52.2
dear 66.6
death 69.8

December 96.1
decide 57.1
deer 91.2
defiance 52.6
degree 63.6
delight 58.2
democracy 50.0
dentist 79.0
describe 52.9
desk 92.5
destroy 52.4
destroyer 50.2
detour 58.5
diamond 52.2
dictionary 70.0
die 93.0
diet 81.3
difference 51.2
different 80.0
dig 64.2
dime 85.2
diner (person) 62.5
dinner 83.7
dinosaur 64.8
directory 52.6
dirt 89.4
dirty 83.0
disappoint 69.8
disappointment 58.5
disease 77.2
dish 86.8
disinfect 61.8
dislike 66.6
disobedient 70.1
disobey 54.0
disrespect 64.2
distance 59.2
divide 68.4
dizzy 66.6
do 64.0
dog 87.6
doll 92.5
dollar 82.2

donkey 95.2
door 81.2
doorknob 60.0
doorstep 54.6
doorway 69.8
dormitory 76.6
dot 63.3
double 55.6
doubtless 78.2
doughnut 66.6
down 66.0
downfall 81.7
downhearted 60.2
downstairs 77.3
dozen 64.2
dragonfly 67.3
draw 90.1
drawing 91.6
dream 84.2
dress 87.3
dresser 56.1
dressmaker 64.6
drink 59.7
drinker 65.4
drip 63.3
drive 83.0
driver 84.1
driveway 77.7
drown 58.5
drummer 66.6
drunkard 71.8
drunkenness 60.6
dry 88.5
dryer 68.6
duck 83.8
due 51.7
dull 51.7
dump 75.4
dunce 54.1
during 62.9
dust 52.1
duty 54.9
dynamite 50.8

each 77.0
eagle 77.4
ear 71.8
early 57.8
earn 59.4
earth 91.2
earthly 74.6
earthquake 59.7
earthworm 77.0
east 79.8
eastern 79.2
easy 80.0
eat 87.8
education 51.3
educational 55.6
eel 56.2
eight 78.9
eighteen 70.1
eighth 89.8
elbow 89.0
elector 62.6
electric 84.9
electrical 84.5
electrician 74.6
elephant 92.9
elevator 62.8
eleven 82.5
else 72.1
elsewhere 61.8
emergency 61.8
employee 67.2
employer 56.4
employment 67.2
empty 54.8
enclose 54.1
encouragement 57.4
end 64.4
engagement 65.4
engine 81.2
English 89.4
enjoy 70.0
enjoyable 54.1
enjoyment 72.5

enlarge 58.0
enter 64.6
equator 77.4
erase 68.5
error 51.7
eruption 52.2
establishment 55.6
even 54.8
evening 73.7
event 50.5
ever 69.6
evergreen 75.6
every 76.2
everybody 77.3
everyday 63.4
everyone 72.5
everything 64.9
everywhere 81.3
evil 70.6
examination 74.2
example 75.2
exchange 67.3
excuse 53.2
exit 68.4
expand 62.9
expedition 60.0
experience 59.7
expert 51.2
explanation 56.4
explore 58.2
explorer 50.9
explosion 57.1
eye 77.4
eyebrow 76.9
eyelash 72.8
eyesight 70.4

face 89.8
fact 60.0
faintness 54.9
fairy 55.6
fall 67.3
false 88.2
family 95.3

famous 64.6
fan 74.1
far 77.4
faraway 75.3
farm 68.4
farmer 77.4
farmhouse 72.5
farther 53.0
fast 67.2
fat 85.8
father 87.4
fatherland 53.7
fatherly 74.5
fault 60.5
favor 54.1
favorite 74.5
fawn 59.6
fear 77.0
fearful 54.8
February 96.0
feed 63.4
feel 74.8
feeling 54.8
female 83.6
fence 61.3
few 79.3
fiddler 54.1
field 73.7
fifteen 89.0
fifth 84.5
fifty 87.0
fight 79.3
fighter 76.6
final 53.7
finally 55.6
finger 80.2
finish (stop) 69.8
fire 78.1
firearm 60.1
fireproof 69.2
firewood 53.8
fireworks 71.7
firing 52.1
first 53.6

fish 79.3
fishery 77.3
fit 61.6
five 83.6
flash 82.4
flashlight 83.6
flatten 52.4
flavor 60.5
flea 62.8
flier 56.8
flirt 57.7
float 61.3
flood 83.6
floor 71.8
florist 56.1
flour 69.3
flower 75.3
flowery 65.4
fluid 53.8
fly 86.2
foam 52.2
fog 81.8
foggy 60.5
foil 50.6
food 94.8
fool 57.4
foolish 50.9
foolishness 79.0
foot 90.8
football 94.2
footlights 54.8
footstool 53.4
footwear 84.5
forbidden 53.4
forehead 50.9
foreleg 53.0
forenoon 61.0
forepaw 55.6
forest 64.4
forever 54.4
forget 59.2
forgiveness 68.0
fork 67.2

forty 71.8
forward 59.4
four 80.2
fourteen 84.6
fourth 78.1
fox 87.3
freedom 63.3
freeze 87.3
freezer 72.9
French 59.4
fresh 56.4
freshman 68.1
freshness 69.6
Friday 87.3
friend 84.6
friendless 67.3
friendly 74.4
fright 56.9
frighten 83.8
frog 96.1
from 56.4
front 66.6
frost 73.7
frosty 81.7
frozen 83.0
fruit 78.9
fry 64.8
fudge 54.1
fuel 50.6
full 51.7
fully 55.6
fun 90.0
fund 67.3
funeral 65.6
fur 85.8
furnish 51.2
furnishings 56.1
furry 51.7
future 65.4
fuzzy 58.0

gallon 69.0
game 88.0

gang 52.2
gangster 57.8
garage 70.1
garbage 51.3
garden 71.8
gardener 57.6
gardenia 52.4
gas 70.0
gate 69.0
gay 51.8
gentle 53.0
gentleness 55.6
geography 84.6
giant 57.6
gift 80.2
gingerbread 76.6
giraffe 87.4
girl 94.2
girlish 78.5
give 60.6
glad 84.1
gladness 58.5
globe 56.9
glory 53.4
glove 84.2
glue 84.9
go 86.4
goat 93.6
godlike 77.3
godmother 86.8
golden 62.4
goldfish 73.7
goldsmith 65.3
golf 84.5
good 78.2
goodness 60.2
goodwill 55.6
goose (bird) 74.6
goose (silly person) 54.8
gorilla 50.5
government 73.7
governor 64.8
grab 53.4

gracious 53.3
grade 89.4
graduate 88.5
grandchild 80.9
grandfather 76.6
grandpa 70.0
grandparent 90.6
grape 95.7
grapefruit 78.8
grass 87.3
grasshopper 74.8
grassy 69.6
grave 50.9
gravel 52.6
gravity 62.5
gravy 66.1
gray 96.5
grayheaded 62.2
graze 53.2
great 54.4
greatness 62.2
green 97.3
greenhouse 76.6
greeting 60.6
greyhound 62.6
grocer 60.8
grocery 71.2
ground 71.6
group 64.1
grow 67.2
guard 62.1
guardian 52.6
guess 54.9
gulf 73.3
gunner 67.3
gunpowder 63.8
guy 57.4
gymnasium 77.7
gymnastics 75.6

hail 58.5
hailstone 63.8
hair 66.0

hairdresser 64.2
hairy 63.2
half 61.3
halfway 63.0
hallway 51.7
ham 88.2
hamburger 94.0
hammer 81.2
hand 82.1
handbag 62.6
handkerchief 61.6
handle 67.3
handsome 83.0
hanging 53.4
happen 70.4
happily 67.4
happiness 53.4
happy 68.9
hard 82.5
hardy 63.4
harmful 70.4
hat 93.0
hate 70.9
have 53.4
hawk 69.8
hay 80.2
hayfield 50.0
haystack 64.8
he 55.6
head 79.6
headache 78.6
headdress 50.2
headlight 77.3
headstrong 50.2
headwater 66.6
health 65.3
healthy 67.3
hear 88.1
hearer 72.5
hearing 74.5
heart 87.0
heartbroken 50.9
heater 57.8

heaven 76.2
heaviness 72.2
heavy 84.2
height 68.8
hell 54.8
hello 54.9
help 71.8
hemisphere 58.6
hen 80.1
henhouse 83.0
her 74.5
here 69.6
heareabout 59.7
hero 65.0
hers 70.4
high 78.1
highland 70.4
highroad 80.9
highway 82.8
hike 67.6
hill 64.2
hilly 57.7
him 63.0
hip 77.0
hippopotamus 57.4
his 62.9
historian 62.8
hive 54.8
hobby 70.8
hockey 61.4
hog 92.1
hole 64.0
holiday 57.7
home 90.5
homeless 57.4
homelike 51.8
homemaker 68.8
homesick 77.7
honest 60.9
honesty 65.3
hook 57.1
hoopskirt 58.6
hop 76.4

hope 72.9
hopeless 72.2
horror 56.2
horse 81.2
horsehair 57.1
horseman 78.9
horseshoe 69.6
hose 55.6
hospital 89.6
hot 93.6
hotel 69.8
hour 75.4
hourly 54.8
house 96.1
household 56.8
housekeeper 74.9
housekeeping 79.8
housetop 73.0
housewife 77.7
how 58.9
hug 56.4
human 68.6
hummingbird 66.6
hundred 90.0
hungry 82.4
hunter 70.0
huntsman 60.0
hurricane 57.4
hurried 59.6
hurriedly 62.4
hurry 85.8
hurt 67.2
husband 80.9

I 83.8
iceberg 54.2
icebox 57.7
iced 80.1
icy 82.5
idea 58.8
if 73.3
ill 82.8
illness 88.2

illustrator 58.4
imaginable 66.0
imaginary 51.0
imaginative 51.7
improve 68.6
improvement 63.6
in 71.8
inch 63.6
incorrect 74.5
independence 58.5
index 65.6
indoor 79.0
indoors 83.7
industrious 57.6
industry 52.4
infect 62.2
infection 63.3
inn 50.9
insect 69.3
instructive 57.1
intelligent 51.4
interesting 54.0
into 73.8
invent 50.5
iodine 52.2
iron 65.0
it 73.7
ivory 57.1

jacket 90.5
jacks 65.6
jail 56.2
January 95.3
jar 79.2
jaw 58.8
jay 51.7
jean 53.4
jelly 80.6
jellyfish 73.8
jet 68.9
jeweler 81.2
jigsaw 57.1
jittery 50.0

job 96.1
jockey 66.1
join 61.8
joke 91.4
joker 70.4
joking 64.9
journey 56.2
joy 77.0
joyful 82.5
joyless 67.3
joyous 67.2
judge 57.7
judgment 52.2
juice 98.1
July 95.3
jump 65.6
June 90.5
junior 83.6
jury 60.6
justify 68.2

kangaroo 83.3
keep 71.6
keeper 60.0
kerchief 52.9
key 50.9
kid 75.4
kill 67.7
killer 60.0
kind 53.7
kindly 65.6
kindness 66.1
kiss 76.1
kitchen 88.5
kite 87.3
kitten 92.5
kitty 84.9
knife 83.0
knight 58.1
knit 51.3
knock 60.2
knot 52.4
knothole 53.4

know 74.6
knowledge 66.1

labor 50.8
ladder 56.4
lady 78.9
ladybug 67.2
lake 86.2
lamb 78.8
lamp 71.0
land 75.8
landing 75.7
landowner 70.9
lane 54.4
language 79.8
large 89.6
last 80.6
late 66.0
laugh 84.5
laughter 65.0
laundress 52.5
laundry 70.8
law 72.9
lazy 91.2
leader 52.1
learn 67.3
leather 71.8
leave 71.8
lemon 83.7
lemonade 84.8
length 65.3
less 60.0
lesson 62.9
let 50.9
letter 84.0
lettuce 73.3
liar 72.2
liberty 87.4
library 97.3
lice 53.0
license 54.6
lick 64.8
lid 56.2

lie 81.2
life 62.2
lifeless 62.5
lifelike 66.1
lifetime 50.0
light 87.4
lighten 83.3
lighthouse 64.5
lightning 83.3
like 63.6
lime (fruit) 72.9
lime (mineral) 51.4
limestone 68.9
limit 50.2
line 52.4
lion 94.5
lipstick 66.6
list 72.8
listen 72.9
little 87.7
live 69.3
liver 61.4
lizard 75.4
lobster 55.6
locker 76.1
log 74.1
lonely 53.6
lonesome 58.6
long 73.7
look 90.0
loose 58.8
lord 53.3
lose 50.8
loser 61.6
loss 59.2
lot 77.3
lotion 56.4
loud 72.8
love 51.7
loveliness 54.6
lovely 83.3
lover 82.4
low 94.9

luggage 62.8
lumber 62.5
lumberman 68.6
lunch 79.0
lung 76.0

machine 72.2
machinist 51.3
mad 82.8
madman 66.6
magazine 57.1
magnet 58.9
maid 60.4
mail 81.8
mailbox 94.4
mailman 86.6
make 73.3
maker 56.4
male 84.8
mama 90.5
mammal 70.4
man 79.0
manager 77.3
many 88.4
map 69.7
maple 68.2
marble 52.5
march 69.6
March 90.8
mark 63.3
market 66.6
marriage 87.3
marry 54.0
marshmallow 51.4
marvelous 58.0
mask 54.9
material 59.2
mathematical 51.7
mathematics 74.1
May 87.7
maybe 71.2
mayor 51.3
maypole 51.7

me 87.0
meal (repast) 82.8
meal (grain) 52.4
mean 57.8
means 69.2
measles 60.4
measure 67.2
meat 84.6
medicine 68.6
meet 65.6
melon 57.9
member 61.8
membership 51.3
memory 54.0
mend 50.9
menu 50.9
merry 82.8
mess 59.2
messenger 53.7
meter 57.7
midday 51.0
middle 70.1
mighty 62.2
mildness 53.4
mile 54.0
milk 85.4
milky 84.9
mill 51.7
miller 56.4
million 89.4
mind 61.6
miner 66.6
mineral 58.1
minute 87.0
mirror 78.5
mischief 54.8
misfortune 54.9
Miss 90.1
mistake 77.3
mistaken 60.2
misunderstand 68.9
mitten 50.9
mix 60.5

moisture 57.8
mole 52.2
mommy 72.4
Monday 95.4
money 82.6
monkey 87.0
monster 72.2
month 83.8
moose 73.7
more 61.8
morning 83.0
mosquito 69.3
moss 58.4
mossy 74.6
most 74.2
moth 71.2
mother 84.0
motherless 59.2
motherly 67.2
motor (drive) 67.0
motor (engine) 67.2
motorcar 84.1
motorist 60.9
mountain 81.7
mouse 83.3
mouthpiece 54.6
move 85.4
movie 75.2
much 80.9
mud 82.8
muddy 62.8
mulberry 55.6
mule 61.3
multiply 55.6
mummy 60.0
murderous 52.9
muscular 59.4
museum 61.8
music 92.2
muskrat 57.1
must 66.6
mustache 57.1
mustard 88.1

my 63.8
mystery 60.8

nail 60.5
name 75.2
nap 50.9
napkin 51.7
narrow 53.0
nation 53.6
natural 69.4
naturalist 54.2
naughty 67.6
near 64.4
nearby 70.1
nearly 60.6
neat 64.2
neck 73.7
necklace 61.3
need 55.6
needle 59.4
needless 63.8
needlework 50.5
Negro 76.4
neighbor 63.4
neighboring 50.5
neighborly 58.9
nephew 72.2
nervous 72.2
nervousness 61.0
nest 80.6
net 60.0
network 50.5
never 60.2
nevermore 79.0
new 67.6
newborn 71.7
news 59.2
newsreel 52.2
next 72.5
nice 79.8
nickel 82.8
nickname 66.6
niece 59.3

night 89.6
nightcap 67.2
nightfall 67.2
nightmare 59.4
nine 92.9
nineteen 63.3
ninety 86.0
no 83.0
nobody 72.9
noise 69.3
noiseless 56.1
noisy 83.8
nomination 53.6
noon 83.0
nor 52.9
normal 64.1
north 79.4
northerly 53.8
nose 87.3
not 72.5
note 77.4
notebook 55.6
notice 59.7
November 88.6
now 70.6
nowhere 65.6
number 65.6
nurse 81.3
nursery 80.9

oak 84.8
oaken 50.9
oatmeal 73.7
oats 54.8
obey 57.4
object 55.6
obliging 54.2
ocean 84.8
October 91.7
octopus 56.1
odd 54.8
of 62.2
offering 55.6

office 77.6
often 71.7
oftentimes 58.8
old 76.5
on 71.7
once 67.7
one 66.6
onion 90.1
only 76.6
opening 52.4
operation (function) 57.6
operation (surgery) 53.4
opposite 81.4
orange 80.9
order (command) 61.0
order (arrange) 69.2
ordinarily 54.8
organization 64.8
oriole 50.0
other 50.5
ought 50.9
ounce 66.0
our 66.1
ourselves 69.0
out 87.4
outer 58.0
outermost 50.0
outlaw 50.6
outnumber 54.6
oven 57.0
over 83.0
overboard 53.5
overcoat 77.4
overeat 52.5
overflow 53.2
overhead 70.4
overjoy 76.6
overland 57.7
overlook 59.4
overpower 77.3
overshoe 83.0
overtime 50.2
overturn 66.0

overweight 73.3
overwork 61.8
owe 62.2
owl 94.5
own 66.0
owner 83.3
ox 66.6
oxygen 80.9
oyster 57.4

page 89.7
pail 62.2
pain 78.1
painful 64.6
paint 76.9
painting 79.8
pair 72.6
pajamas 81.8
pal 61.0
palm 64.8
pan 61.3
pancake 88.5
papa 69.7
papoose 50.0
parade 75.6
paragraph 68.9
paralyzed 50.5
parent 85.2
park 53.2
parrot 72.5
part 80.2
particularly 50.9
party 78.8
pass (go by) 60.5
past 60.5
paste 58.1
path 52.2
patrolman 57.8
paw 67.2
pay 90.6
payment 79.8
pea 73.3
peace 62.4

peach 80.6
peanut 86.6
pear 81.2
pecan 51.0
pencil 90.4
penny 98.0
people 78.1
perfect 58.6
perfection 54.4
perfume 56.8
perhaps 56.8
period 51.8
permit 67.3
person 87.8
pet 88.6
phone 84.8
phonograph 62.2
photo 75.0
photograph 80.9
photographer 80.9
physical 53.3
pick 50.2
pickle 58.6
picnic 51.4
picture 94.0
piece 75.6
pig 90.0
pigeon 54.0
pigtail 52.1
pile 62.2
pill 64.2
pillow 51.7
pin 54.8
pine 83.7
pineapple 76.4
pink 86.6
pint 60.5
pioneer 55.6
pitch 56.4
plain (clear) 57.1
plain (land) 51.0
plan 54.9
plane 78.6

plant 66.6

plantation 72.8

planter 75.4

plastic 60.6

plate (dish) 72.9

plate (cover) 53.8

play 87.8

playful 79.4

playground 79.3

playhouse 51.8

playmate 51.8

plaything 88.2

pleasant 66.1

please 71.4

pleasure 57.8

pledge 68.5

plowman 54.1

plum 85.6

plumber 70.4

plural 50.2

plus 59.7

pocket 83.0

pocketbook 63.6

poetry 62.4

poisonous 60.2

polar 54.8

police 67.7

policeman 91.7

polish 60.0

political 58.5

politician 55.6

pond 66.6

pony 90.0

poodle 67.2

pool (water) 88.1

pool (game) 79.4

poor 64.9

poorhouse 77.7

popcorn 77.7

popular 71.6

pork 74.1

port 60.8

postage 67.2

postcard 60.2

postman 85.2

postmaster 69.3

pot 54.2

potato 94.9

pound 72.5

powerful 74.1

powerless 60.9

practice 66.0

pray 81.7

preacher 53.0

preserve 55.6

presidency 55.6

president 67.2

press 55.6

pressure 53.2

prevent 55.6

priest 67.8

prince 63.4

princess 83.8

principal 60.6

print 76.0

printer 71.6

prison 77.7

prisoner 51.2

prize 67.8

problem 64.8

process 57.8

productive 50.6

progress 54.6

progressive 56.2

proper 54.1

protection 52.4

proud 76.0

prove 74.2

prune 59.7

public 50.9

publisher 61.6

pump 72.8

pumpkin 84.6

punishable 67.3

puppy 98.0

purple 84.9

purse 65.3

push 64.2

pussy 70.1

put 62.4

quart 55.6

quarter 60.5

quarterback 55.6

queen 91.8

queer 70.1

question 73.3

quick 78.8

quickly 70.6

quickness 52.1

quicksand 55.6

quiet 67.7

quit 75.0

rabbit 94.1

raccoon 85.4

race 80.9

racer 58.8

rag 73.3

railroad 90.9

railway 88.2

rain 81.2

rainbow 77.4

rainfall 70.1

rainy 91.7

raisin 70.8

ranch 68.0

rancher 68.0

rapid 53.2

rapidly 50.9

raspberry 63.6

rat 88.5

ray 54.1

read 74.6

real 66.1

realize 63.2

really 59.7

receive 50.2

red 97.3

refresh 51.2
refuse 50.9
regret 50.9
regular 69.6
reheat 62.1
rejoin 56.1
relationship 61.8
relative 57.7
remember 54.6
remind 50.9
reminder 54.9
remove 69.4
rent 79.2
repair 60.0
repeat 58.1
replacement 57.7
report 53.2
reporter 71.8
reprint 55.6
Republican 53.2
respecting 52.6
rest 83.0
restaurant 61.2
restless 60.8
restlessness 58.4
retire 58.6
return 75.3
review 74.6
rheumatism 56.4
rib 71.4
rice 80.0
rich 84.2
ride 74.5
rider 69.2
right 74.6
ring 79.7
rise 56.2
risk 56.4
river 88.2
road 85.4
roadway 87.4
roar 52.6
robbery 51.8

robin 84.9
robot 51.4
rocky 55.6
rodeo 50.0
romance 54.2
roof 74.6
roofing 71.6
roommate 80.9
rooster 97.4
root 71.0
rope 57.0
rose 85.7
rough 69.7
round 66.6
route 80.9
row 52.2
rower 53.2
rug 89.0
rule 66.1
run 50.2
rush 56.2
rye 62.1

sack 54.6
sad 90.0
sadden 65.4
saddle 50.0
sadness 69.0
safeguard 54.2
safety 64.4
sail 65.4
sailboat 86.6
sailor 81.3
saint 62.5
salad 73.3
sale 73.8
salesman 72.9
salesmanship 69.8
saleswoman 76.9
salmon 66.0
salty 66.6
same 68.8
sample 60.2

sand 80.1
sandwich 90.5
Saturday 70.1
saucepan 53.3
sausage 62.2
save 89.6
saver 58.1
savings 70.6
savior 50.2
saw 74.8
sawdust 60.0
sawmill 60.0
say 65.3
scare 68.1
scholar 52.9
schoolboy 80.9
schoolhouse 78.9
schoolmaster 79.8
schoolroom 63.0
science 54.9
scientist 60.8
scissors 68.6
scold 56.2
score 76.5
scrapbook 62.8
scratch 56.2
scream 51.2
screw 50.2
sea 95.2
seal 76.6
seaman 64.2
seaplane 70.1
searchlight 58.6
seashore 71.6
seasick 66.0
seaside 66.6
season 56.2
seat 72.5
seaweed 62.4
second 80.2
secrecy 52.1
secret 51.3
see 97.8

seed 84.1	shoot 61.3	sixty 73.3
seedling 62.8	shop 76.1	size 54.6
seek 54.2	shopkeeper 75.3	skate 57.6
seesaw 60.0	shopper 56.2	skeleton 74.5
self 54.8	shopping 65.0	ski 81.3
selfish 54.0	shoreline 63.8	skillful 54.0
sell 61.0	short 71.7	skin 83.0
semicircle 56.1	shoulder 68.9	skinny 51.8
send 55.6	shout 56.8	skip 60.9
senior 72.5	shovel 56.1	skirt 84.2
sense 54.8	show 70.8	skunk 84.9
sentence 77.3	shower (rain) 64.2	sky 70.9
separate 50.2	shower (bathe) 74.8	skyscraper 67.3
September 96.5	showman 57.8	slacks 56.2
service 60.2	shrimp 66.6	slap 68.4
set 50.9	shut 69.6	slave 52.2
settler 53.2	shyness 51.4	sleep 81.2
seven 81.2	sick 74.9	sleeper 56.2
seventh 83.0	sicken 71.4	sleepless 74.2
seventy 66.6	sickly 75.4	sleepwalker 73.8
sew 76.6	sickness 64.9	sleepy 83.6
sewing 91.6	side 55.6	sleeveless 55.6
sex 66.6	signal 56.1	sleigh 53.7
shade 56.2	signature 71.7	slip 55.6
shadow 71.7	silence 52.5	slipper 55.6
shake 51.2	silk 69.8	slop 50.5
shameful 52.5	silkworm 62.5	sloppy 50.9
shampoo 87.4	silly 77.3	slow 89.6
shark 70.1	silver 60.6	small 92.2
sharp 57.6	silverware 87.2	smallpox 64.1
shave 73.3	silvery 63.6	smart 71.7
she 95.6	simply 54.0	smell 57.4
sheep 83.7	sin 64.9	smile 56.2
sheet 50.8	since 52.6	smog 75.4
shellac 51.0	sing 74.1	smoke 70.5
shellfish 70.4	singer 62.5	smoker 56.9
shepherd 84.4	sink 62.5	smokestack 59.7
sheriff 67.0	sister 89.0	smooth 54.0
shine 84.9	sit 71.4	snail 77.7
shiny 70.6	six 86.6	sniff 57.6
ship 89.0	sixpence 71.7	snow 85.8
shoe 98.1	sixteen 72.9	snowbank 53.7
shoemaker 81.7	sixth 91.4	snowflake 65.0

snowy 81.3
soak 63.4
soapsuds 58.0
society (all people) 54.6
society (community) 59.7
soft 89.7
soften 54.0
soil 59.6
soldier 82.2
some 73.3
someday 70.4
someone 67.7
sometimes 55.6
somewhere 69.3
son 86.0
song 68.4
songster 59.7
sonny 64.1
soon 90.5
sore 69.6
soreness 53.6
sorrow 54.6
sorrowful 66.6
sorry 66.1
sound 65.6
soup 88.5
south 86.6
southern 58.6
souvenir 52.0
spaghetti 57.8
spank 59.7
sparrow 56.9
speak 77.3
speaker 70.6
special 52.2
speech 74.5
speechless 67.8
speedily 60.6
spell 74.6
spend 62.2
spendthrift 51.8
spider 69.8
spin 54.0

spinach 69.2
splash 68.1
spoil 51.4
spokesman 57.1
spoon 87.0
sport 78.1
sportsman 54.1
spot 61.8
spotless 53.4
spotlight 65.4
spray 71.4
spring 84.9
springtime 87.8
sprinkle 62.2
spy 86.9
spyglass 74.4
square 52.4
squeeze 56.1
squirrel 86.0
stair 53.2
stamp (mark) 56.1
start 77.2
starve 60.8
statesman 67.3
station 57.1
stay 74.8
steak 77.3
steal 62.2
steamship 69.8
steer 74.8
stem 50.2
step 78.5
stepfather 77.0
stepmother 76.1
stew 59.4
steward 58.9
stick 55.6
stiff 57.6
stilts 63.3
stink 58.1
stockholder 50.2
stocking 77.0
stomach 86.2

stone 74.4
stop 71.0
store 82.4
storekeeper 69.8
storm 80.9
stormy 72.1
story 69.8
stove 86.6
strangeness 62.2
straw 70.1
strawberry 90.9
stream 67.0
street 92.0
strike 55.6
stroke 55.6
strong 74.8
student 72.2
studio 67.3
study 81.4
style 54.9
submarine 54.1
subtract 66.6
subtraction 60.5
subway 77.3
such 55.6
sudden 58.4
suffer 51.7
suffix 52.4
suit 77.7
suitcase 67.6
sum 53.8
summer 69.0
sun 66.6
Sunday 78.5
sundown 65.6
sunflower 82.4
sunless 61.0
sunlight 80.6
sunny 73.8
sunset 70.1
sunshine 81.8
sunshiny 85.8
superintendent 62.4

supermarket 71.6
supervisor 59.7
supper 72.2
support 67.3
sure 61.6
surely 62.2
surprise 61.6
swamp 75.2
sweater 77.4
sweep 70.6
sweeper 78.5
sweeten 61.8
sweetheart 81.4
swim 94.0
swing 71.7
sword 56.9
syllable 70.1
syrup 52.5

table 89.7
tablecloth 74.8
tablespoon 83.3
tablet 66.1
tableware 72.8
tack 54.0
take 58.9
talk 70.4
talker 77.0
tall 77.0
tan 75.7
tang 53.3
tape 59.6
tasteless 68.9
tasty 62.1
tax 77.7
taxation 64.6
taxi 68.1
tea 83.7
teach 67.3
teacher 95.2
team 87.2
teamwork 53.7
tease 64.5

teaspoon 65.2
teens 79.7
telegram 55.6
telegraph 52.2
telephone 86.5
telescope 65.4
tell 85.7
temperature 56.4
ten 76.0
tender 52.6
tennis 80.6
tent 62.4
terrible 55.6
test 58.4
testament 68.2
testimony 56.2
textbook 68.2
thank 59.7
thankful 50.5
thankfulness 62.2
thankless 63.6
theater 65.6
their 73.3
there 88.5
thereby 56.2
thermometer 69.8
thief 58.2
thieve 50.0
thin 86.0
think 76.5
thinker 56.2
third 79.4
thirst 69.7
thirsty 65.6
thirty 64.1
thoughtful 61.6
thoughfulness 52.2
thousand 86.2
three 78.1
thrill 52.2
throat 86.2
throw 51.4
thumb 85.8

thunder 53.2
thunderbolt 61.8
thundercloud 64.2
thunderous 59.6
Thursday 97.6
thy 54.0
ticket 67.2
tiger 88.0
tight 52.9
time 65.0
timepiece 68.1
tiny 68.4
tissue 54.2
title (name) 78.1
title (privilege) 57.8
toast 90.0
toaster 60.6
tobacco 79.0
today 82.6
toe 83.8
toilet 82.8
tomato 79.3
tomorrow 88.2
ton 62.2
tongue 62.4
tonight 67.3
too 56.4
toothache 82.1
toothpick 67.6
tornado 69.6
touch 61.0
tourist 52.5
towel 76.6
town 50.5
township 59.2
toy 83.0
track 53.6
tractor 60.0
trade 57.7
trader 52.2
trail 51.2
trailer 78.6
train 90.9

trainer 51.2
training 50.9
traveler 59.7
treasure 74.1
treasurer 53.8
tree 90.6
triangle 54.0
trip 68.4
troop 61.6
trophy 54.1
trouble 73.3
truck 68.1
true 69.8
truly 66.6
truthful 55.6
tub 52.0
Tuesday 87.8
tuna 77.7
turkey 70.9
turn 72.5
turtle 83.8
twelve 88.2
twenty 80.9
twice 71.7
twin 81.8
twinkle 50.0
twirl 66.0
two 84.4
type 76.1
typewriter 69.0
typist 64.6

ugly 78.1
umbrella 81.8
unashamed 82.1
unbecoming 67.6
unborn 72.6
uncle 80.9
unclean 77.7
uncover 54.1
under 76.1
underground 76.0
underline 61.8

undersell 54.9
understand 62.8
undone 76.1
undress 58.8
unemployed 60.0
unequal 55.6
unfailing 56.2
unfair 55.6
unfit 61.8
unfold 62.2
unfriendly 77.0
ungrateful 62.2
unguarded 56.8
unhappiness 67.2
unhappy 90.0
unharmed 56.8
unhealthful 74.1
unhealthy 71.8
unheard 74.1
unhurt 74.1
uniform 64.1
unimportant 50.0
unkind 62.8
unkindness 52.2
unlawful 67.3
unlearned 73.7
unlike 54.9
unlikely 58.6
unlock 76.5
unlovely 64.1
unlucky 67.7
unnamed 76.1
unnatural 50.0
unopened 72.0
unpaid 55.6
unpleasant 66.4
unreal 79.4
unsatisfactory 63.8
unsuccessful 72.1
unsuspected 51.0
unsuspecting 52.2
untaught 67.7
until 61.6

unto 51.7
untrained 56.4
untroubled 50.0
untrue 77.2
unwelcome 61.6
unwilling 70.0
up 64.9
upholster 50.9
upland 70.1
upon 69.4
upper 69.3
uppermost 56.8
uproar 56.2
upside 84.1
upstairs 88.5
upward 59.8
us 86.0
useless 64.4

vacation 52.5
valentine 65.6
vegetable 92.8
verb 56.9
very 90.0
village 60.8
vinegar 65.7
violinist 54.0
visit 90.0
visitor 64.2
vitamin 65.2
vocabulary 69.3
voice 56.4
volt 51.3
vote 73.7
voter 69.8
voyage 50.5

wagon 70.1
waist 63.0
wait 91.3
waitress 60.5
wake 82.4
wakeful 64.6

waken 69.8
walk 90.0
walker 74.1
wall 74.1
wallet 70.1
walnut 59.7
want 68.6
warehouse 57.8
warfare 62.4
warm 79.8
warmth 72.5
warn 54.9
warning 62.6
wash 91.2
washbowl 70.4
washer 82.4
washing 85.4
washroom 73.3
wasp 66.0
waste 60.2
wasteful 55.6
watch 88.2
watchdog 66.0
watchman 55.6
watchtower 66.6
waterfall 69.6
waterway 86.8
waterworks 65.6
watery 66.6
wave 67.2
way 62.5
wayside 68.9
we 66.0
weak 87.4
weaken 61.8
wear 57.8
web 52.1
wed 55.6
Wednesday 98.1
weed 74.4
week 85.4
weekend 94.9
weekly 69.6

weep 57.3
weigh 87.4
weight 78.4
weighty 87.4
west 64.1
western 55.6
wet 81.3
whale 74.6
whalebone 66.1
whaler 53.3
wheat 70.4
wheel 74.6
when 76.6
where 77.4
whereabouts 52.2
wherever 68.1
which 54.8
while 65.4
whirlpool 60.6
whirlwind 79.0
white 83.0
who 83.0
whoever 73.8
whole 54.4
whom 78.2
whose 85.2
why 65.6
wide 62.2
wildcat 80.6
wildfire 52.2
will 59.2
willing 50.9
wind 91.7
windmill 76.0
window 76.1
windowpane 59.7
windy 80.1
wine 64.6
wing 78.5
wink 51.4
winner 80.1
winter 88.2
wipe 57.1

wire 67.3
wireless 57.6
wish 75.6
witch 80.9
witchcraft 52.4
within 63.3
without 74.2
wizard 66.6
wolf 86.6
woman 85.3
womanhood 57.7
womanly 66.6
wonderful 62.4
wood 71.8
woodchuck 62.2
woodcraft 65.7
woodcutter 85.2
wooded 70.4
wooden 50.0
woodland 92.9
woodpecker 82.9
woodsman 55.6
woodwork 87.4
woody 84.9
wool 56.4
woolen 71.0
woolly 55.6
workman 65.6
workmanship 63.3
workroom 82.2
workshop 59.7
world 73.3
worm 82.4
worth 52.4
wrapper 60.0
wreck 57.7
wrestle 53.0
wrestler 51.4
write 83.3
writer 55.6
wrong 76.4

yard 53.8

yarn 54.8	yolk 68.2	zebra 82.2
year 93.0	you 64.0	zero 78.8
yell 58.1	young 81.8	zoo 90.8
yellow 100.0	youngster 71.8	
yesterday 89.8	youth 71.4	

V
Words by Part of Speech and Earliest Age Known

All words are arranged according to the following parts of speech: nouns (N), verbs (V), adjectives (J), adverbs (D), interjections (I), conjunctions (C), function nouns (FN), noun determiners (ND), pronouns (R), and prepositions (P). For each part of speech the words are presented alphabetically, and are followed by the earliest age at which the words are known. For convenience, only the first age of each two-year age group is listed: 8, 10, 12, 14, and 16 years.

NOUNS

a
abbreviation 16
account 16
acorn 16
acre 16
act (of a show) 14
activity 14
actor 14
addition 16
address 12
adventure 16
age 16
agreement 16
aid 14
air 14
aircraft 14
airplane 10
airport 12
airway 16
alcohol 16
alligator 12
alphabet 14

America 12
American 12
amount 16
angel 14
animal 14
ant 12
apartment 14
ape 14
apple 10
approval 16
April 12
apron 14
arctic 16
arithmetic 12
arm 12
army 12
arrangement 16
arrow 16
art 16
artist 14
aspirin 16

astronomy 16
athletics 16
atlas 16
atmosphere 16
attendance 16
aunt 12
author 14
auto 14
autograph 12
autumn 16
avenue 14
award 14
ax 14

b
babe 12
baboon 16
baby 12
babyhood 16
back 16
bacon 12
bacteria 16

bag 12
baggage 14
baker 12
bakery 12
ball 12
ballet 16
balloon 10
ballroom 16
banana 10
bank (for money) 10
bank (of a river) 12
bankbook 14
banker 12
baptism 14
barber 12
barn 12
barometer 16
base 16
baseball 10
basement 14
basketball 10
bat (stick) 14
bath 12
bathroom 12
batter (mix) 16
battery 14
battlefield 16
bay 14
beach 16
beak 16
bean 12
bear 10
beard 14
beauty 16
beaver 14
bed 16
bedclothes 16
bedroom 12
bee 14
beef 12
beefsteak 12
beehive 16
beer 12
beet 14

beetle 14
beginner 14
bell 14
belt 12
bench 14
berry 12
bib 16
Bible 12
bigness 14
bill (charges) 16
billboard 16
billion 12
biography 16
bird 10
birthday 12
birthplace 14
blackberry 12
blackbird 14
blackness 14
blacksmith 12
blade 16
blanket 14
blessing 16
blindness 16
blizzard 14
blockhouse 16
bloodhound 16
bloom 14
blossom 14
blouse 10
blueberry 12
bluebird 12
bluejay 12
board 14
boardinghouse 14
boat 10
bobcat 14
body 12
bomb 14
bomber 16
bonfire 16
book 12
bookkeeper 16
bookrack 12

bookseller 14
bookshelf 14
boot 10
boss 14
bottle 12
bottom 14
boundary 16
bouquet 14
bowl 12
bowling 12
box 12
boxer (fighter) 16
boy 12
brain 16
branch (tree) 14
bravery 16
bread 10
breakfast 14
breast 16
breath 14
breeze 14
brick 14
bride 16
bridegroom 16
bridge 14
brightness 12
brilliance 16
brook 16
broom 12
broomstick 16
brownie (cake) 10
brush 16
bucket 16
buckshot 14
buckskin 12
buffalo 16
bug 14
bugle 16
builder 16
building 12
bull 12
bullet 16
bulletin 16
bum 16

bump 16
bumper 16
bundle 16
bunny 8
burro 16
bus 14
business 14
butter 14
butterfly 14
buyer 14

C cab 14
cabbage 12
cabin 12
cactus 16
cafe 14
cage 16
calendar 14
calf 12
camel 10
camera 12
camp 12
campus 14
canal 14
cancer 16
candle 14
candlestick 14
candy 12
cane 16
canoe 14
canyon 16
cap 8
capital 14
captain 12
car 14
card 12
cardboard 14
cardinal 16
career 16
cargo 14
carpenter 16
carrot 12
cart 16
cartoon 16

cartoonist 16
case (box) 16
cash 14
cashier 14
castle 16
cat 10
catcher (player) 16
catfish 12
cattle 12
cauliflower 16
caution 14
cavern 12
celery 12
cemetery 16
cent 12
center 14
century 16
cereal 14
ceremony 16
chair 14
champion 14
championship 14
change (money) 12
chapter 14
checkers 16
cheek 16
cheese 10
chemistry 16
cherry 10
chest 14
chick 16
chickadee 14
chicken 12
chieftain 16
child 10
chin 16
chip 16
chipmunk 12
chocolate 12
choir 16
chorus 16
church 12
churchman 14
churchyard 14

cigar 14
cigarette 14
cinnamon 16
circle 12
circulation 16
circus 12
city 12
civics 16
class 14
classmate 14
classroom 10
clerk 16
clippers 16
clock 8
closet 14
cloth 14
clothes 12
cloud 12
cloudburst 14
clown 12
club 14
clubhouse 16
coachman 16
coal 16
coast 16
coat 12
cocoa 12
coconut 12
coffee 12
coin 12
collar 14
collection 16
college 12
collie 14
colony 16
colt 14
column 16
comb 10
combat 12
comeback 14
comma 14
commandment 16
commissioner 16
communism 16

community 14
company 16
compass 16
condemnation 16
congress 14
constitution 16
contentment 16
cookie 12
cooler (appliance) 16
cooperation 16
copper 14
corn 14
corner 16
cornstarch 16
cost 12
costume 14
cottonwood 14
country 14
courthouse 14
cousin 12
cow 10
cowboy 14
cowhide 14
crab 14
cracker 10
cradle 16
craft 16
craftsman 16
cranberry 14
crayfish 12
crayon 12
cream 10
credit 16
crop 16
crossroads 16
crossword 14
crow 12
crowd 16
crown 16
cub 14
cuckoo 14
cup 12
cupful 16
customer 16

cutter 16
cutworm 14

d daddy 10
daisy 16
dam 14
damage 14
dancer 14
danger 16
darkness 12
darling 14
date 16
daughter 12
day 12
daylight 12
deafness 14
dear 14
death 14
December 10
deer 12
defiance 16
degree 14
delight 16
democracy 16
dentist 10
desk 10
destroyer (ship) 16
detour 16
diamond 16
dictionary 12
diet 14
difference 16
dime 12
diner (person) 16
diner (place) 14
dinner 12
dinosaur 16
directory 16
dirt 12
disappointment 14
disease 16
dish 12
disrespect 16
distance 16

dividend 14
dog 12
doll 10
dollar 12
donkey 12
door 10
doorknob 16
doorstep 16
doorway 12
dormitory 14
dot 16
doughnut 14
dove 14
downfull 14
dozen 14
dragonfly 14
drawing 10
dream 14
dresser 16
dressmaker 14
drinker 16
driver 12
driveway 12
drummer 14
drunkard 14
drunkenness 14
dryer 16
duck 10
dunce 14
dust 16
duty 16
dynamite 16

e eagle 10
ear 12
earth 12
earthquake 14
earthworm 14
east 14
education 16
eel 16
eight 10
eighteen 10
eighty 14

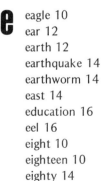

elbow 14
elector 16
electrician 14
elephant 10
elevator 14
eleven 12
emergency 16
employee 16
employer 16
employment 16
end 14
encouragement 16
engagement 16
engine 14
engineer 14
English 14
enjoyment 14
equator 16
error 16
eruption 16
establishment 16
evening 14
event 16
evergreen 14
examination 16
example 16
exit 14
experience 16
expert 16
expedition 16
explanation 16
explorer 16
explosion 16
eye 12
eyebrow 14
eyelash 16
eyesight 14

f

face 12
fact 16
faintness 16
fairy 16
faith 14
family 12

farm 14
farmer 10
farmhouse 14
father 12
fatherland 16
fault 16
favor 16
fawn 16
February 10
feeling 16
female 14
fence 16
fiddler 16
field 12
fifteen 8
fifty 12
fighter (soldier) 14
finger 12
finish 14
fire 12
firearm 16
firewood 14
fireworks 14
firing (shooting) 16
fish 12
fishery 16
five 10
flash 12
flashlight 12
flavor 16
flea 14
flier 16
floor 14
florist 16
flour 14
flower 12
fluid 14
foam 16
fog 14
foil 16
food 12
fool 16
foolishness 14
foot 12

football 10
footlights 16
footstool 16
footwear 12
forehead 12
foreleg 14
forenoon 16
forepaw 14
forest 12
forgiveness 16
fork (road) 14
forty 12
four 12
fourteen 12
fox 10
freedom 16
freezer 12
French 16
freshman 16
freshness 16
Friday 10
friend 14
fright 16
frog 12
frost 14
fruit 14
fudge 14
fuel 14
fun 10
fund 16
funeral 14
fur 12
furnish 16
furnishings 14
future 16

g

gallon 14
game 12
gang 16
gangster 16
garage 12
garbage 16
garden 10
gardener 14

gardenia 14
gas 14
gate 12
gentleness 14
geography 14
gift 12
gingerbread 14
giraffe 12
girl 12
gladness 16
globe 14
glory 16
glove 12
glue 12
goat 12
godmother 12
goldfish 12
goldsmith 16
golf 12
goodness 16
goodwill 16
goose 12
goose (silly person) 16
gorilla 16
government 14
governor 14
grade 12
grandchild 14
grandfather 12
grandpa 12
grandparent 10
grape 12
grapefruit 12
grass 12
grasshopper 14
grave 14
gravel 16
gravity 14
gravy 16
greatness 16
greenhouse 12
greeting 14
greyhound 16
grocer 14

grocery 12
ground 14
group 14
guardian 16
gulf 14
gunner 14
gunpowder 16
guy 16
gymnasium 12
gymnastics 14

h hail 16
hailstone 16
hair 12
hairdresser 12
hallway 16
ham 12
hamburger 12
hammer 12
hand 14
handbag 14
handkerchief 14
hanging 16
hangman 14
happiness 14
hat 12
hawk 14
hay 12
hayfield 14
haystack 14
head 14
headache 14
headdress 16
headlight 14
headwater 14
health 14
hearer 12
hearing 12
heart 12
heater 14
heaven 14
heaviness 16
heel 14
height 14

hell 16
hemisphere 16
hen 12
henhouse 12
hero 14
highland 14
highroad 14
highway 12
hill 16
hip 16
hippopotamus 14
historian 14
hive 16
hobby 16
hockey 16
hog 14
hole 14
holiday 14
home 12
homemaker 14
honesty 14
hook 16
hoopskirt 14
horror 16
horse 10
horsehair 14
horseman 14
horseshoe 14
hose (pipe) 16
hospital 10
hotel 14
hour 14
house 10
household 14
housekeeper 14
housekeeping 12
housetop 12
housewife 14
hummingbird 14
hundred 12
hunter 14
huntsman 14
hurricane 16
husband 14

i
iceberg 16
icebox 14
idea 14
illness 12
illustrator 16
improvement 14
inch 14
independence 16
index 14
industry 16
infection 14
inn 14
insect 12
iodine 16
iron 14
isle 14

j
jacket 12
jacks 14
jail 16
January 10
jar 14
jaw 16
jay 14
jean (cloth) 16
jelly 10
jellyfish 10
jet 12
jeweler 14
jigsaw 14
job 12
jockey 16
joke 12
joker 14
journey 16
joy 16
judgment 16
juice 10
July 10
June 12
jury 16

k
kangaroo 12
keeper 14

kerchief 16
key 14
kid 14
killer 16
kindness 14
kitchen 12
kite 10
kitten 10
kitty 12
knife 14
knight 16
knothole 16
knowledge 14

l
ladder 16
lady 14
ladybug 14
lake 12
lamb 10
lamp 12
land 14
landing 16
landowner 16
lane 16
language 14
laugh 12
laughter 14
laundress 16
laundry 14
law 12
leader 16
leather 14
lemon 12
lemonade 12
length 14
lesson 16
letter 12
lettuce 14
liar 16
liberty 14
library 12
lice 16
license 16
lid 16

lie 14
life 14
lifetime 16
light 10
lighthouse 16
lightning 12
lime (fruit) 14
lime 16
limestone 16
limit 16
line 16
lion 12
lip 14
lipstick 16
list 14
liver 16
lizard 14
lobster 16
locker 12
log 12
longitude 14
lookout 12
lord 16
loser 14
loss 16
lotion 16
love 16
loveliness 14
lover 12
luggage 16
lumber 14
lumberman 14
lunch 14
lung 14

m
machine 14
machinist 16
madman 14
magazine (holder) 16
magnet 16
maid 16
mail 10
mailbox 8
mailman 12
maker 16

male 14
mama 10
mammal 12
man 14
manager 14
map 14
maple 14
marble 16
March 12
mark 14
marriage 14
marshmallow 16
mask 14
material 16
mathematics 14
May 12
mayor 16
maypole 16
meal 12
meal (grain) 16
measles 16
meat 12
medicine 14
melon 14
member 16
membership 16
memory 16
menu 16
mess 16
messenger 16
meter (instr.) 16
midday 16
middle 14
mildness 16
mile 16
milk 10
mill 14
miller 16
million 12
mind 16
miner 14
mineral 16
minute 12
mirror 12

mischief 16
misfortune 16
miss 12
mistake 14
mitten 12
moisture 16
mole 16
mommy 8
Monday 10
money 14
monkey 10
monster 16
month 12
moose 10
morning 12
mosquito 16
moss 16
moth 14
mother 14
motor 16
motorcar 12
motorist 16
mountain 12
mouse 10
mouth 14
mouthpiece 16
movie 12
mud 16
mulberry 16
mule 16
mummy (body) 16
museum 16
music 14
muskrat 12
mustache 16
mustard 14
mystery 14

n nail 14
name 12
nap 16
napkin 16
nation 12
naturalist 16

neck 14
necklace 16
needle 14
needlework 16
Negro 14
neighbor 14
nephew 16
nervousness 16
nest 12
net 16
network 16
news 16
newsreel 16
nickel (coin) 12
nickname 16
niece 14
night 12
nightcap 14
nightfall 14
nightmare 16
nine 12
nineteen 12
ninety 12
noise 12
nomination 16
noon 10
north 14
nose 12
note 14
notebook 16
November 10
number 16
nurse 10
nursery 10
nut 14

o oak 14
oatmeal 12
oats 16
object 16
ocean 12
October 12
octopus 14
offering 16

office 12
officer 14
one 16
onion 12
opening 16
operation (function) 16
operation (surgery) 16
orange 10
organization 16
oriole 16
ounce 16
outlaw 16
oven 14
overcoat 14
overflow 16
overshoe 12
overtime 16
overwork 16
owl 10
owner 16
ox 16
oxygen 16
oyster 14

p page (book) 10
pail 14
paint 12
painting 14
pair 16
pajamas 14
pal 14
palm 16
pan 12
pancake 10
papa 14
papoose 16
paragraph 14
parent 12
park 16
parrot 12
part 14
party 12
path 16
patrolman 16

paw 14
payment 14
pea 12
peace 14
peach 12
peanut 12
pear 10
pecan 14
pencil 12
penny 12
people 12
perfection 16
perfume 16
period 14
permit 16
person 14
pet 10
phonograph 14
photo 14
photograph 16
photographer 16
pickle 14
picnic 14
picture 10
piece 14
pig 10
pigeon 16
pigtail 16
pile 16
pill 12
pillow 14
pin 14
pine 14
pineapple 12
pint 16
pioneer 16
plain 16
plan 16
plane (air) 12
plant 14
plantation 16
planter 14
plate 14
play (fun) 12

playground 10
playhouse 16
playmate 14
plaything 10
pleasure 16
plowman 16
plum 12
plumber 16
pocket 12
pocketbook 14
poetry 16
point 14
police 16
policeman 10
politician 16
pond 12
pony 10
poodle 16
pool 10
pool (game) 16
poorhouse 14
popcorn 12
pork 12
port (harbor) 16
postage 14
postcard 14
postman 12
postmaster 14
postscript 14
pot 16
potato 10
pound 14
practice 16
preacher 16
presidency 16
president 14
press (newspapers) 16
pressure 16
priest 16
prince 14
princess 14
print 14
printer 16
prison 16

prisoner 16
prize 16
problem 14
process 16
progress 16
protection 16
prune 16
publisher 16
pump 16
pumpkin 14
puppy 10
purse 14
pussy 14

q quart 16
quarter 16
quarterback 16
queen 12
question 12
quickness 14
quicksand 16

r rabbit 10
raccoon 14
racer 12
rag 16
railroad 12
railway 10
rain 10
rainbow 12
rainfall 16
raisin 14
ranch 12
rancher 12
raspberry 14
rat 12
ray 16
relationship 16
relative 16
reminder 16
rent 14
replacement 16
report 14
reporter 14

restaurant 16
restlessness 16
rheumatism 16
rib 14
rice 12
rider 14
ring 14
risk 16
river 12
road 12
roadway 10
robbery 16
robin 10
robot 16
rodeo 16
romance 16
roof 14
roofing 14
roommate 14
rooster 12
root 12
rope 16
rose 12
route 14
row 16
rower 16
rug 12
rye 16

s sack 16
saddle 14
sadness 16
safety 16
sail 16
sailboat 12
sailor 12
saint 16
salad 10
sale 12
salesman 14
salesmanship 16
saleswoman 14
salmon 16
sand 14

sandwich 12
Saturday 14
saucepan 16
sausage 14
saver 14
savings 16
savior 16
saw 14
sawdust 16
sawmill 16
scale 14
scholar 16
schoolboy 12
schoolhouse 12
schoolmaster 10
schoolroom 14
science 16
scientist 14
scissors 14
scrapbook 14
screw 16
sea 10
seal (animal) 12
seaman 14
seaplane 14
searchlight 16
seashore 14
seaside 14
season 14
seat 16
seaweed 16
secrecy 16
secret 16
seed 12
seedling 14
self 16
seller 14
semicircle 16
sense 16
sentence 14
September 12
seriousness 14
service 16
set 16

settler 14
seven 12
seventy 14
sewing 12
sex 14
shade 16
shadow 12
shark 16
sheep 12
sheet 14
shellac 16
shellfish 14
shepherd 14
sheriff 14
ship 12
shipyard 14
shoe 10
shoemaker 14
shop 14
shopkeeper 14
shopper 14
shopping 14
shoreline 16
shoulder 16
shovel 14
shower (rain) 14
showman 16
shrimp 14
shyness 16
sickness 14
side 16
signal 14
signature 16
silence 16
silk 14
silkworm 14
silver 14
silverware 14
sin 14
singer 16
sink 14
sister 12
six 10
sixpence 14

sixteen 14
sixty 16
size 16
skeleton 16
skin 14
skirt 10
skunk 12
sky 12
skyscraper 16
slacks 16
slave 16
sleep 14
sleeper 16
sleepwalker 14
sleigh 14
slipper 14
smallpox 16
smog 16
smoker 16
smokestack 14
snail 12
snow 12
snowbank 14
snowflake 14
soapsuds 14
society (people) 16
society (community) 16
soil 16
soldier 12
son 12
song 12
songster 14
sonny 16
soreness 16
sorrow 16
sound 14
soup 10
south 12
souvenir 16
spaghetti 16
sparrow 16
speaker 14
speech 14
spendthrift 14

spider 12
spinach 16
spokesman 16
spoon 12
sport 12
sportsman 16
spot 16
spotlight 14
springtime 12
spy 14
spyglass 16
square 16
squirrel 12
stair 16
statesman 16
station 16
steak 14
steamship 14
stem (plant) 16
stepfather 12
stepmother 14
steward 16
stick 12
stilts 14
stockholder 14
stocking 14
stomach 14
stone 12
store 10
storekeeper 16
storm 12
story 16
stove 14
strangeness 16
straw 16
strawberry 10
stream 14
street 12
stroke 14
student 14
studio 14
style 16
submarine 16
subtraction 14

subway 14
suffix 16
suit 12
suitcase 16
sum 16
summer 12
sun 14
Sunday 10
sundown 14
sunflower 10
sunlight 14
sunset 16
sunshine 12
superintendent 16
supermarket 14
supervisor 14
supper 14
swamp 14
sweater 14
sweeper 14
sweetheart 12
sword 16
syllable 16
syrup 14

t table 12
tablecloth 12
tablespoon 14
tablet 16
tableware 14
tack 16
tag 14
talker 14
tang 16
tape 14
taxation 14
taxi 14
tea 12
teacher 10
team 14
teamwork 16
teaspoon 12
teens 14
telegram 16

telescope 16
temperature 16
temptation 14
ten 12
tennis 14
tent 14
testament 16
testimony 16
textbook 16
thankfulness 16
theater 16
thermometer 14
thief 16
thinker 14
thirst 14
thirty 14
thought 14
thoughtfulness 16
thousand 12
three 12
thrill 16
throat 14
thumb 12
thunder 16
thunderbolt 14
thundercloud 12
Thursday 12
ticket 14
tiger 12
time 16
timepiece 16
tissue 16
title (name) 14
title (privilege) 16
toast 14
toaster 14
tobacco 14
today 12
toe 12
toilet 14
tomato 14
tomorrow 12
ton 14
tongue 14

tonight 14
toothache 14
toothpick 16
tornado 14
tourist 16
towel 12
town 16
township 16
toy 12
track 14
tractor 14
trader 16
trailer 14
train 12
trainer 16
training 16
trash 14
traveler 14
treasure 16
treasurer 16
tree 12
triangle 16
trip 14
troop 14
trophy 16
truck 12
tub 14
Tuesday 10
tuna 16
turkey 12
turtle 12
twelve 12
twenty 10
twin 12
two 10
typewriter 14
typist 16

u umbrella 14
uncle 12
unhappiness 14
uniform 16
unkindness 16
upland 16

uproar 16
upside 12

V vacation 16
valentine 12
vegetable 12
verb 16
village 14
vinegar 16
violet 14
violinist 16
visitor 14
vitamin 14
vocabulary 14
voice 14
volt 16
vote 14
voter 14
voyage 16

W wagon 16
waist 16
waitress 16
walker 12
wall 12
wallet 16
walnut 16
warehouse 14
warfare 16
warmth 14
warning 14
washbowl 14
washer 14
washing 12
washroom 12
wasp 16

watchdog 16
watchman 16
watchtower 14
waterfall 14
waterway 12
waterworks 16
wave 14
way 14
wayside 14
web 14
Wednesday 10
weed 14
week 12
weekend 10
weight 14
west 16
whale 14
whalebone 16
whaler 16
wheat 14
wheel 14
while 16
whirlpool 14
whirlwind 14
wildcat 12
wildfire 16
wind 8
windmill 14
window 12
windowpane 16
wine 16
wing 12
winner 14
winter 12
wire 14
wireless 16

witch 12
witchcraft 14
wizard 16
wolf 12
woman 12
womanhood 14
wood 14
woodchuck 14
woodcraft 14
woodcutter 12
woodland 10
woodpecker 12
woodsman 14
woodwork 10
wool 12
workman 14
workmanship 16
workroom 12
workshop 16
world 14
worm 12
worth 16
wrapper 16
wrestler 14
writer 16

Y yard 12
yarn 16
year 12
yolk 16
youngster 14
youth 14

Z zebra 10
zero 14
zoo 12

VERBS

a ache 16
add 14
adopt 16

agree 14
alarm 16
amaze 14

answer 14
arrive 16
ask 12

b

bake 12
balance 16
bathe 14
beat 14
beautify 14
become 14
begin 14
begone 16
behave 16
believe 14
bite 16
bleed 12
bless 14
blindfold 14
blow 12
blowout 16
boating 12
boil 14
bother 16
brake 14
breathe 14
brighten 14
bring 12
bud 14
build 14
burn 12
buy 14

c

call 14
care 16
catch 14
cause 16
change 14
chase 16
check 16
chew 14
choose 16
chop 16
cleanse 14
climb 12
clothe 10
color 10
come 14
commission 16

complain 16
contact 16
cook 10
correct 14
count 14
crawl 14
crow 16
cram 16
crush 14
cry 16
curl 12
curve 16
cut 14

d

dampen 14
dance 12
darken 16
daydream 14
deaden 16
deafen 14
deal 16
decide 16
describe 16
destroy 16
die 12
dig 14
disappoint 16
disinfect 16
dislike 16
disobey 16
divide 16
do 16
double 16
draw 12
dress 12
drink 16
drip 14
drive 14
drown 14
dump 16

e

earn 16
eat 10
enclose 16

enjoy 16
enlarge 14
enter 16
erase 16
exchange 16
excuse 16
expand 16
explore 16

f

fall 14
fan 12
fear 16
feed 14
feel 14
fight 12
finish 14
fit 16
flatten 16
flirt 16
float 16
flood 14
fly 12
forget 14
freeze 14
frighten 12
fry 16

g

give 14
go 12
grab 16
graduate 14
graze 16
grow 12
guard 16
guess 16

h

handle 14
happen 16
hate 14
have 16
hear 12
help 16
hike 16
hop 10

hope 14
hug 16
hurry 14
hurt 16

i
improve 16
infect 16
invent 16

j
join 16
joking 12
judge 16
jump 14
justify 16

k
keep 12
kill 16
kiss 14
knit 16
knock 16
knot 14
know 12

l
labor 16
lead 14
learn 14
leave 14
let (allow) 16
lick 16
lighten 14
listen 12
live 14
look 8
lose 14

m
make 16
march 14
market 16
marry 16
means 16
measure 14
meet 14
mend 16
misunderstand 14

mix 16
motor 14
move 14
multiply 16
must 16

n
need 16
notice 16

o
obey 14
order (command) 16
order (arrange) 14
ought 14
outnumber 16
outrun 12
overeat 16
overjoy 14
overlook 12
overpower 14
overspread 14
overturn 16
owe 16
own 14

p
pain 16
parade 12
pass 14
paste 14
pay 12
phone 12
pick 14
pitch 16
plate 16
please 14
pledge 14
polish 14
pour 14
pray 10
preserve 14
prevent 16
prove 16
push 12
put 16

q
quit 14

r
race 12
raise 14
read 14
realize 16
receive 16
refresh 16
refuse 16
regret 16
reheat 16
rejoin 16
remember 16
remind 16
remove 16
repair 16
repeat 16
reprint 16
rest 12
retire 16
return 14
review 14
ride 14
rise 16
roar 14
rub 14
rule 16
run 16
rush 14

s
sadden 16
safeguard 16
sample 16
save 14
say 14
scare 16
scold 16
score 14
scratch 16
scream 14
see 8
seek 16
seesaw 14
sell 14

send 16
separate 16
sew 14
shake 14
shampoo 12
shave 16
shine 12
shoot 16
shout 14
show 14
shower (bathe) 12
shut 14
sicken 14
sing 12
sit 14
skate 12
ski 12
skip 14
slap 16
slip 14
slop 14
smell 16
smile 14
smoke 12
sniff 16
soak 14
soften 16
spank 16
speak 14
spell 14
spend 14
spin 16
splash 16
spoil 16
spray 14
spring 12
sprinkle 16
squeeze 14
stamp 16
start 14

starve 14
stay 14
steal 16
steer 14
step 14
stew 14
stink 16
stop 14
strike 16
study 12
subtract 14
suffer 16
support 16
surprise 16
sweep 14
sweeten 16
swim 10
swing 16

t take 14
talk 14
tax 14
teach 16
tease 16
telegraph 16
telephone 12
tell 12
test 16
thank 14
thieve 16
think 14
throw 16
touch 14
trade 14
trail 16
trouble 14
try 14
turn 14
twinkle 16
twirl 16

type 12

u uncover 14
underline 16
undersell 16
understand 16
undress 14
unfold 16
unlock 14
unpack 14
upholster 16
use 14

v visit 12

w wait 12
wake 12
waken 16
walk 10
want 14
warn 16
wash 10
waste 16
watch 10
weaken 16
wear 14
wed 16
weep 16
weigh 14
will 16
wink 14
wipe 16
wish 14
worry 14
wrap 14
wreck 16
wrestle 16
write 10

y yell 16

ADJECTIVES

a
accidental 16
additional 16
adult 14
afire 14
afraid 10
aged 14
ago 14
airy 14
alive 16
allowable 14
alphabetical 14
angry 12
athletic 14
awake 14
away 14
awful 12

b
bad 8
bald 16
beaten 16
beautiful 10
best 12
better 12
big 12
bigger 12
black 10
blank 16
blind 14
blond 14
bloodshot 12
blue 8
boyish 16
breakable 16
breathless 14
breezy 14
bright 12
broke 16
brotherly 14
brown 8
bushy 14
busy 12

c
calm 14
capital 14
careless 16
charming 16
cheap 16
cheerful 16
circulatory 16
civil 14
clean 16
clear 12
cloudless 14
cloudy 14
coastal 16
cold 12
colored 12
colorful 14
comfortable 14
complete 16
constitutional 16
crazy 14
creamy 14
cute 12

d
daily 14
dangerous 14
dark 12
dead 12
deadly 14
deaf 12
different 14
dirty 12
disobedient 16
dizzy 16
downhearted 16
dry 12
due 16
dull 16

e
earthly 16
eastern 16
easy 12
educational 16

eighth 12
electric 14
electrical 12
else 16
empty 16
enjoyable 16
enthusiastic 14
even 16
everyday 16
evil 14

f
false 12
famous 16
far 12
faraway 12
farther 16
fast 14
fat 12
fatherly 12
favorite 14
fearful 16
fifth 12
final 16
fireproof 12
first 16
flat 14
flowery 16
foggy 16
foolish 14
forbidden 16
fourth 12
fresh 16
friendless 16
friendly 12
front 16
frosty 14
frozen 14
full 12
furry 16
fuzzy 16

g
gay 16

gentle 16
giant 14
girlish 12
glad 14
godlike 16
golden 14
good 14
gracious 16
grassy 14
gray 8
grayheaded 14
great 16
green 8

h
hairy 14
handsome 12
happy 14
hard 14
hardy 12
harmful 14
hateful 14
headstrong 16
healthy 16
heartbroken 16
heavy 14
high 14
hilly 16
homeless 16
homelike 14
homesick 12
honest 16
hopeless 16
hot 10
human 14
hungry 12
hurried 16

i
iced 12
icy 12
ill 12
imaginable 14
imaginary 16
imaginative 16
incorrect 16

indoor 12
industrious 14
instructive 16
intelligent 16
interesting 16
ivory 16

j
jittery 16
joyful 14
joyless 16
joyous 16
junior 14

k
kind 14
kindly 16

l
large 10
last 12
late 14
lazy 12
less 16
lifeless 16
lifelike 16
little 12
lonely 16
lonesome 16
long 16
loose 16
loud 14
lovely 12
low 12
lukewarm 14

m
mad 12
manly 14
marvelous 16
mathematical 12
mean 14
merry 12
mighty 16
milky 12
mistaken 14
moist 14
more 16

mossy 16
motherless 16
motherly 14
muddy 12
murderous 16
muscular 16

n
nameless 14
narrow 16
natural 16
naughty 16
nearby 14
neat 16
needless 16
neighboring 16
neighborly 16
nervous 16
new 16
newborn 12
next 16
nice 12
noiseless 16
noisy 12
normal 16

o
oaken 12
obliging 16
odd 16
old 12
open 14
opposite 14
other 16
outer 14
outermost 16
overweight 16

p
painful 16
paralyzed 16
past 14
perfect 16
physical 14
pink 12
plain 16
plastic 14

playful 12
pleasant 16
pleasurable 14
plural 16
poisonous 14
polar 14
political 16
poor 16
popular 16
possible 14
powerful 14
powerless 16
princely 14
principal 16
productive 16
progressive 16
proper 16
proud 14
public 16
punishable 16
purple 10

q queer 16
quick 14
quiet 14

r rainy 12
rapid 16
real 12
red 8
regular 14
Republican 16
restless 16
rich 12
right 14
rocky 16
rough 14
round 12

s sad 8
salty 16
same 16
seasick 16
second 12

selfish 16
senior (older) 16
seventh 10
shameful 16
sharp 14
shiny 14
short 12
sick 14
sickly 16
silly 12
silvery 16
sixth 10
skillful 16
skinny 14
sleepless 14
sleepy 10
sleeveless 16
sloppy 16
slow 10
small 12
smart 16
smooth 16
snowy 10
soft 12
sore 14
sorrowful 14
sorry 12
southern 16
special 16
speechless 16
spotless 16
stiff 14
stormy 14
strong 12
such 16
sudden 16
sunless 16
sunny 12
sunshiny 14
sure 16

t tall 12
tan 14
tasteless 16

tasty 14
tender 16
terrible 16
thankful 16
thankless 14
thin 10
third 14
thirsty 14
thoughtful 14
thunderous 14
tight 14
tiny 14
true 12
truthful 14

u ugly 14
unashamed 16
unbecoming 16
unborn 16
unclean 14
underground 12
undone 14
unemployed 16
unequal 16
unfailing 14
unfair 14
unfit 16
unfriendly 14
ungrateful 16
unguarded 16
unhappy 10
unharmed 16
unhealthful 16
unhealthy 14
unheard 16
unhurt 14
unimportant 16
unkind 14
unlawful 16
unlearned 14
unlike 16
unlikely 16
unlovely 14
unlucky 14

unnamed 14
unnatural 16
unopened 16
unpaid 16
unpleasant 16
unreal 16
unsatisfactory 16
unsuccessful 14
unsuspected 16
unsuspecting 16
untaught 14
untrained 16
untroubled 16
untrue 14
unwelcome 16
unwilling 14
upper 14
uppermost 16

useful 14
useless 16

v victorious 14
voiceless 14

w wakeful 12
warm 10
wasteful 16
watery 16
weak 12
weedy 14
weekly 12
weighty 12
western 14
wet 14

white 10
whole 16
wide 16
willing 16
windy 12
womanly 14
wonderful 16
wooded 12
wooden 16
woody 10
woolen 16
woolly 16
worthless 14
wrong 12

y yearly 14
yellow 8
young 12

ADVERBS

a about 16
afar 14
again 14
alike 16
almost 14
aloud 14
anyhow 16
anywhere 14
asleep 14
assuredly 16
awhile 14

b before 14
beyond 16
busily 14

c clockwise 16

d doubtless 14
down 16
downstairs 12

e early 14
elsewhere 16
ever 16
evermore 14
everywhere 12

f finally 16
forever 16
forward 16
fully 16

h half 16
halfway 16
happily 14
here 14
hereabout 16
hourly 14
how 16
hurriedly 14

i indoors 12

l lot 12

m maybe 14

n near 14
nearly 14
never 14
nevermore 14
northerly 16
not 12
now 14
nowhere 16

o often 14
oftentimes 16
once 14
only 14
ordinarily 16
out 14
overboard 14
overhead 14

overland 16

p particularly 16
perhaps 16

q quickly 14

r rapidly   14
really 16

s simply 16
since 16
someday 14

somewhere 14
sometimes 16
soon 14
speedily 16
surely 16

t there 14
thereby 16
too 14
truly 16
twice 16

u upstairs 12

upward 16

v very 12

w when 12
where 12
whereabouts 14
why 14
within 16

y yesterday 12

INTERJECTIONS

amen 14
hello 16

CONJUNCTIONS

and 14
because 16
if 16

nor 16
until 14

whenever 14
wherever 14

FUNCTION NOUNS

another 16
both 14
each 14
few 14

hers 12
his 12
many 12
most 14

much 16
neither 12
some 14

NOUN DETERMINERS

a 14
an 16

every 12
no 10

PRONOUNS

anybody 14
anyone 14
everybody 12
everyone 14
everything 12
he 14
her 12
him 14
I 14

it 14
me 10
my 16
nobody 14
our 14
ourselves 14
she 8
someone 12
their 12

thy 16
us 10
we 14
which 16
who 12
whoever 14
whom 14
whose 12
you 14

PREPOSITIONS

above 14
after 12
behind 16
below 16
beside 16
by 16
during 16

from 16
in 12
into 14
like 14
of 16
on 14
over 12

plus 16
respecting 16
under 14
unto 16
up 14
upon 16
without 14

VI
Words by Topical Classification, Part of Speech and Earliest Age Known

The words presented here have been grouped into 147 categories, arranged according to the scheme outlined in the third section of Chapter III. Within a category, words are arranged alphabetically and are followed by part of speech, earliest age at which known, and any other categories to which the words may have been assigned. For example, under ACTIONS, 02 BATHE, one can find "washer N 14: 71d,90f." This means that "washer" (i.e., one who washes) is a noun, that it is known at least by the 14- 15-year-old group, and that it has been classified also under OBJECTS, 71 PEOPLE,Roles, d. General, and under OBJECTS, 90 STRUC-TURES,Houses, f.Washing.

ACTIONS

01 AFFECT

amaze V 14
disappoint V 16
frighten V 12
overjoy V 14
please V 14
sadden V 16
scare V 16
surprise V 16: 22
tease V 16

02 BATHE

bathe V 14
cleanse V 14
shampoo V 12
shave V 12
shower V 12
wash V 10
washer N 14: 71d,90f

03 CHANGE

beautify V 14
build V 14
cause V 16
change V 14
correct V 14
erase V 16: 62b
improve V 16
invent V 16
make V 16
overspread V 14
refresh V 16
separate V 16
soften V 16
wrap V 14

04 COMMUNICATE

alarm V 16
answer V 14
call V 14
complain V 16
crow V 16

describe V 16
phone V 12
say V 14
scold V 16
shout V 14
sing V 12
speak V 14
speech N 14
talk V 14
telegraph V 16
telephone V 12
tell V 12
warn V 16
warning N 14

05 DAMAGE

crush V 14
damage N 14
deaden V 16
deafen V 14
destroy V 16
hurt V 16
kill V 16: 64
spoil V 16
weaken V 16
wreck V 16

06 GIVE & TAKE

adopt V 16
exchange V 16
furnish V 16: 90d
give V 14
grab V 16
receive V 16
remove V 16
take V 14

07 GROW

become V 14
bud V 14
double V 16
enlarge V 14

expand V 16
grow V 12
outnumber V 16
unfold V 16

08 HIT

beat V 14
bump N 16
chop V 16
flatten V 16
knock V 16
push V 12
scratch V 16
slap V 16
spank V 16
strike V 16

09 JOIN

join V 16
knot V 14
marry V 16: 55b
meet V 14
mix V 16
rejoin V 16
sew V 14: 80
wed V 16: 55b

10 JUDGE

ask V 12
choose V 16
decide V 16
guess V 16
judge V 16
measure V 14
pick V 14
prove V 16
sample V 16
seek V 16
test V 16
try V 14
weigh V 14

11 MOVE

arrive V 16
begone V 16
climb V 12
come V 14
crawl V 14
curl V 12
dance V 12
drip V 14
enter V 16
fall V 14
fly V 12: 88b
go V 12
hike V 16,
hurry V 14
leave V 14
march V 14
move V 14
parade V 12
pass V 14
return V 14
rise V 16
rush V 14
shake V 14
sit V 14
slip V 14
spin V 16
spring V 12
step V 14
trail V 16
turn V 14
twirl V 16
visit V 12
walk V 10

12 PERCEIVE

look V 8
lookout N 12
notice V 16
overlook V 12
see V 8
watch V 10

13 PRESERVE

guard V 16: 64
have V 16
keep V 12
lose V 14
mend V 16
own V 14
preserve V 14
protection N 16
repair V 16
safeguard V 16
safety N 16
save V 14

14 REMEMBER

forget V 14
memory N 16
remember V 16
remind V 16
reminder N 16
souvenir N 16

15 SHINE

brighten V 14
darken V 16
lighten V 14
shine V 12

twinkle V 16

16 STOP & START

begin V 14
brake V 14
finish V 14
prevent V 16
quit V 14
shut V 14
start V 14
stay V 14
stop V 14
wait V 12

17 THINK

arrangement N 16
believe V 14
daydream V 14
idea N 14
justify V 16
know V 12
learn V 14
plan N 16
realize V 16
review V 14
study V 12
think V 14
thought N 14
understand V 16

18 TOUCH & SMELL

feel V 14
handle V 14
hug V 16
kiss V 14
lick V 16
rub V 14
smell V 16
sniff V 16
squeeze V 14
stink N 16
touch V 14

19 USE

bring V 12
cram V 16
divide V 16
do V 16
dump V 16
order V 14
put V 16
raise V 14
repeat V 16
send V 16
show V 14
use V 14
waste V 16

ATTRIBUTES

20 ACTIVITY

alive J 16
breezy J 14
busily D 14
busy J 12
calm J 14
dead J 12
fast J 14

hurried J 16
hurriedly D 14
lifeless J 16
lifelike J 16
quick J 14
quickly D 14
rapid J 16
rapidly D 14
slow J 10

speedily D 16
stormy J 14: 67h
sudden J 16

21 BRIGHTNESS

bright J 12
dark J 12
dull J 16

shiny J 14
silvery J 16: 24
spotless J 16
sunless J 16
sunny J 12: 67h
sunshiny J 14: 67h

22 CERTAINTY

accidental J 16
almost D 14
assuredly D 16
due J 16
doubtless D 14
hopeless J 16
imaginable J 14
maybe D 14
nearly D 14
needless J 16
not D 12
ordinarily D 16
particularly D 16
perhaps D 16
possible J 14
really D 16
sure J 16
surely D 16
surprise V 16: 0l
truly D 16
unlikely J 16
unsuspected J 16

23 CLARITY

clear J 12
fuzzy J 16
plain J 16

24 COLOR

black J 10
blond J 14
bloodshot J 12
blue J 8

brown J 8
colored J 12
colorful J 14
golden J 14
grassy J 14
gray J 8
green J 8
ivory J 16
milky J 12
pink J 12
purple J 10
red J 8
silvery J 16: 21
snowy J 10
tan J 14
yellow J 8
white J 10

25 DANGER

danger N 16
dangerous J 14
deadly J 14
harmful J 14
murderous J 16: 64
poisonous J 14
risk N 16
unguarded J 16: 64

26 DIRECTION

clockwise D 16
down D 16
eastern J 16
forward D 16
northerly D 16
overboard D 14
southern J 16
upward D 16
western J 14

27 DISTANCE

afar D 14

away J 14
beyond D 16
far J 12
faraway J 12
farther J 16
hereabout D 16
limit N 16
near D 14
nearby J 14
neighboring J 16
next J 16
out D 14
otermost J 16

28 EVALUATION

awful J 12
bad J 8
beautiful J 10
best J 12
better J 12
clean J 16
comfortable J 14
cute J 12
dirty J 12
earthly J 16
enjoyable J 16
evil J 14
false J 12
favorite J 14
foolish J 14
good J 14
handsome J 12
homelike J 14
honest J 16: 64
incorrect J 16: 70c
interesting J 16
lovely J 12
marvelous J 16
mistaken J 14: 70c
natural J 16
neat J 16
nice J 12
normal J 16

perfect J 16
pleasant J 16
proper J 16
queer J 12
real J 12
right J 14
silly J 12
simply D 16
sloppy J 16
terrible J 16
true J 12
truthful J 14
ugly J 14
unbecoming J 16
unclean J 14
unfailing J 14
unfair J 14
unfit J 16
unimportant J 16
unlovely J 14
unnatural J 16
unpleasant J 16
unsatisfactory J 16
untrue J 14
unwelcome J 16
useful J 14
useless J 16
wonderful J 16
worthless J 14
wrong J 12: 70c

29 FLAVOR

salty J 16
tang N 16
tasteless J 16
tasty J 14

30 GENERAL

beauty N 16
bigness N 14
distance N 16
flavor N 16

greatness N 16
heaviness N 16
height N 14
length N 14
loveliness N 14
perfection N 16
pressure N 16
quickness N 14
seriousness N 14
sex N 14
size N 16
temperature N 16
warmth N 14
weight N 14
worth N 16

31 HARDNESS

hard J 14
plastic J 14
soft J 12
stiff J 14

32 HUMANNESS

broke J 16
brotherly J 14
careless J 16
charming J 16
crazy J 14
disobedient J 16
dizzy J 16
friendless J 16
friendly J 12
gentle J 16
gracious J 16
hateful J 14
headstrong J 16
imaginative J 16
intelligent J 16
kind J 14
kindly J 16
lazy J 12
lonely J 16

naughty J 16
obliging J 16
playful J 12
poor J 16
princely J 14: 60b, 67e
rich J 12
selfish J 16
skillful J 16
smart J 16
thankful J 16
thoughtful J 14
unashamed J 16
unfriendly J 14
ungrateful J 16
unkind J 14
unlucky J 14
unsuccessful J 14
unwilling J 14
willing J 16

33 LOUDNESS

loud J 14
noiseless J 16
noisy J 12
quiet J 14
thunderous J 14
unheard J 16
voiceless J 14

34 NOTORIETY

famous J 16
mystery N 14
nameless J 14
popular J 16
secrecy N 16
secret N 16
underground J 12
unnamed J 14

35 NUMEROSITY

additional J 16

blank J 16
complete J 16
empty J 16
full J 12
fully D 16
half D 16
lot D 12
more J 16
often D 14
once D 14
only D 14
plural J 16
too D 14
twice D 16
very D 12
wasteful J 16
whole J 16

36 POSITION

about D 16
anywhere D 14
base N 16
bottom N 14
center N 14
corner N 16
downstairs D 12
east N 14
elsewhere D 12
end N 14
everywhere D 12
halfway D 16
here D 14
indoor J 12
outer J 14
overhead D 14
middle N 14
north N 14
nowhere D 16
side N 16
somewhere D 14
south N 12
there D 14
upper J 14

uppermost J 16
upside N 12
upstairs D 12
west N 16
within D 16

37 PRIMACY

capital J 14
championship N 14
first J 16
front J 16
principal J 16
victorious J 14

38 SHAPE

ball N 12
circle N 12
dot N 16
flat J 14
globe N 14
hemisphere N 16
mark N 14
point N 14
ring N 14
round J 12
semicircle N 16
sharp J 14
skinny J 14
spot N 16
square N 16
thin J 10
triangle N 16
wheel N 14

39 SIMILARITY

alike D 16
balance V 16
different J 14
else J 16
even J 16
odd J 16

opposite J 14
other J 16
replacement N 16
same J 16
special J 16
such J 16
unequal J 16
unlike J 16

40 SIZE

big J 12
bigger J 12
giant J 14
great J 16
high J 14
large J 10
less J 16
little J 12
long J 12
loose J 16
low J 12
narrow J 16
short J 12
small J 12
tall J 12
tight J 14
tiny J 14
wide J 16

41 STRENGTH

athletic J 14
breakable J 16
easy J 12
hardy J 12
manly J 14
mightly J 16
muscular J 16
powerful J 14
powerless J 16
strong J 12
tender J 16
weak J 12

42 TEMPERATURE

cold J 12
hot J 10
iced J 12
icy J 12
lukewarm J 14
warm J 10

43 TEMPORALITY

again D 14
ago J 14
awhile D 14
before D 14
daily J 14
early D 14
ever D 16
evermore D 14
everyday J 16
final J 16
finally D 16
forever D 16

fresh J 16
freshness N 16
last J 12
late J 14
never D 14
nevermore D 14
new J 16
now D 14
oftentimes D 16
old J 12
past J 14
regular J 14
soon D 14
weekly J 12
yearly J 14

44 TEXTURE

bushy J 14
creamy J 14
flowery J 16
furry J 16
hairy J 14

mossy J 16
oaken J 12: 77
rocky J 16
rough J 14
smooth J 16
wooden J 16: 77
woolen J 16: 52
woolly J 16: 52

45 WEIGHT

fat J 12
heavy J 14
overweight J 16
weighty J 12

46 WETNESS

dry J 12
moist J 14
watery J 16: 67j
wet J 14: 67j

OBJECTS

47 ANIMALS, Air

blackbird N 14
bluebird N 12
bluejay N 12
cardinal N 16
chick N 16
chickadee N 14
chicken N 12
crow N 12
cuckoo N 14
dove N 14
duck N 10
eagle N 10
goose N 12
hawk N 14

hen N 12
hummingbird N 14
jay N 14
oriole N 16
owl N 10
parrot N 12
pigeon N 16
robin N 10
rooster N 12
sparrow N 16
woodpecker N 12

48 ANIMALS, Enclosures

beehive N 16
cage N 16

hive N 16
nest N 12
net N 16: 81
web N 14

49 ANIMALS, General

animal N 14
bird N 10
bug N 14
fish N 12: 67j
insect N 12
mammal N 12
pet N 10
watchdog N 16

50 ANIMALS, Insects

ant N 12
bee N 14
beetle N 14
butterfly N 14
dragonfly N 14
flea N 14
grasshopper N 14
ladybug N 14
lice N 16
mosquito N 16
moth N 14
spider N 12
wasp N 16

51 ANIMALS, Land

ape N 14
baboon N 16
bear N 10
beaver N 14
bloodhound N 16
bobcat N 14
buffalo N 16
bull N 12
bunny N 8
burro N 16
calf N 12
camel N 10
cat N 10
cattle N 12: 67a
chipmunk N 12
collie N 14
colt N 14
cow N 10
cub N 14
cutworm N 14
deer N 12
dinosaur N 16
dog N 12
donkey N 12
earthworm N 14
elephant N 10
fawn N 16

fox N 10
giraffe N 12
goat N 12
gorilla N 16
greyhound N 16
hippopotamus N 14
hog N 14
horse N 10: 67e
kangaroo N 12
kitten N 10
kitty N 12
lamb N 10
lion N 12
lizard N 14
mole N 16
monkey N 10
moose N 10
mouse N 10
mule N 16
muskrat N 12
ox N 16
pig N 10
pony N 10
poodle N 16
puppy N 10
pussy N 14
rabbit N 10
raccoon N 14
rat N 12
sheep N 12
silkworm N 14
skunk N 12
snail N 12
squirrel N 12
tiger N 12
wildcat N 12
wolf N 12
woodchuck N 14
worm N 12
zebra N 10

52 ANIMALS, Products

buckskin N 12

cowhide N 14
horsehair N 14
leather N 14
saddle N 14: 67a
whalebone N 16: 67j
wool N 12
woolen J 16: 44
woolly J 16: 44

53 ANIMALS, Water

alligator N 12
catfish N 12
crab N 14
crayfish N 12
eel N 16
frog N 12
goldfish N 12
jellyfish N 10
lobster N 16
octopus N 14
oyster N 14
salmon N 16
seal N 12
shark N 16
shellfish N 14
shrimp N 14
tuna N 16
turtle N 12
whale N 14

54 CONCEPTS, Closure

boundary N 16
cut V 14
enclose V 16
exit N 14
hole N 14
open J 14
opening N 16
part N 14
piece N 14
uncover V 14
undone J 14

unlock V 14
unopened J 16

55 CONCEPTS, Events

a. General

adventure N 16
emergency N 16
event N 16
happen V 16
operation N 16
process N 16

b. Social

birthday N 12
ceremony N 16
engagement N 16
funeral N 14
holiday N 14
marriage N 14
marry V 16: 09
wed V 16: 09

c. Travel

baggage N 14: 81, 86
comeback N 14
expedition N 16
explore V 16
explorer N 16: 67e,
   71e
journey N 16
landing N 16
suitcase N 16: 81, 86
tourist N 16: 71d
traveler N 14: 67e,
   71d
trip N 14
unpack V 14
vacation N 16: 61d,
   62b, 68d
voyage N 16
walker N 12: 71d

56 CONCEPTS, Groups

a. General

collection N 16
column N 16: 83
group N 14
mess N 16
network N 16
pile N 16
row N 16
set N 16
world N 14: 67d

b. Social

choir N 16: 60a
class N 14
club N 14: 68d
colony N 16: 67e
community N 14: 63
company N 16
congress N 14: 63,
   67e
crowd N 16
gang N 16
jury N 16: 64
membership N 16
organization N 16
party N 12: 68d
people N 12: 63
society (all people)
   N 16: 63
society (community)
   N 16
team N 14: 68b
troop N 14: 69

57 CONCEPTS, Number

zero N 14
one N 16
two N 10
second J 12
three N 12
third J 14

four N 12
fourth J 12
five N 10
fifth J 12
six N 10
sixth J 10
seven N 12
seventh J 10
eight N 10
eighth J 12
nine N 12
ten N 12
eleven N 12
twelve N 12
fourteen N 12
fifteen N 8
sixteen N 14
eighteen N 10
nineteen N 12
twenty N 10
thirty N 14
forty N 12
fifty N 12
sixty N 16
seventy N 14
eighty N 14
ninety N 12
hundred N 12
thousand N 12
million N 12
billion N 12

58 CONCEPTS, Physical States

a. Change

activity N 14
afire J 14
age N 16
blowout V 16
bonfire N 16
burn V 12
circulation N 16
difference N 16

earthquake N 14
eruption N 16
explosion N 16
fire N 12
improvement N 14
progress N 16
progressive J 16
wildfire N 16

b. General

electric J 14
electrical J 12
fireproof J 12
physical J 14
smoke V 12

c. Light

blackness N 14
brightness N 12
brilliance N 16
darkness N 12
daylight N 12
flash N 12
ray N 16
shade N 16
shadow N 12
sunlight N 14

d. Sound

aloud D 14
noise N 12
roar V 14
scream V 14
silence N 16
sound N 14
uproar N 16
voice N 14
yell V 16

59 CONCEPTS, Time

a. Days

Sunday N 10
Monday N 10
Tuesday N 10

Wednesday N 10
Thursday N 12
Friday N 10
Saturday N 14

b. General

calendar N 14: 83
century N 16: 83
clock N 8: 83
date N 16
day N 12: 83
future N 16
hour N 14: 83
lifetime N 16
minute N 12: 83
month N 12: 83
period N 14: 83
since D 16
someday D 14
sometimes D 16
time N 16
timepiece N 16: 83
today N 12
tomorrow N 12
tonight N 14
week N 12: 83
weekend N 10
while N 16
year N 12: 83
yesterday D 12

c. Hours

evening N 14
forenoon N 16
hourly D 14
midday N 16
morning N 12
night N 12
nightfall N 14
noon N 10
sundown N 14
sunset N 16: 67h

d. Months

January N 10

February N 10
March N 12
April N 12
May N 12
June N 12
July N 10
September N 12
October N 12
November N 10
December N 10

e. Seasons

autumn N 16
season N 14
springtime N 12
summer N 12
winter N 12

60 INSTITUTIONS, The Arts

a. Entertainment

act N 14
actor N 14: 71e
ballet N 16
choir N 16: 56b
chorus N 16
circus N 12
clown N 12: 71e
dancer N 14: 71e
drummer N 14: 71e
fiddler N 16: 71e
footlights N 16
movie N 12
music N 14
playhouse N 16
rodeo N 16
showman N 16: 71e
singer N 16: 71e
song N 12
songster N 14: 71e
theater N 16
ticket N 14
violinist N 16: 71e
writer N 16: 71e

b. Fantasy

castle N 16: 67e, 89
crown N 16: 67e
dream N 14
fairy N 16
hero N 14
imaginary J 16
knight N 16: 67e
lord N 16: 67e
monster N 16
nightmare N 16
prince N 14: 67e
princely J 14: 32, 67e
princess N 14: 67e
queen N 12: 67e
treasure N 16
unreal J 16
witch N 12
witchcraft N 14
wizard N 16

c. Graphics

artist N 14: 71e
cartoon N 16
cartoonist N 16: 71e
draw V 12
drawing N 10
illustrator N 16: 71e
newsreel N 16
painting N 14
photo N 14
photograph N 16
photographer N 16: 71e
picture N 10
studio N 14: 90c

61 INSTITUTIONS, Business

a. Finance

account N 16
bank N 10
bankbook N 14
banker N 12: 71e
bill N 16
bookpeeper N 16: 71e
cashier N 14: 71e
credit N 16
dividend N 14
fund N 16
loss N 16
owner N 16: 71d
payment N 14
rent N 14
savings N 16
spendthrift N 14: 71d
stockholder N 14
treasurer N 16
unpaid J 16

b. Money

cash N 14
cent N 12
change N 12
coin N 12
dime N 12
dollar N 12
nickel N 12
money N 14
penny N 12
sixpence N 14

c. Sales

bookseller N 14: 71e
buy V 14
buyer N 14
cargo N 14
cheap J 16
cost N 12
customer N 16
deal V 16
market V 16
owe V 16
pay V 12
sale N 12
salesman N 14: 71e
salesmanship N 16
saleswoman N 14: 71e
sell V 14
seller N 14: 71e
shop N 14: 89
shopkeeper N 14: 71e
shopper N 14
shopping N 14
spend V 14
store N 10: 89
storekeeper N 16: 71e
style N 16
trade V 14
trader N 16: 67e, 71e
undersell V 16

d. Work

boss N 14
business N 14
career N 16
duty N 16
earn V 16
employee N 16
employer N 16
establishment N 16
industrious J 14
industry N 16
job N 12
labor V 16
manager N 14
office N 12: 90c
overtime N 16
overwork N 16
productive J 16
retire V 16
superintendent N 16
supervisor N 14
unemployed J 16
vacation N 16: 55c, 62b, 68d
workman N 14: 71e
workmanship N 16
workroom N 12: 90c
workshop N 16: 90c

62 INSTITUTIONS, Education

a. Courses

astronomy N 16
chemistry N 16
civics N 16
education N 16
English N 14: 67f
French N 16: 67f
geography N 14
government N 14
poetry N 16: 62d
science N 16
sewing N 12
woodcraft N 14

b. General

alphabetical J 14
art N 16
attendance N 16
book N 12: 62d
color V 10
craft N 16
dictionary N 12: 62d
educational J 16
erase V 16: 03
examination N 16
example N 16
experience N 16
explanation N 16
fact N 16
grade N 12
graduate V 14
instructive J 16
knowledge N 14
lesson N 16
practice N 16
problem N 14
question N 12
read V 14
report N 14
spell V 14
teach V 16

textbook N 16: 62d
training N 16
unlearned J 14
untaught J 14
untrained J 16
vacation N 16: 55c, 61d, 68d

c. Locations

campus N 14: 91
classroom N 10
college N 12: 89
dormitory N 14
gymnasium N 12
locker N 12
schoolhouse N 12: 89
schoolroom N 14

d. Reading Matter

atlas N 16: 67d, 67j
author N 14: 71e
billboard N 16
biography N 16: 67e
book N 12: 62b
bulletin N 16
dictionary N 12: 62b
directory N 16
index N 14
letter N 12
list N 14
mail N 10
menu N 16: 82c
news N 16
note N 14
poetry N 16: 62a
postcard N 14
postscript N 14
press N 16
print N 14
reprint V 16
romance N 16
scrapbook N 14
story N 16
telegram N 16

textbook N 16: 62b
valentine N 12

e. Roles See Roles, Education

f. Writing

card N 12
check V 16
crayon N 12
notebook N 16
page N 10
paste V 14
pencil N 12
postage N 14
stamp V 16
tablet N 16
tag N 14
type V 12
underline V 12
write V 10

63 INSTITUTIONS, Government

American N 12: 67e
capital N 14: 67e
city N 12: 91
civil J 14
commission V 16
commissioner N 16
communism N 16: 67e
community N 14: 56b
congress N 14: 56b, 67e
constitution N 16: 67e
constitutional J 16: 67e
country N 14: 67d, 91
courthouse N 14: 89
democracy N 16: 67e
downfall N 14: 67e
elector N 16
fatherland N 16: 91
freedom N 16: 67e
governor N 14: 67e
independence N 16: 67e

leader N 16: 67e, 71d
liberty N 14: 67e
life N 14
loser N 14: 71d
mayor N 16
nation N 12: 91
nomination N 16
peace N 14
people N 12: 56b
political J 16
politician N 16: 71e
presidency N 16
president N 14: 67e
public J 16
Republican J 16
rule V 16: 67e
society (all people)
   N 16: 56b
speaker N 14
spokesman N 16
statesman N 16: 67e
tax V 14: 67e
taxation N 14: 67e
title N 16
town N 16: 91
township N 16: 91
village N 14: 91
vote N 14
voter N 14
winner N 14: 71d

64 INSTITUTIONS, Law

allowable J 14
commandment N 16: 66
condemnation N 16
forbidden J 16
gangster N 16
guard V 16: 13
hanging N 16
hangman N 14
honest J 16: 28
jail N 16: 89
judgment N 16

jury N 16: 56b
keeper N 14: 71e
kill V 16: 05
killer N 16
law N 12
license N 16
lie N 14
murderous J 16: 25
outlaw N 16
patrolman N 16: 71e
permit N 16
police N 16
policeman N 10: 71e
prison N 16: 89
prisoner N 16
punishable J 16
robbery N 16
sheriff N 14: 71e
spy N 14
steal V 16
testimony N 16
thief N 16
thieve V 16
unguarded J 16: 25
unlawful J 16
watchman N 16: 71e

65 INSTITUTIONS, Medicine

ache V 16
aspirin N 16
bacteria N 16
bleed V 12: 72d
blind J 14: 72d
blindness N 16
cancer N 16
deaf J 12: 72d
deafness N 14
death N 14
dentist N 10: 71e
die V 12: 72d
diet N 14
disease N 16

disinfect V 16
eyesight N 14
faintness N 16
headache N 14
health J 16
healthy J 16: 72d
hospital N 10: 89
ill J 12: 72d
illness N 12
infect V 16
infection N 14
iodine N 16
measles N 16
medicine N 14
mummy N 16
nurse N 10: 71e
operation N 16
pill N 12
pain V 16: 72d
painful J 16: 72d
paralyzed J 16: 72d
rheumatism N 16
seasick J 16: 72d
sick J 14: 72d
sicken V 14
sickly J 16: 72d
sickness N 14
smallpox N 16
soreness N 16
stroke N 14
toothache N 14
unhealthful J 16
unhealthy J 14: 72d
vitamin N 14

66 INSTITUTIONS, Religion

angel N 14
baptism N 14
Bible N 12
bless V 14
blessing N 16
cemetery N 16: 91

church N 12: 89
churchman N 14
churchyard N 14: 91
commandment N 16: 64
faith N 14
godlike J 16
grave N 14: 91
heaven N 14
hell N 16
pray V 10
preacher N 16
priest N 16
saint N 16
savior N 16
sin N 14
temptation N 14
testament N 16

67 INSTITUTIONS,
   Science

a. Agriculture
   barn N 12: 89
   blacksmith N 12: 71e
   cattle N 12: 51
   cowboy N 14: 67e,
      71e
   crop N 16
   dig V 14
   farm N 14: 91
   farmer N 10: 71e
   farmhouse N 14: 89
   field N 12: 91
   graze V 16: 82c
   greenhouse N 12: 89
   hay N 12
   hayfield N 14: 91
   haystack N 14
   henhouse N 12: 89
   plantation N 16: 91
   planter N 14: 71e
   plowman N 16: 71e
   ranch N 12: 91
   rancher N 12: 71e

saddle N 14: 52
seed N 12
seedling N 14
shepherd N 14: 71e
straw N 16
tractor N 14
weed N 14
weedy J 14

b. Anatomy
   arm N 12
   back N 16
   beak N 16
   beard N 14
   body N 12
   brain N 16
   breast N 16
   breath N 14
   cheek N 16
   chest N 14
   chin N 16
   circulatory J 16
   ear N 12
   elbow N 14
   eye N 12
   eyebrow N 14
   eyelash N 16
   face N 12
   finger N 12
   foot N 12
   forehead N 12
   foreleg N 14
   forepaw N 14
   fur N 12
   hair N 12
   hand N 14
   head N 14
   heart N 12
   heel N 14
   hip N 16
   jaw N 16
   lip N 14
   lung N 14
   mind N 16

mouth N 14
mustache N 16
neck N 14
nose N 12
paw N 14
pigtail N 16
rib N 14
shoulder N 16
skeleton N 16
skin N 14
stomach N 14
throat N 14
thumb N 12
toe N 12
tongue N 14
waist N 16
wing N 12

c. Forestry
   board N 14: 90d
   branch N 14: 75
   camp N 12: 91
   forest N 12
   knothole N 16
   log N 12
   lumber N 14: 90d
   lumberman N 14: 71e
   sawdust N 16
   sawmill N 16: 89
   stick N 12
   tree N 12
   watchtower N 14:
      67e, 89
   wood N 14
   woodcutter N 12:
      71e
   wooded J 12
   woodland N 10
   woodsman N 14: 71e
   woody J 10

d. Geography
   America N 12: 67e
   arctic N 16

atlas N 16: 62d, 67j
bank (river) N 12
bay N 14
beach N 16: 67j
brook N 16
canal N 14
canyon N 16
cavern N 12
coast N 16: 67j
coastal J 16: 67j
country N 14: 63, 91
dam N 14
earth N 12
equator N 16: 67j
ground N 14
gulf N 14: 67j
headwater N 14
highland N 14
hill N 16
hilly J 16
iceberg N 16: 67j
isle N 14
lake N 12
land N 14
longitude N 14: 67j
map N 14
mountain N 12
muddy N 12
ocean N 12: 67j
overland D 16
plain N 16
polar J 14: 67j
pond N 12
pool N 10
river N 12
sea N 10: 67j
seashore N 14: 67j
seaside N 14
shoreline N 16: 67j
snowbank N 14
stream N 14
swamp N 14
upland N 16
waterfall N 14

waterway N 12
wave N 14: 67j
whirlpool N 14
world N 14: 56a

e. History

America N 12: 67d
American N 12: 63
army N 12: 69
arrow N 16: 68c
ballroom N 16: 68d,
   89
battlefield N 16: 69
biography N 16: 62d
blockhouse N 16: 69
cabin N 12: 89
capital N 14: 63
castle N 16: 60b,
   89
chieftain N 16: 69
coachman N 16: 71e
colony N 16: 56b
communism N 16: 63
congress N 14: 56b,
   63
constitution N 16: 63
constitutional J 16:
   63
cowboy N 14: 67a,
   71e
crown N 16: 60b
democracy N 16: 63
downfall N 14: 63
explorer N 16: 55c,
   71e
fight V 12: 69
freedom N 16: 63
governor N 14: 63
gunpowder N 16: 69
highroad N 14: 92
hoopskirt N 14: 80
horse N 10: 51
horseshoe N 14: 68c
independence N 16: 63

inn N 14: 89
knight N 16: 60b
landowner N 16: 71e
leader N 16: 63, 71d
liberty N 14: 63
lighthouse N 16: 67j,
   89
lord N 16: 60b
Negro N 14: 71d
nightcap N 14: 80
officer N 14: 69
overturn V 16: 69
pioneer N 16: 71d
president N 14: 63
prince N 14: 60b
princely J 14: 32,
   60b
princess N 14: 60b
queen N 12: 60b
rule V 16: 63
settler N 14: 71d
slave N 16: 71d
soldier N 12: 69
statesman N 16: 63
sword N 16: 69
tax V 14: 63
taxation N 14: 63
trader N 16: 61c,
   71e
traveler N 14: 55c,
   71d
uniform N 16: 80
warfare N 16: 69
watchtower N 14:
   67c, 89
whaler N 16: 67j,
   71e

f. Linguistics

abbreviation N 16
alphabet N 14
chapter N 14
comma N 14
English N 14: 62a

French N 16: 62a
language N 14
paragraph N 14
sentence N 14
suffix N 16
syllable N 16
verb N 16
vocabulary N 14

g. Mathematics

add V 14
addition N 16
amount N 16
arithmetic N 12
count V 14
mathematical J 12
mathematics N 14
multiply V 16
number N 16
pair N 16
quarter N 16
subtract V 14
subtraction N 14
sum N 16

h. Meteorology

air N 14
airy J 14
atmosphere N 16
barometer N 16: 83
blizzard N 14
breeze N 14
cloud N 12
cloudburst N 14
cloudless J 14
cloudy J 14
flood V 14
fluid N 14
fog N 14
foggy J 16
freeze V 14
frost N 14
frosty J 14
frozen J 14

gas N 14
gravity N 14
hail N 16
hailstone N 16
hurricane N 16: 67j
lightning N 12
moisture N 16
overflow N 16
oxygen N 16
rain N 10
rainbow N 12
rainfall N 16
rainy J 12
shower N 14
sky N 12
smog N 16
snow N 12
snowflake N 14
storm N 12
stormy J 14: 20
sun N 14
sunny J 12: 21
sunset N 16: 59c
sunshine J 12
sunshiny J 14: 21
thermometer N 14: 83
thunder N 16
thunderbolt N 14
thundercloud N 12
tornado N 14
whirlwind N 14
wind N 8
windy J 12

i. Mineralogy

coal N 16
copper N 14
diamond N 16
dirt N 12
dust N 16
goldsmith N 16: 71e
gravel N 16
iron N 14
jeweler N 14: 71e

lime N 16
limestone N 16
marble N 16
miner N 14: 71e
mineral N 16
mud N 16
plate V 16
quicksand N 16
sand N 14
silver N 14
soil N 16
stone N 12

j. Oceanography

atlas N 16: 62d, 67d
beach N 16: 67d
boat N 10: 88a
coast N 16: 67d
coastal J 16: 67d
compass N 16: 83
equator N 16: 67d
fish N 12: 49
fishery N 16: 91
float V 16: 68a
foam N 16: 90f
gulf N 14: 67d
hurricane N 16: 67h
iceberg N 16: 67d
lighthouse N 16: 67e, 89
longitude N 14: 67d
ocean N 12: 67d
polar J 14: 67d
port N 16: 91
pump N 16: 84
sail N 16: 87
sailboat N 12: 88a
sailor N 12: 71e
saver N 14: 85
sea N 10: 67d
seaman N 14: 71e
seashore N 14: 67d
seaweed N 16: 75
ship N 12: 88a

shipyard N 14: 91
shoreline N 16: 67d
steamship N 14: 88a
submarine N 16: 88a
watery J 16: 46
wave N 14: 67d
wet J 14: 46
whalebone N 16: 52
whaler N 16: 67e,
   71e

68 INSTITUTIONS, Sports

a. Action

blindfold V 14: 68c
catch V 14
chase V 16
contact V 16
curve V 16
float V 16: 67j
hop V 10
jump V 14
outrun V 12
pitch V 16
race V 12
run V 16
score V 14
seesaw V 14
skate V 12
ski V 12
skip V 14
swim V 10
swing V 16
throw V 16
wrestle V 16

b. Athletes

boxer N 16
catcher N 16
champion N 14
horseman N 14
huntsman N 14
jockey N 16: 71e

quarterback N 16
racer N 12
rider N 14
rower N 16
sportsman N 16
team N 14: 56b
wrestler N 14

c. Games and Toys

arrow N 16: 67e
athletics N 16
balloon N 10
baseball N 10
basketball N 10
bat N 14
blindfold V 14: 68a
boating V 12
bowling N 12
bugle N 16
checkers N 16
crossword N 14
doll N 10
football N 10
fun N 10
game N 12
golf N 12
gymnastics N 14
hobby N 16
hockey N 16
horseshoe N 14: 67e
jacks N 14
jigsaw N 14
joke N 12
kite N 10
maypole N 16
park N 10: 68d, 91
play (fun) N 12
playground N 10: 68d,
   91
playmate N 14: 71d
plaything N 10
pool (game) N 16
sport N 12
stilts N 14

tennis N 14
toy N 12

d. Recreation

ballroom N 16: 67e,
   89
club N 14: 56b
clubhouse N 16: 89
fireworks N 14: 85
museum N 16: 89
park N 16: 68c, 91
party N 12: 56b
picnic N 14: 82c
playground N 10: 68c,
   91
vacation N 16: 55c,
   61d, 62b
zoo N 12: 91

69 INSTITUTIONS, Warfare

army N 12: 67e
battlefield N 16: 67e
beaten J 16
blockhouse N 16: 67e
bomb N 14
bomber N 16
buckshot N 14
bullet N 16
captain N 12
chieftain N 16: 67e
combat N 12
destroyer N 16
fight V 12: 67e
fighter (soldier) N 14
firearm N 16
firearm (shooting) N 16
gunner N 14
gunpowder N 16: 67e
lead V 14
magazine N 16
officer N 14: 67e
order V 16

overpower V 14
overturn V 16: 67e
shoot V 16
soldier N 12: 67e
sword N 16: 67e
troop N 14: 56b
warfare N 16: 67e

70 PEOPLE, Behavior

a. Assistance

agree V 14
agreement N 16
aid N 14
cooperation N 16
encouragement N 16
excuse V 16
favor N 16
greeting N 14
help V 16
let (allow) V 16
offering N 16
service N 16
support V 16
teamwork N 16

b. Awards

approval N 16
award N 14
gift N 12
glory N 16
prize N 16
trophy N 16

c. Errors

error N 16
fault N 16
incorrect J 16: 28
mischief N 16
misfortune N 16
mistake N 14
mistaken J 14: 28
misunderstand V 14
wrong J 12: 28

d. Intention

behave V 16
disobey V 16
hope V 14
means (intends) V 16
must V 16
need V 16
obey V 14
ought V 14
pledge V 14
refuse V 16
want V 14
will V 16
wish V 14

71 PEOPLE, Roles

a. Age

adult J 14
aged J 14
babe N 12
baby N 12
babyhood N 16
child N 10
grayheaded J 14
junior J 14
kid N 14
newborn J 12
papoose N 16
person N 14
senior J 16
teens N 14
unborn J 16
young J 12
youngster N 14
youth N 14

b. Education

beginner N 14
classmate N 14
expert N 16
freshman N 16
historian N 14
scholar N 16

schoolboy N 12
schoolmaster N 10
student N 14
teacher N 10
thinker N 14
trainer N 16: 71e

c. Family

aunt N 12
bride N 16
bridegroom N 16
cousin N 12
daddy N 10
daughter N 12
family N 12
father N 12
fatherly J 12
godmother N 12
grandchild N 14
grandfather N 12
grandpa N 12
grandparent N 10
household N 14
husband N 14
mama N 10
mommy N 8
mother N 14
nephew N 16
niece N 14
papa N 14
parent N 12
relative N 16
sister N 12
son N 12
stepfather N 12
stepmother N 14
twin N 12
uncle N 12
visitor N 14

d. General

bum N 16
darling N 14
dear N 14

diner (person)
   N 16: 82c
drinker N 16: 82c
driver N 12: 88b
drunkard N 14
dunce N 14
fool N 16
friend N 14
goose (silly person)
   N 16
guardian N 16
joker N 14
leader N 16: 63, 67e
liar N 16
loser N 14: 63
lover N 12
madman N 14
member N 16
motherless J 16
motorist N 16: 88b
Negro N 14: 67e
neighbor N 14
owner N 16: 61a
pal N 14
pioneer N 16: 67e
playmate N 14: 68c
relationship N 16
roommate N 14
settler N 14: 67e
slave N 16: 67e
sleeper N 16
sleepwalker N 14
smoker N 16
spendthrift N 14: 61a
sweetheart N 12
talker N 14
tourist N 16: 55c
traveler N 14: 55c, 67e
walker N 12: 55c
washer N 14: 02,
   90f
winner N 14: 63

e. Occupation

   actor N 14: 60a

artist N 14: 60c
author N 14: 62d
baker N 12: 82b
banker N 12: 61a
barber N 12
blacksmith N 12: 67a
bookkeeper N 16: 61a
bookseller N 14: 61c
builder N 16
carpenter N 16
cartoonist N 16: 60c
cashier N 14: 61a
clerk N 16
clown N 12: 60a
coachman N 16: 67e
cowboy N 14: 67a, 67e
craftsman N 16
cutter N 16
dancer N 14: 60a
dentist N 10: 65
dressmaker N 14
drummer N 14: 60a
electrician N 14
engineer N 14: 88b
explorer N 16: 55c, 67e
farmer N 10: 67a
fiddler N 16: 60a
flier N 16: 88b
florist N 16
gardener N 14
goldsmith N 16: 67i
grocer N 14: 82d
hairdresser N 12
homemaker N 14
housekeeper N 14
housewife N 14
hunter N 14
illustrator N 16: 60c
Jeweler N 14: 67i
jockey N 16: 68b
keeper N 14: 64
landowner N 16: 67e
laundress N 16: 90f
lumberman N 14: 67c

machinist N 16
maid N 16
mailman N 12
maker N 16
messenger N 16
miller N 16
miner N 14: 67i
naturalist N 16
nurse N 10: 65
patrolman N 16: 64
photographer N 16: 60c
planter N 14: 67a
plowman N 16: 67a
plumber N 16
policeman N 10: 64
politician N 16: 63
postman N 12
postmaster N 14
printer N 16
publisher N 16
rancher N 12: 67a
reporter N 14
sailor N 12: 67j
salesman N 14: 61c
saleswoman N 14: 61c
scientist N 14
seaman N 14: 67j
seller N 14: 61c
shepherd N 14: 67a
sheriff N 14: 64
shoemaker N 14
shopkeeper N 14: 61c
showman N 16: 60a
singer N 16: 60a
songster N 14: 60a
steward N 16
storekeeper N 16: 61c
trader N 16: 61c, 67e
trainer N 16: 71b
typist N 16
violinist N 16: 60a
waitress N 16: 82c
watchman N 16: 64
whaler N 16: 67e, 67j

woodcutter N 12: 67c
woodsman N 14: 67c
workman N 14: 61d
writer N 16: 60a

f. Sex

boy N 12
boyish J 16
female N 14
girl N 12
girlish J 12
guy N 16
lady N 14
male N 14
man N 14
Miss N 12
motherly J 14
sonny N 16
woman N 12
womanhood N 14
womanly J 14

72 PEOPLE, States

a. Emotional

afraid J 10
angry J 12
bother V 16
care V 16
cheerful J 16
contentment N 16
delight N 16
disappointment N 14
dislike V 16
downhearted J 16
enjoy V 16
enjoyment N 14
enthusiastic J 14
fear V 16
fearful J 16
flirt V 16
fright N 16
gay J 16

glad J 14
gladness N 16
happily D 14
happiness N 14
happy J 14
hate V 14
heartbroken J 16
homesick J 12
horror N 16
jittery J 16
joking V 12
joy N 16
joyful J 14
joyless J 16
joyous J 16
laugh N 12
laughter N 14
lonesome J 16
love N 16
mad J 12
mean J 14
merry J 12
neighborly J 16
nervous J 16
nervousness N 16
pleasure N 16
proud J 14
regret V 16
restless J 16
restlessness N 16
sad J 8
sadness N 16
shyness N 16
sorrow N 16
sorrowful J 14
sorry J 12
speechless J 16
strangeness N 16
thank V 14
trouble V 14
unhappiness N 14
unhappy J 10
untroubled J 16
worry V 14

b. General

bravery N 16
caution N 14
defiance N 16
disrespect N 16
drunkenness N 14
feeling N 16
foolishness N 14
forgiveness N 16
gentleness N 14
goodness N 16
goodwill N 16
homeless J 16
honesty N 14
human J 14
kindness N 14
mildness N 16
pleasurable J 14
shameful J 16
thankfulness N 16
thankless J 14
thoughtfulness N 16
thrill N 16
unharmed J 16
unkindness N 16
unsuspecting J 16

c. Identity

autograph N 12
name N 12
nickname N 16
self N 16
signature N 16
title (name) N 14

d. Physical

asleep D 14
awake J 14
bald J 16
bleed V 12: 65
blind J 14: 65
blow V 12
breathe V 14
breathless J 14

cry V 16
deaf J 12: 65
die V 12: 65
drown V 14
healthy J 16: 65
hear V 12
hearer N 12
hearing N 12
hungry J 12
ill J 12: 65
listen V 12
live V 14
nap N 16
pain V 16: 65
painful J 16: 65
paralyzed J 16: 65
rest V 12
seasick J 16: 65
sense N 16
sick J 14: 65
sickly J 16: 65
sleep N 14
sleepless J 14
sleepy J 10
smile V 14
sore J 14
starve V 14
suffer V 16
thirst N 14
thirsty J 14
unhealthy J 14: 65
unhurt J 14
wake V 12
wakeful J 12
waken V 16
weep V 16
wink V 14

73 PLANTS, Flowers

daisy N 16
gardenia N 14
rose N 12

sunflower N 10
violet N 14

74 PLANTS, Fruits & Berries

apple N 10
banana N 10
blackberry N 12
blueberry N 12
cherry N 10
coconut N 12
cranberry N 14
grape N 12
grapefruit N 12
lemon N 12
lime N 14
melon N 14
orange N 10
peach N 12
pear N 10
pineapple N 12
plum N 12
prune N 16
pumpkin N 14
raisin N 14
raspberry N 14
strawberry N 10
tomato N 14

75 PLANTS, General

bloom N 14
blossom N 14
branch N 14: 67c
flower N 12
grass N 12
moss N 16
plant N 14
root N 12
seaweed N 16: 67j
stem N 16

76 PLANTS, Nuts & Grains

acorn N 16
corn N 14
oats N 16
peanut N 12
pecan N 14
rice N 12
rye N 16
walnut N 16
wheat N 14

77 PLANTS, Products

bouquet N 14
cigar N 14
cigarette N 14
oaken J 12: 44
tobacco N 14
wooden J 16: 44

78 PLANTS, Trees

cactus N 16
cottonwood N 14
evergreen N 14
maple N 14
mulberry N 16
oak N 14
palm N 16
pine N 14

79 PLANTS, Vegetables

bean N 12
beet N 14
cabbage N 12
carrot N 12
cauliflower N 16
celery N 12
lettuce N 14
onion N 12
pea N 12

potato N 10
spinach N 16

80 PRODUCTS,
Clothing

apron N 14
belt N 12
bib N 16
blouse N 10
boot N 10
cap N 8
clothe V 10
clothes N 12
coat N 12
collar N 14
costume N 14
dress V 12
fit V 16
footwear N 12
glove N 12
handbag N 14: 86
handkerchief N 14
hat N 12
headdress N 16
hoopskirt N 14: 67e
jacket N 12
kerchief N 16
knit V 16
mitten N 12
nightcap N 14: 67e
overcoat N 14
overshoe N 12
pajamas N 14
pocket N 12
pocketbook N 14: 86
purse N 14: 86
sew V 14: 10
shoe N 10
skirt N 10
slacks N 16
sleeveless J 16
slipper N 14
stocking N 14

suit N 12
sweater N 14
undress V 14
uniform N 16: 67e
wear V 14

81 PRODUCTS,
Containers

bag N 12
baggage N 14: 55c, 86
bottle N 12: 90e
bowl N 12: 90e
box N 12: 90d
bucket N 16: 90e
bundle N 16
case N 16: 86
cup N 12: 90e
jar N 14: 90e
luggage N 16: 86
net N 16: 48
pail N 14: 90e
pan N 12: 90e
pot N 16: 90e
sack N 16
saucepan N 16: 90e
suitcase N 16: 55c, 86
tub N 14: 90d

82 PRODUCTS, Food

a. Beverages

alcohol N 16
beer N 12
cocoa N 12
coffee N 12
cream N 10
juice N 10
lemonade N 12
milk N 10
soup N 10
tea N 12
wine N 16

b. Cooking

bake V 12
baker N 12: 71e
boil V 14
cook V 10
fry V 16
pour V 14
reheat V 16
stew V 14
sweeten V 16: 82f

c. Eating

bite V 16
breakfast N 14
cafe N 14: 89
chew V 14
diner (place) N 14: 89
diner (person) N 16:
   71d
dinner N 12
drink V 16
drinker N 16: 71d
eat V 10
feed V 14
graze V 16: 67a
lunch N 14
meal N 12
menu N 16: 62d
overeat V 16
picnic N 14: 68d
restaurant N 16: 89
supper N 14
waitress N 16: 71e

d. General

bakery N 12: 80
batter N 16
berry N 12
bread N 10
butter N 14
cereal N 14
cheese N 10
cinnamon N 16
cornstarch N 16

flour N 14
food N 12
fruit N 14
gravy N 16
grocer N 14: 71e
grocery N 12: 89
kitchen N 12: 90c
meal (grain) N 16
meat N 12
mustard N 14
nut N 14
oatmeal N 12
pancake N 10
pickle N 14
popcorn N 12
salad N 10
sandwich N 12
spaghetti N 16
supermarket N 14: 89
toast N 14
vegetable N 12
vinegar N 16
yolk N 16

e. **Meat**

bacon N 12
beef N 12
beefsteak N 12
ham N 12
hamburger N 12
liver N 16
pork N 12
sausage N 14
steak N 14

f. **Sweets**

brownie N 10
candy N 12
chocolate N 12
cookie N 12
cracker N 10
doughnut N 14
fudge N 14

gingerbread N 14
jelly N 10
marshmallow N 16
sweeten V 16: 82b
syrup N 14

83 PRODUCTS,
   Instruments &
   Measures

acre N 16
barometer N 16: 67h
calendar N 14: 59b
century N 16: 59b
clock N 8: 59b
column N 16: 56a
compass N 16: 67j
cupful N 16
day N 12: 59b
degree N 14
dozen N 14
gallon N 14
hour N 14: 59b
inch N 14
line N 16
meter N 16
mile N 16
minute N 12: 59b
month N 12: 59b
ounce N 16
period N 14: 59b
pint N 16
pound N 14
quart N 16
scale N 14
spyglass N 16
telescope N 16
thermometer N 14: 67h
timepiece N 16: 59b
ton N 14
volt N 16
week N 12: 59b
year N 12: 59b

84 PRODUCTS,
   Machines & Tools

ax N 14
battery N 14
blade N 16
camera N 12
clippers N 16
engine N 14: 88b
flashlight N 12
hammer N 12
headlight N 14
knife N 14
machine N 14
magnet N 16
motor N 16
needle N 14
pump N 16: 67j
robot N 16
saw N 14
scissors N 14
searchlight N 16
shovel N 14
spotlight N 14
typewriter N 14
windmill N 14

85 PRODUCTS, Misc.
   Objects

bell N 14
bumper N 16
cardboard N 14
chip N 16
dynamite N 16
fireworks N 14: 68d
object N 16
saver N 14: 67j
signal N 14
wrapper N 16

86 PRODUCTS,
   Personal Effects

baggage N 14: 55c, 81

cane N 16
case N 16: 81
comb N 10
handbag N 14: 80
key N 14
lipstick N 16
lotion N 16
luggage N 16: 81
mask N 14
mouthpiece N 16
necklace N 16
perfume N 16
pocketbook N 14: 80
purse N 14: 80
suitcase N 16: 55c, 81
tissue N 16
toothpick N 16
umbrella N 14
wallet N 16

87 PRODUCTS, Textiles

cloth N 14
jean (cloth) N 16
material N 16
rag N 16
sail N 16: 67j
sheet N 14
silk N 14
tent N 14

88 PRODUCTS, Transportation

a. Mode

aircraft N 14
airplane N 10
auto N 14
boat N 10: 67j
bus N 14
cab N 14
canoe N 14
car N 14
cart N 16

elevator N 14
jet N12
motorcar N 12
plane N 12
railroad N 12
railway N 10
sailboat N 12: 67j
seaplane N 14
ship N 12: 67j
sleigh N 14
steamship N 14: 67j
submarine N 16: 67j
subway N 14
taxi N 14
trailer N 14
train N 12
truck N 12
wagon N 16

b. Operation

drive V 14
driver N 12: 71d
engine N 14: 84
engineer N 14: 71e
flier N 16: 71e
fly V 12: 11
motor V 14
motorist N 16: 71d
ride V 14
steer V 14

89 STRUCTURES, Buildings

bakery N 12: 82d
ballroom N 16: 67e, 68d
barn N 12: 67a
boardinghouse N 14
building N 12
cabin N 12: 67e
cafe N 14: 82c
castle N 16: 60b, 67e
church N 12: 66
clubhouse N 16: 68d

college N 12: 62c
courthouse N 14: 63
diner (place) N 14: 82c
farmhouse N 14: 67a
garage N 12
greenhouse N 12: 67a
grocery N 12: 82d
henhouse N 12: 67a
hospital N 10: 65
hotel N 14
house N 10
inn N 14: 67e
jail N 16: 64
lighthouse N 16: 67e, 67j
mill N 14
museum N 16: 68d
poorhouse N 14
prison N 16: 64
restaurant N 16: 82c
sawmill N 16: 67c
schoolhouse N 12: 62c
shop N 14: 61c
skyscraper N 16
store N 10: 61c
supermarket N 14: 82d
warehouse N 14
watchtower N 14: 67c, 67e

90 STRUCTURES, Houses

a. Appliances

cooler N 16
dryer N 16
fan V 12
freezer N 12
heater N 14
icebox N 14
lamp N 12
oven N 14
phonograph N 14
stove N 14

sweeper N 14
toaster N 14
wireless N 16

b. Furniture

bed N 16
bench N 14
bookrack N 12
bookshelf N 14
chair N 14
cradle N 16
desk N 10
dresser N 16
finish N 14
footstool N 16
furnishings N 14
light N 10
rug N 12
seat N 16
table N 12
upholster V 16
woodwork N 10

c. Parts

address N 12
apartment N 14
basement N 14
bathroom N 12
bedroom N 12
closet N 14
door N 10
doorstep N 16
doorway N 12
driveway N 12: 92
fence N 16
floor N 14
garden N 10: 91
gate N 12
hallway N 16
home N 12: 91
housetop N 12
kitchen N 12: 82d
laundry N 14: 90f

library N 12
mailbox N 8
nursery N 10
office N 12: 61d
roof N 14
smokestack N 14
stair N 16
studio N 14: 60c
toilet N 14
wall N 12
washroom N 12
window N 12
windowpane N 16
workroom N 12: 61d
workshop N 16: 61d
yard N 12: 91

d. Supplies

bath N 12
board N 14: 67c
box N 12: 81
brick N 14
doorknob N 16
fuel N 14
furnish V 16: 06
glue N 12
hook N 16
hose N 16
ladder N 16
lid N 16
lumber N 14: 67c
nail N 14
paint N 12
roofing N 14
rope N 16
screw N 16
shellac N 16
sink N 14
tack N 16
tape N 14
tub N 14: 81
washbowl N 14
waterworks N 16
wire N 14

e. Wares

bedclothes N 16
blanket N 14
bottle N 12: 81
bowl N 12: 81
broom N 12
broomstick N 16
brush N 16
bucket N 16: 81
candle N 14
candlestick N 14
cup N 12: 81
dish N 12
firewood N 14
foil N 16
garbage N 16
housekeeping N 12
indoors D 12
jar N 14: 81
mirror N 12
napkin N 16
needlework N 16
pail N 14: 81
pan N 12: 81
pillow N 14
pin N 14
plate N 14
polish V 14
pot N 16: 81
saucepan N 16: 81
silverware N 14
spoon N 12
sweep V 14
tablecloth N 12
tablespoon N 14
tableware N 14
teaspoon N 12
towel N 12
trash N 14
yarn N 16

f. Washing

dampen V 14
foam N 16: 67j

laundress N 16: 71e
laundry N 14: 90c
slop V 14
soak V 14
soapsuds N 14
splash V 16
spray V 14
sprinkle V 16
washer N 14: 02, 71d
washing N 12
wipe V 16

91 STRUCTURES,
Locations
airport N 12
birthplace N 14
camp N 12: 67c
campus N 14: 62c
cemetery N 16: 66
churchyard N 14: 66
city N 12: 63
country N 14: 63, 67d

farm N 14: 67a
fatherland N 16: 63
field N 12: 67a
fishery N 16: 67j
garden N 10: 90c
grave N 14: 66
hayfield N 14: 67a
home N 12: 90c
nation N 12: 63
park N 16: 68c, 68d
plantation N 16: 67a
playground N 10: 68c, 68d
port N 16: 67j
ranch N 12: 67a
shipyard N 14: 67j
station N 16
town N 16: 63
township N 16: 63
village N 14: 63
yard N 12: 90c
zoo N 12: 68d

92 STRUCTURES,
Thoroughfares

airway N 16
avenue N 14
bridge N 14
crossroads N 16
detour N 16
driveway N 12: 90c
fork N 14
highroad N 14: 67e
highway N 12
lane N 16
path N 16
road N 12
roadway N 10
route N 14
street N 12
track N 14
way N 14
wayside N 14

VII
Words by Definition
and Topical Classification

In this chapter all of the words have been placed in alphabetical order. Directly following each word is a topical classification code. For example, the word "abbreviation" is followed by the code "(67f)". This refers to the classification: *67 INSTITUTIONS, Science, f. Linguistics*, shown in Chapter VI. In the event that a word has not been classified in Chapter VI, it will be followed by the notation "(UNCL)" which is short for unclassified.

The topical classification code is followed by four choices: three decoys and the definition of the word (italics). The choices are presented in their original order.

a (UNCL): food, *one*, way, eating

abbreviation (67f): sleeping rooms, meal, *shortened form*, make a hole

about (36): tune, fruit, road, *around*

above (UNCL): *higher place*, way, weather, not fine

accidental (22): study of numbers, in the time between, *happening by chance*, tobacco for smoking

account (61a): collection of animals, *record of money*, center part, filling for pies

ache (65): not certain, *be in pain*, to a lower floor, not quiet

acorn (76): dry earth, *nut*, unhappy, not clear

acre (83): strong rope, car on a train, sharp watch, *measure of land*

act (60a): *part of a show*, one who loses, neither hot nor cold, giving to the poor

activity (58a): *movement*, juice, leaf, show

actor (60a, 71e): sea spirit, animal, fasten, *performer*

add (67g): pay close attention, not fixed, *put together*, cake

addition (67g): always, tree, *summing up*, strong

additional (35): musical instrument, *extra*, gun, fall behind

address (90c): part of a ticket, sliding down of soil, *place where mail is sent*, not willing to work

adopt (06): place for cartridges, division of an army, done by magic, *take for your own* adult (71a): food, young animal, worth remembering, *grown-up*

adventure (55a): valley, crowd, *happening*, humble

afar (27): line through the center, one thousand, *a long way off*, take care of

afire (58a): killer, not certain, *burning*, strong

afraid (72a): light, *frightened*, tag, nearness

after (UNCL): *later*, carriage, whip, not fine

again (43): trust with, *once more*, help in trouble, friendship

age (58a): false story, *time of life*, looking alive, never stopping

aged (71a): dead, keep on, tower, *old*

ago (43): fortune, squeak, *past*, lame person

agree (70a): pillow, *think alike*, build, handle

agreement (70a): religious service, large quantity, helping to make beautiful, *understanding between persons*

aid (70a): gentle, living, *help*, small

air (67h): get away from, opening in a wall, *gases around the earth*, not long ago

aircraft (88a): tardy, idleness, *plane*, flour

airplane (88a): blood poisoning, make a hole, *flying machine*, not tight

airport (91): machine for weaving, die under water, *station for planes*, work of art

airway (92): middle, *route*, house, young woman

airy (67h): way, train, young, *breezy*

alarm (04): possibly, big, boss, *warn*

alcohol (82a): rob, leather trousers, *liquor*, title

alike (39): more cold than hot, *in the same way*, place where two lines meet, time of being a man

alive (20): liver, road, *living*, young animals

alligator (53): decide, cushion, *animal*, hat

allowable (64): bravery, farm, *permissible*, guide

almost (22): *nearly*, vegetable, large city, middle

aloud (58d): paper giving powers, spot on the skin, day of the week, *in a clear voice*

alphabet (67f): animal, packed, friendship, *letters*

alphabetical (62b): part of the day, be made of, like a mother, *letters in order*

amaze (01): give, cloth, *surprise*, light

amen (UNCL): person who runs away, *word at end of prayer*, part of a continent, material left by natural means

America (67d): telegram, Monday, Christmas, *United States*

American (63, 67e): *citizen of United States*, time of being a man, car on a train, make a mistake

amount (67g): insect, player, parent, *sum*

an (UNCL): family, light, *one*, stop

and (UNCL): high hill, *as well as*, game, dead body

angel (66): speak low, *winged being,* silly, make cold

angry (72a): corn, *mad,* humble, group

animal (49): bring up to date, free from dirt, *any living being,* office worker

another (UNCL): *one more,* school, put together, wrong

answer (04): *speak in return,* looking glass, very small, not black or white

ant (50): copy, *insect,* mix, bright

anybody (UNCL): care for the hands, in any way, *any person,* self important

anyhow (UNCL): *in any way,* greater part, use a tool, any living person

anyone (UNCL): grand, meeting, tell a secret, *some person*

anywhere (36): not high, think about, letter box, *at some place*

apartment (90c): more cold than hot, great number, of the sea, *set of rooms*

ape (51): soldier, *monkey,* company, wolf

apple (74): *fruit,* foggy, duck, cover

approval (70b): hole, baggage, *praise,* boat

April (59d): color, jump, not beg, *month*

apron (80): box, house, man, *bib*

arctic (67d): *at the north pole,* gathering of people, flash of electricity, person who lied

arithmetic (67g): keep in mind, *art of numbers,* a sea spirit, put to death

arm (67b): *part of the body,* woman who milks cows, wall to hold back water, take care of

army (67e, 69): set free, *group of soldiers,* school for children, of the teeth

arrangement (17): oil, dog, *plan,* fake

arrive (11): box, tools, cat, *come*

arrow (67e, 68c): animal, trust, soldier, *stick*

art (62b): stream, gentleman, *skill,* insect

artist (60c, 71e): sail, break, smallest, *painter*

ask (10): open, *question,* floor, storm

asleep (72d): *at rest,* harm, bits of thread, not safe

aspirin (65): not big, exciting, weed, *drug*

assuredly (22): bunch, *certainly,* wind, lonely

astronomy (62a): belonging to me, paper giving powers, *science dealing with stars,* front of a gun

athletic (41): put into service, good to eat, *physically strong,* telling one's sins

athletics (68c): things inside, *games and sports,* set of keys, touch with the lips

atlas (62d, 67d, 67j): public official, *book of maps,* young cat, work into shape

atmosphere (67h): sofa, kindness, varnish, *air*

attendance (62b): draw off, *being present,* huge snake, wrap up

aunt (71c): covered part of a truck, *sister of one's mother or father,* one of the edges of the map, table showing days of the year author (62d, 71e): person who seeks office, *person who writes books,* piece of wood, time of being a man

auto (88a): glass, *car,* stick, gun

autograph (72c): mix, *signature,* food, boat

autumn (59e): valley, sweetheart, couch, *season*

avenue (92): strong liking, fish, chief, *street*

awake (72d): *not sleeping,* heavenly body, fixed time, worker who builds

award (70b): *prize,* cover, money, instant

away (27): *gone,* wrong, player, fish

awful (28): *very bad,* make rough, take care of, run after

awhile (43): *for a short time,* stop the breath, person who sells, grain ground up

ax (84): *tool,* mother, dress, postman

babe (71a): bird, get, land, *baby*

baboon (51): joke, fruit, *monkey,* cut

baby (71a): happily, fill again, *young child,* go by

babyhood (71a): face of a baby, part of a telephone, stop up the mouth, *time of being a baby*

back (67b): *rear,* steam, warm, pour

bacon (82e): fight, *meat,* word, organ

bacteria (65): movable, *germs,* shine, loosen up

bad (28): answer, package, faint light, *not good*

bag (81): *sack,* grandfather, change, see

baggage (55c, 81, 86): *suitcases,* stones, honor, new arrival

bake (82b): be glad, *cook,* dark hours, fur

baker (71e, 82b): *person who makes bread,* frozen drop of rain, get the meaning of, at this time

bakery (82d, 89): *bread shop,* small bag, spring back, in the middle

balance (39): hunting for facts, ground beef, *make equal,* science of government

bald (72d): study again, *without hair,* possession, firmness

ball (38): in some measure, *anything round,* sounding together, rise up again

ballet (60a): *dance,* empty, decent, poems

balloon (68c): *toy,* glory, polite, author

ballroom (67e, 68d, 89): small bag, *dance hall,* make free, hold close

banana (74): *fruit,* part, water, get up

bank (61a): *place for keeping money,* light at front, end of a fork, line of things

bank (67d): *side of a river,* going well together, offer of marriage, go with speed

bankbook (61a): story book, pull, *account book,* blow

banker (61a, 71e): *person who runs a bank,* the woman spoken about, fond of fighting, the bank of a river

baptism (66): *church admission,* family, somewhat purple, fixed time barber (71e): person who belongs to the same family, powder that goes off with noise, *person whose business is cutting hair*, son of one's brother or sister

barn (67a, 89): place where water is stored, expecting to receive what one wants, *building for storing cows and horses*, a word that says no

barometer (67h, 83): system for sending messages, *instrument for measuring pressure*, part of the forehead, person paying rent

base (36): *bottom*, happen, person, foolish

baseball (68c): *a game*, from, left, true

basement (90c): insect, cream, ready, *cellar*

basketball (68c): stare, toilet, large, *a game*

bat (68c): *stick*, cabin, gas, move

bath (90d): dig, *tub*, woman, pot

bathe (02): *wash*, charming, bird, close

bathroom (90c): school room, *room*, a rope, one fourth

batter (82d): sheltering, give off rays, high birth, *cooking mixture*

battery (84): sheep, room for children, dislike, *electric cell*

battlefield (67e, 69): *theater of war*, spots on the skin, absence without leave, made of oak

bay (67d): over, quick, rock, *gulf*

beach (67d, 67j): cross, metal, *shore*, stretched

beak (67b): welcome, *bird's bill*, worthy of trust, gas

bean (79): cure, pot, smile, *vegetable*

bear (51): answer, promise, *animal*, hall

beard (67b): in a bad temper, person who gathers news, *hair on a man's face*, one who shares

beat (08): make known, *strike*, look, barber

beaten (69): plenty, passage, *defeated*, possibly

beautiful (28): ready, fish, *pretty*, bay

beautify (03): get up, whistle, *make beautiful*, beautiful dress

beauty (30): take away, make well, checks or stripes, *good looks*

beaver (51): play, clear, *animal*, attention

because (UNCL): *for*, pipes, spoil, hasty

become (07): a gas, mailman, not smooth, *change into*

bed (90b): globe, value, *cot*, dance

bedclothes (90e): vegetables, *linen*, tall, grain

bedroom (90c): way of showing truth, bow of colors, *room to sleep in*, no more room

bee (50): *insect*, bag, sorry, fur

beef (82e): *meat*, inn, chickens, say

beefsteak (82e): like better, stand for, every hour, *slice of meat*

beehive (48): *house for bees*, dark point, hurt by bees, feel angry

beer (82a): yet, go on, come back, *drink*

beet (79): *plant*, jokes, sounds, through

beetle (50): wit, stream, *insect*, blow

before (43): act of buying, street, *earlier than*, chase

begin (16): color, slipped stitches, *start*, player

beginner (71b): *starter*, overshoes, business, steal

begone (11): wash the throat, *go away*, student, making over

behave (70d): cat, happy, give up, *act*

behind (UNCL): for many, piece of metal, study again, *in the rear*

believe (17): stare, neither side, *trust*, fence

bell (85): *alarm*, wagon, boy, cook

below (UNCL): remember, *under*, rock, leather

belt (80): in the open air, make fresh again, *leather worn around body*, being to blame

bench (90b): warm, large, *seat*, too

berry (82d): hold, *fruit*, bucket, answer

beside (UNCL): friend, proper, top part, *near*

best (28): sharp pain, chair, *most good*, without a head

better (28): umbrella, a deep sound, *more good*, forgive

beyond (27): *farther away*, warm over, a greeting, practice

bib (80): *apron*, stay, laid, rider

Bible (66): give back, *a book*, half a globe, Merry Christmas

big (40): *large*, go back, light blow, brave

bigger (40): *larger*, fish, true, path

bigness (30): dangerous, *greatness*, shell, lightness

bill (61a): stealing, tall, *charges*, foot

billboard (62d): vegetable, love, *sign*, country

billion (57): *thousand million*, merry, top part, admirer

biography (62d, 67e): move one thing, sprinkle, *life history*, without money

bird (49): crush, *animal*, player, owner

birthday (55b): written order, *day when born*, run into, time of day

birthplace (91): a man, woman or child, place where people play, *place where a person is born*, a row side by side

bite (82c): *chew*, doctor, blush, ring

black (24): *color*, plate, leap, hole

blackberry (74): opening, poems, true, *fruit*

blackbird (47): *bird*, level, bird's nest, way out

blackness (58c): honor, animal, kindness, *darkness*

blacksmith (67a, 71e): do harm in return, rules of health, *man who shoes horses*, more than enough

blade (84): desire for food, raised flooring, *cutting edge*, save for later blank (35): shaky, promise, *empty*, tramp

blanket (90e): foolish, owner, dig, *cover*

bleed (65, 72d): make smooth, expecting to receive, *lose blood*, thing needed

bless (66): *make holy*, foolish, bang, flower

blessing (66): well-liked, stiff, harbor, *a prayer*

blind (65, 72d): make a loud noise, *not able to see*, person held by an enemy, something to do with mail

blindfold (68c): *cover the eyes*, part of a plant, fixed time, a measure

blindness (65): *lack of sight*, every hour, line of things, cause to flow

blizzard (67h): *snow storm*, part left over, dance, old ship

blockhouse (67e, 69): away, order, *fort*, give

blond (24): *fair-haired*, keeping safe, move quickly, children's wear

bloodhound (51): boat, cost, song, *dog*

bloodshot (24): *red*, steal, courage, speak

bloom (75): *flower*, measure, old, settle

blossom (75): player, *flower*, shine, not used

blouse (80): *shirt*, steam, animal, evening

blow (72d): bad dream, *breathe hard*, bring together, talk wildly

blowout (58a): truly, *explode*, night, never

blue (24): sorry, *color*, silent, receive

blueberry (74): take away, hand over, twelve o'clock, *fruit*

bluebird (47): birdhouse, direction, *bird*, answer

bluejay (47): icy, look, danger, *bird*

board (67c, 90d): finish school, ice for skating, *piece of wood*, man who rows

boardinghouse (89): *hotel*, religious, metal, willing

boat (67j, 88a): welcome, *ship*, dangerous, business

boating (68c): happen, cheating, smell, *sailing*

bobcat (51): catsup, father, *wild cat*, leave out

body (67b): shine, thick line, *person*, single

boil (82b): *cook*, sports, not shut, hole

bomb (69): belonging to us, *container with explosives*, person who writes, rough person

bomber (69): steal, farthest, *airplane*, hold

bonfire (58a): frozen, strip, fear, *blaze*

book (62b, 62d): give off rays, floating platform, *written sheets of paper*, catching of the breath

bookkeeper (61a, 71e): wind, pocket knife, *clerk*, tracks

bookrack (90b): young goose, *bookcase*, possibly, swift

bookseller (61c, 71e): sweet smell, ice cream, *salesman*, large

bookshelf (90b): *bookcase*, stones, bookshop, amount

boot (80): visitor, *shoe*, understand, medicine

boss (61d): *chief*, gain, heavenly, web

both (UNCL): bad dream, rule, person who sells, *two together*

bother (72a): *trouble*, evening, make neat, say

bottle (81, 90e): answer, *jar*, tree, numbers

bottom (36): figure, *lowest part*, unpleasant, covering

boundary (54): for the night, harshness, *limiting line*, great wait

bouquet (77): *bunch of flowers*, take a share, by means of, put out of sight

bowl (81, 90e): clothing, *dish*, true, joy

bowling (68c): repeat, *a game*, mailman, shout at

box (81, 90d): teacher, insect, *case*, value

boxer (68b): *man who fights*, give off rays, keep from happening, person held by enemy

boy (71f): railroad, *male child*, chase, hold close

boyish (71f): *youthful*, confused, moist, path

brain (67b): cushion, sorry, limp, *mind*

brake (16): *stop*, family, surface, notice

branch (67c, 75): worthy of trust, place for the sick, *part of a tree*, cause to flow

bravery (72b): *without fear*, shaky, view, ten times ten

bread (82d): tear, extra, wash, *food*

breakable (41): way of stepping, take away from, sheet of paper, *easily broken*

breakfast (82c): *a meal*, love story, plant, bring together

breast (67b): large, *chest*, bird, for many

breath (67b): person whose duty it is to keep order, get the meaning of the printed word, the spirt of one who is dead, *air drawn into and out of the lungs*

breathe (72d): head of the church, being liked by most people, *draw air into the lungs*, person who makes things

breathless (72d): speak well of, *out of breath*, make pure, great size

breeze (67h): *wind*, put back, kept, eat fast

breezy (20): *windy*, polite, metal, miner

brick (90d): make, *block of clay*, dig out, carry along

bride (71c): make many holes in, *woman just married*, study of words, keep busy

bridegroom (71c): small person, chance of harm, slope of a road, *man just married*

bridge (92): hole where a dead body is buried, son of one's son or daughter, one who takes parts on stage, *something across a river or road*

bright (21): not smooth, *giving light*, drug, snake

brighten (15): *shine*, government, person, welcome

brightness (58c): corn, move, sure, *shining*

brilliance (58c): waste, clay, *brightness*, channel

bring (19): speed, protect, visitor, *carry*

broke (32): pile of hay, warm over, *out of money,* somewhat purple

brook (67d): peak, step, *stream,* boil

broom (90e): *brush,* pig, be glad, in order

broomstick (90e): *handle,* necessary, case, happiness

brotherly (32): *friendly,* reduce, certainly, famous

brown (24): *color,* eat, cry, time

brownie (82f): small berry, do again, in no place, *chocolate cake*

brush (90e): *broom,* of old, brain, correct

bucket (81, 90e): further, prepared, dig, *pail*

buckshot (69): *bullet,* authority, school, bake

buckskin (52): grandmother, learn, *leather,* take

bud (07): think over, *begin to grow,* extra time, say hello

buffalo (51): row, priest, *ox,* greet

bug (49): rain, red, artist, *insect*

bugle (68c): somewhat, *trumpet,* baby, meat

build (03): divide, *make,* judge, interest

builder (71e): take place, voyage, *maker,* gone by

building (89): soft, *house,* be glad, paths

bull (51): connect, land, hundred, *male animal*

bullet (69): put in the earth, man, woman or child, turn in a circle, *lead shot from a gun*

bulletin (62d): a gas, breathing, *news report,* gloomy

bum (71d): *beggar,* dish, flooring, place

bump (08): merry, strip off, *heavy knock,* tower

bumper (85): *bars that protect a car,* pay for the use of, near the north pole, part of a plant

bundle (81): boat, house, land, *package*

bunny (51): *rabbit,* quickly, ugly, owned

burn (58a): slip stitches, *be on fire,* small bird, on neither side

burro (51): give up, *donkey,* boy, funny

bus (88a): study again, one way, *large automobile,* fooling

bushy (44): letter, partly, *growing thickly,* fish scales

busily (20): *actively,* idea, feed, gladly

business (61d): turn, trouble, rooms, *job*

busy (20): stove, *working,* leather, chance

butter (82d): for the night, *fat from cream,* young from an egg, cut and dry grass

butterfly (50): fear, not sick, *insect,* lasting

buy (61c): come together again, have not, *get by paying,* give a loud cry

buyer (61c): *shopper,* drawing, plenty, robber

by (UNCL): happy, purse, poems, *near*

cab (88a): one, *car*, older, spoon

cabbage (79): *vegetable*, late, join, run

cabin (67e, 89): mark the skin, look at closely, get caught, *small house*

cactus (78): *plant*, machine, order, seasoning

cafe (82c, 89): *eating house*, automobile for hire, piece of soil, chew and swallow

cage (48): end part, *place closed in*, sharp weapon, one or the other

calendar (59b, 83): lines on which music is written, man who takes care of engines, *table showing days of the year*, say it must be done

calf (51): *young cow*, bet, small, be happy

call (04): carve, science, *speak*, rise

calm (20): very good, *quiet*, cook, bathroom

camel (51): rock, skin, death, *animal*

camera (84): day of the week, pointed piece of wood, *machine for taking pictures*, steam that escapes

camp (67c, 91): *group of tents*, teacher of reading, sudden attack, make clear

campus (62c, 91): *school grounds*, in fashion, small amount, lose color

canal (67d): sunset, *channel*, children, open

cancer (65): like a father, a single thing, believe guilty without proof, *growth in the body*

candle (90e): easily bent, *stick of wax*, stay on top, move through the air

candlestick (90e): due, *holder*, quick, loving

candy (82f): open, *sweet*, whip, servant

cane (86): *stick*, mark, share, neat

canoe (88a): *boat*, food, always, we

canyon (67d): shoe, holder, small, *valley*

cap (80): honest, wealth, porch, *hat*

capital (63, 67e): full of anger, move quickly over, *seat of government*, break a law

capital (37): select, *chief*, clear, tool

captain (69): time, *chief*, sight, get

car (88a): meeting, beat, *automobile*, listen

card (62f): useful, direction, *paper*, pleasant

cardboard (85): turn over to, let fall, *stiff paper*, let dry

cardinal (47): wine, platform, *bird*, set

care (72a): baseball, *worry*, beat, bad

career (61d): bathe, sweep, *occupation*, stirred

careless (32): raise the shoulders, for what reason, to an end, *done without thought*

cargo (61c): fashion, attack, juice, *freight*

carpenter (71e): *worker who builds*, part of the face, person who sings, skill in a worker

carrot (79): *plant*, shut, jerk, fire

cart (88a): *wagon*, ships, smooth, not true

cartoon (60c): melt ore, *drawing*, flowers, thread

cartoonist (60c, 71e): failure, *artist*, flood, fist

case (81, 86): pardon, *box*, smell, shape

cash (61b): ship, *money*, cloth, part

cashier (61a, 71e): cut with something sharp, can hold no more, front of the neck, *person in charge of money*

castle (60b, 67e, 89): eight, for sale, wear out, *building*

cat (51): wise, dull, choose, *animal*

catch (68a): made of paper, helpful act, *take and hold*, as many as needed

catcher (68b): bursting, order, animal, *player*

catfish (53): feel full, fish cake, waste, *fish*

cattle (51, 67a): more far, *animals*, shape, papers

cauliflower (79): *vegetable*, hut, grave, badly

cause (03): praise, throw, piece of wood, *make happen*

caution (72b): contest, *being careful*, metal sheets, seacoast

cavern (67d): very, clown, *cave*, blind

celery (79): *vegetable*, fish, trousers, hit

cemetery (66, 91): *graveyard*, envelope, pry, typewriter

cent (61b): *coin*, friend, needed, come

center (36): *middle*, banjo, interested, warm

century (59b, 83): moving stairway, not hard, *one hundred years*, deprive of weapons

cereal (82d): all time, south, happening, *grain*

ceremony (55b): open, below, test, *service*

chair (90b): told, join, fashion, *seat*

champion (68b): *winner*, new, deer, rowboat

championship (37): not normal, raised floor, angry look, *first place*

change (03): not fresh, frightened, throw up, *make different*

change (61b): suffer hunger, central government, lump on skin, *money returned*

chapter (67f): *division of a book*, flood of water, filling much space, start a lawsuit against

charming (32): cry out, *pleasing*, broom, building

chase (68a): potato, *run after*, remains, folks

cheap (61c): pay honor, killing, covered with fur, *costing little*

check (62f): fortune, stirred up, *mark*, many trees

checkers (68c): showing, way out, lady, *a game*

cheek (67b): repeat the sound, come to an end, *side of the face*, hold out against

cheerful (72a): wise, band, head, *glad*

cheese (82d): throat, leave, *food*, lose

chemistry (62a): sure, power, *science*, ranch

cherry (74): farm, *fruit*, horse, air

chest (67b): edge of a road, *part of a person's body*, say it must be done, shaking of the ground

chew (82c): direction of the sunrise, *crush with the teeth*, using too much, begin to grow

chick (47): *young chicken*, closet, chicken farm, sounding again

chickadee (47): division, result, *bird*, spray

chicken (47): walk through water, *young hen*, one or the other, at the end

chieftain (67e, 69): defeat, shame, *leader*, spot

child (71a): hollow holder, give work, having a taste, *boy or girl*

chin (67b): *front of the lower jaw*, not to be depended upon, make unable to get air, send out of one's country

chip (85): *piece*, show, spill, more

chipmunk (51): fall, every one, *squirrel*, take out

chocolate (82f): *candy*, swallow, who, strange

choir (56b, 60a): *singers*, weak, teach, fast

choose (10): form, older, *pick*, six

chop (08): time, raise, *cut*, being

chorus (60a): pen, duty, knee, *song*

church (66, 89): *house of prayer*, without ending, day of the week, word meaning you

churchman (66): cabbage, *minister*, reason, plant

churchyard (66, 91): yard stick, machine, each one, *graveyard*

cigar (77): *tobacco for smoking*, look at closely, part of the foot, known to be true

cigarette (77): along the ocean, person who aids, *tobacco for smoking*, showing no favor

cinnamon (82d): higher, lie, *spice*, fooling

circle (38): useful, *ring*, far, we

circulation (58a): *going around*, freedom, farm, dark place

circulatory (67b): germs used to protect a person, *having to do with circulation*, cloth worn around the shoulders, circle the wide world

circus (60a): time, death, *show*, blow

city (63, 91): fish, melt, lives, *town*

civics (62a): *study of rights of citizens*, day of the week, number of people working together, move through the air

civil (63): in a house, good enough, *of a citizen*, giving thanks

class (56b): fish, *group*, climb, also

classmate (71b): different from the rule, class of four-footed animals, wagon pulled by an automobile, *member of the same class*

classroom (62c): weakness, bedroom, drug, *schoolroom*

clean (28): price of a ticket, *free from dirt*, have faith in, work for others

cleanse (02): brave, hot, oil, *bathe*

clear (23): clock, weak, burn, *clean*

clerk (71e): come upon, *office worker*, open to question, not fast

climb (11): not important, ships sailing, *go up*, all people

clippers (84): clown, *shears*, streams, game

clock (59b, 83): surprise, wound, *watch*, stool

clockwise (26): *a direction*, because of, not allowed, give up

closet (90c): very large, strong wind, very much, *room for clothes*

cloth (87): *rag*, liberty, bird, porch

clothe (80): *dress*, week, fruit, doctor

clothes (80): strip of leather, hides the face, *coverings for the body*, cold enough for frost

cloud (67h): *smoke in the air*, work very hard, face of a watch, money to pay for clothes

cloudburst (67h): rapid movement, fond of study, covered with fur, *sudden rainfall*

cloudless (67h): *clear*, material, wrinkle, look at

cloudy (67h): of that kind, two rain clouds, *covered with clouds*, place with grape vines

clown (60a, 71e): *man who makes people laugh*, get in return for work, part of a word, form thread into a thing

club (56b, 68d): *group*, listen, alive, nut

clubhouse (68d, 89): river, grow, *hall*, side

coachman (67e, 71e): machine, walk, ocean, *driver*

coal (67i): ax, hire, *fuel*, improve

coast (67d, 67j): as many as needed, coming and going, known to a few, *land along the ocean*

coastal (67d, 67j): education, alike, *shore*, fear

coat (80): flower, mistake, *jacket*, state

cocoa (82a): a letter, gray, *a drink*, game

coconut (74): favor, machine, deep, *fruit*

coffee (82a): born, cloth, *a drink*, good-bye

coin (61b): quick, wild, animal, *money*

cold (42): shirt, meat, paper, *chilly*

collar (80): not the same, *band around the neck*, coming before others, let be seen

collection (56a): hard stone, *bringing together*, not lucky, poor health

college (62c, 89): quiet, *school*, outline, rush

collie (51): much, wave, *dog*, people

colony (56b, 67e): pure, *settlement*, send, charm

color (62b): walk, *paint*, act, parent

colored (24): part of the face, having three parts, one more than five, *not black or white*

colorful (24): snow, *bright*, worry, cloth

colt (51): one that sleeps, piece of music, coming before, *young horse*

column (56a, 83): move through the air, *division on a page*, piece that has broken, two times ten comb (86): *rubber with teeth used to arrange the hair,* writing or saying the letters of a word, word that tells what is or was done, clothes worn under a suit or a dress

combat (69): *fight,* wood, small, dirt

come (11): chair, *move toward,* very sad, other place

comeback (55c): sudden, clean, *return,* worm

comfortable (28): power, *satisfied,* bird, whole

comma (67f): *a mark,* fifth, same, eye

commandment (64, 66): sleep, *law,* open, man

commission (63): *put into service,* make a mark, can be seen, unfair play

commissioner (63): cook, *official,* book, sausage

communism (63, 67e): food, *social organization,* not probable, plant

community (56b, 63): from then till now, *group of people,* take out, put into

company (56b): *group of people,* will not let, ill will, lights in the front

compass (67j, 83): boat moved by steam, up and down, *instrument for showing direction,* not all of a thing

complain (04): *talk about pains,* woman on an airplane, at what time, turn into ice

complete (35): cream, magic, drop, *whole*

condemnation (64): dull, clearly, *judgment,* leather

congress (56b, 63, 67e): cut of meat, one more than five, *national law making body,* like a father

constitution (63, 67e): hair, quiet, *laws,* tool

constitutional (63, 67e): *lawful,* restlessly, water, south

contact (68a): plant food, *make a connection,* not thought of, strong lights

contentment (72a): *satisfaction,* sled, dishes, raised floor

cook (82b): *prepare food,* move round, put out, leave

cookie (82f): tooth, power saw, *flat cake,* false

cooler (90a): short, character, imagined, *refrigerator*

cooperation (70a): small trees, *working together,* most distant, going down

copper (67i): endless, alone, *metal,* gift

corn (76): tower, *grain,* single, shooting

corner (36): thin strip of wood, *place where two lines meet,* without a name, light from a fire

cornstarch (82d): telescope, success, *flour,* spot

correct (03): *make right,* kind of shoe, base, about

cost (61c): frighten, sweet smell, very large, *price paid*

costume (80): piece, porch, *dress,* liberty

cottonwood (78): helper, *tree,* much, loving

count (67g): *name numbers in order,* where the wilds begin, cloth worn about the shoulders, group of houses

country (63, 67d, 91): sight, furniture, *land,* writing

courthouse (63, 89): food shop, pipes, shame, *a building*

cousin (71c): *son or daughter of an uncle or aunt,* car that runs on rails in the street, place where goods are kept for sale, look long with the eyes wide open

cow (51): bring, many, air, *animal*

cowboy (67a, 67e, 71e): *man who looks after cattle,* room of a painter, will not let water through, house on a farm

cowhide (52): slipping, *leather,* gray, quick

crab (53): wind, touch, saw, *animal*

cracker (82f): *food,* where, small, beginning

cradle (90b): *baby's bed,* west, point, dry land

craft (62b): *art,* platform, thrifty, water

craftsman (71e): accustom to food, *skilled workman,* man chosen, improve the flavor

cram (19): woman, *stuff,* used, for

cranberry (74): every, get, blueberry, *berry*

crawl (11): belonging to you, cause to go, *move slowly,* time to come

crayfish (53): area, *animal,* thoughtful, curly

crayon (62f): *stick for drawing,* part of an egg, covered with fur, put into play

crazy (32): cough, bottom, *foolish,* village

cream (82a): day before today, hold no more, *part of milk,* wearing old clothes

creamy (44): turned into ice, with no cream, *like cream,* once a year

credit (61a): hat for the head, officer of the law, *trust in future payments,* stray away from

crop (67a): ugly, flame, *plants,* smoke

crossroads (92): *intersection,* ridge, burn, meal

crossword (68c): seven, hook, *puzzle,* layer

crow (47): have, arm, *bird,* coat

crow (04): war, *boast,* milk, nose

crowd (56b): in that way, *large number of people,* having too much water, draw into the nose

crown (60b, 67e): give food to, find the answer, *head covering,* flat tire

crush (05): skin, *squeeze,* quest, animal

cry (72d): grape, lovely, rise, *weep*

cub (51): *young animal,* large spoon, a long way, of the sun

cuckoo (47): *bird,* weapon, average, torn

cup (81, 90e): travel, slice, *dish,* fear

cupful (83): make go from home or country, look long with the eyes wide open, cup the hands around the ball, *as much as a cup can hold*

curl (11): time, jump, *roll,* week

curve (68a): baby, power, *bend,* long

customer (61c): pain in a tooth, strong wine, *person who buys,* plant food

cut (54): fruit, weak, highest, *open*

cute (28): tumble, *pretty,* shooting, waste

cutter (71e): one more than four, buy something, *person who cuts*, cut the cake

cutworm (51): crown, exciting, *caterpillar*, engine

daddy (71c): table, freedom, poor, *father*

daily (43): *every day*, iron block, shake up, push out

daisy (73): *flower*, join, smart, picture

dam (67d): *wall to hold back water*, space below roof, feeling in the skin, being liked by people

damage (05): *harm*, toy, spot, sure

dampen (90f): carrier, written, lips, *moisten*

dance (11): hair on man's face, person in newspaper work, *move in time with music*, word used instead of a noun

dancer (60a, 71e): *person who dances*, part of a machine, give little care to, dance away the night

danger (25): give away, something brought in, *chance of harm*, bad dream

dangerous (25): life history, in a house, *not safe*, night clothes

dark (21): not anything, *without light*, dog, make angry

darken (15): figure, lost, bird, *dim*

darkness (58c): oak, *shade*, red, meaning

darling (71d): *person much loved*, slice of beef, man who rows, making better

date (69b): cloth worn around the body, part of money paid, play that is sung, *time when something happens*

daughter (71c): also, work, stop, *child*

day (59b, 83): man who shoes horses, *time between sunrise and sunset*, part of the face, no longer at bat

daydream (17): not able to see, stream of water, shaped like an egg, *think about pleasant things*

daylight (58c): cover the eyes, a very short time, *light of the sun*, without any light

dead (20): *without life*, windy, sheet of paper, time of joy

deaden (05): block of clay, *make dull*, night clothes, a drink

deadly (25): inside of the hand, *causing death*, deaden the pain, giving life

deaf (65, 72d): short stiff hair, *not able to hear*, sheet of glass, give a good reason

deafen (05): out of money, breathe hard, frozen water, *deprive of hearing*

deafness (65): deaf cat, *being deaf*, crush, thought

deal (61c): *buy and sell*, chocolate cake, stupid person, small room

dear (71d): agree, copy, *darling*, rider

death (65): record of money, having some fault, *end of life*, soft and pale

December (59d): *month*, arrange, really, handwriting

decide (10): take for your own, done in a house, *make up one's mind*, turn into stone

deer (51): *animal*, ash, believe, public

defiance (72b): special right, *refusing to obey*, month of the year, fruit of a tree degree (83): at the north pole, write in haste, *unit for measuring temperature,* piece of metal

delight (72a): sickness, *pleasure,* eight, helper

democracy (63, 67e): *government run by the people,* fertile spot in the desert, put in a class, for a short time

dentist (65, 71e): *doctor,* set, bug, drip

describe (04): not long ago, lift the head, weapon, *tell about*

desk (90b): space, *table,* better, food

destroy (05): make happy, *break to pieces,* added to, turn the head

destroyer (69): *warship,* include, bars, cook

detour (92): mailman, seventh month, kind of hawk, *roundabout way*

diamond (67i): miner, *stone,* correct, friend

dictionary (62b, 62d): *book that explains,* getting no help, think highly of, act of buying

die (65, 72d): in a book, move, purple, *stop living*

diet (65): easily set on fire, in the air, move by pressing against, *special selection of food*

difference (58a): time at bat, *amount of being different,* close up to, of a different color

different (39): put in, *not the same,* person who acts, piece of metal

dig (67a): *turning over the ground,* of the navy, thing made known, station for planes

dime (61b): male donkey, tank for fish, *ten cents,* a new kind

diner (71d, 82c): every night, frozen water, on fire, *person eating*

diner (82c, 89): bow the head, *eating place,* cooled, completely

dinner (82c): *meal,* case, law, right

dinosaur (51): loop, *animal,* real, busy

directory (62d): grain, *list,* hotel, surprise

dirt (67i): *mud,* quick, smile, wrong

dirty (28): body of water, asking questions, very old, *not clean*

disappoint (01): *fail to satisfy,* fried eggs, make drunk, clapping hands

disappointment (72a): hole, *failure,* force, come near

disease (65): bundle, *sickness,* performer, listener

dish (90e): fried, reason, sack, *plate*

disinfect (65): *destroy germs,* forgive, make more, stick

dislike (72a): lookout, set in, radio signal, *hate*

disobedient (32): *refusing to obey,* pocket knife, strip of water, be a member of

disobey (70d): for each hundred, asking many questions, *pay no attention to,* liquid for drinking

disrespect (72b): jail, brother, *rudeness,* foreign

distance (30): heed, musician, trash, *length*

divide (19): flower, water, borrow, *separate*

dividend (61a): move up and down, divide the pie, freedom from war, *number to be divided*

dizzy (32): extra, fixed, cent, *foolish*

do (19): very thin, lift the head, *carry out*, of a flower

dog (51): side, rather, choose, *animal*

doll (68c): medicine, line, who, *toy*

dollar (61b): easily made angry, bunch of flowers, *one hundred cents*, swelling of the skin

donkey (51): *animal*, newspaper, breath, dish

door (90c): draw air into the lungs, take parts on the stage, time of joy, *opening in a wall*

doorknob (90d): windy, *handle*, nice, group

doorstep (90c): person, enough, steal, *stair*

doorway (90c): part of a harness, piece of ground, *opening in a wall*, strip of water

dormitory (62c): make very hot, small bag, put in, *sleeping rooms*

dot (38): hot, ask, *spot*, friendly

double (07): plan, *make twice*, dark color, thing

doubtless (22): knitted, yellow, horse, *surely*

doughnut (82f): bang, tricks, ox, *cake*

dove (47): carriage, *bird*, value, people

down (26): picture of a person, *to a lower place*, swell outward, putting in prison

downfall (63, 67e): bud, money, *drop*, frog

downhearted (72a): protect, perhaps, *sad*, really

downstairs (36): having to do with workers, *to a lower floor*, bars that protect a car, push out the lips

dozen (83): land, white, however, *twelve*

dragonfly (50): stream, upper, name, *insect*

draw (60c): one time, sweet smell, *make a picture*, flying machine

drawing (60c): surprise, *picture*, bird, warm

dream (60b): *something seen during sleep*, a measure of length, branch on a tree, put into order

dress (80); first letter, coverings of grain, last longer than, *put clothes on*

dresser (90b): away, *furniture*, kid, run

dressmaker (71e): a dress for a doll, a food made of flour, bundle of things wrapped together, *person whose work is making dresses*

drink (82c): *take in*, pull, dark hair, loving

drinker (71d, 82c): cut in pieces, *one who drinks*, drink the milk, plan for spending

drip (11): do tricks, male animal, small stone, *fall in drops*

drive (88b): father, *make go*, small spring, borrow on

driver (71d, 88b): feeling in the skin, short still hair, *person who drives*, cannot drive

driveway (90c, 92): ask, *road*, line, both

drown (72d): *die under water*, not outside, board for notice, round fruit

drummer (60a, 71e): *musician*, nervous, rear, famous

drunkard (71d): forming pictures in the mind, a very young child, garment worn in bed, *person who drinks too much*

drunkenness (72b): foreign, monkey, *intoxication*, again

dry (46): cannot be done, *not wet*, on the top, not either

dryer(90a): *machine that removes water*, person who invests money, woman just married, group of sentences

duck (47): supposing, *bird*, different, needed

due (22): clear, *expected*, germ, night

dull (21): money paid, *not sharp*, at bat, very little

dump (19): *throw down*, search, tub, loss of power

dunce (71d): father or mother, wooden stick, *stupid person*, with water

during (UNCL): and, love, *while*, heart

dust (67i): pocket knife, walk on, time of joy, *dry earth*

duty (61d): sprinkle, jar, *work*, nice

dynamite (85): squeeze, lining, *explosive*, depart

each (UNCL): keep guard, plane station, *every one*, chair leg

eagle (47): pail, *bird*, the, rush

ear (67b): car on a train, house for a dog, *part of the body*, arranged in order

early (43): sudden wonder, *in the beginning*, set of keys, figure out

earn (61d): put a child to death, word at end of prayer, more than one calf, *get in return for work*

earth (67d): bee, clerk, king, *land*

earthly (28): *worldly*, merrily, avenue, four-footed animal

earthquake (58a): *shaking of the ground*, citizen of United States, school for children, four-footed animal

earthworm (51): women, worker, wine, *worm*

east (36): run for public office, coming once a year, *the direction of the sunrise*, room where food is cooked

eastern (26): *toward the east*, rub with oil, east or west, work into shape

easy (41): go home, bow down, be seen, *not hard*

eat (82c): *chew and swallow food*, thing that knocks, think very highly of, low point of land

education (62a): winner, movies, shrunken, *teaching*

educational (62b): place where arms are kept, take care of a place, *having to do with education*, an educator of children

eel (53): dish, *fish*, calf, buzz

eight (57): not long ago, *one more than seven*, on land or sea, food for plants

eighteen (57): *eight more than ten*, drug for headaches, matter for a court, a girl of eight

eighth (57): *next after seventh*, lend a hand, tell the truth, Indian baby

eighty (57): hot melted rock, make sure or certain, *eight times ten*, be the eighth one

elbow (67b): *bend of the arm*, fight on horseback, large damp cave, to hear or see

elector (63): rude, pack, queen, *voter*

electric (58b): elephant, elbow bend, *of electricity*, an elder electrical (58b): *electric*, eleven, eldest, either

electrician (71e): top of a room, an evergreen tree, *person who repairs wiring*, tell a fairy tale to

elephant (51): *animal*, think, sudden, rich

elevator (88a): *machine for carrying*, an oak tree, free from doubt, flying in planes

eleven (57): a wide street, keep away from, many farm animals, *one more than ten*

else (39): hip, knee, rat, *other*

elsewhere (36): *in some other place*, free from dirt, a breathing organ, give some help

emergency (55a): hair on a horse, *need for immediate action*, front of the lower jaw, young boy or girl

employee (61d): tiny simple plants, a female horse, *person who works*, ways of living

employer (61d): cannot, *boss*, defeat, unmarried

employment (61d): coin, boot, wig, *job*

empty (35): feel surprise about, notes of music, study of numbers, *with nothing in it*

enclose (54): a locksmith, steep rock, *shut in*, afternoon

encouragement (70a): throw water out, *something that gives hope*, in the middle of, tobacco for smoking

end (36): his own, *last part*, bread shop, of the mind

engagement (55b): on the upper floor, *promise to marry*, at the coast, miles traveled

engine (84, 88b): does, copy, *machine*, burn

engineer (71e, 88b): tower, *driver*, bluejay, cave

English (62a, 67f): stage, *language*, rowboat, thief

enjoy (72a): help a friend, give an order, *be happy with*, hole in the earth

enjoyable (28): *pleasant*, cocktail, forty, otherwise

enjoyment (72a): crowbar, ponies, *pleasure*, having

enlarge (07): bad luck, *make greater*, save money, something nice

enter (11): ran away, *go into*, red apple, male deer

enthusiastic (72a): repeated blows, *eagerly interested*, center part, dead body

equator (67d, 67j): *imaginary circle around the earth*, sand at the mouth of rivers, a bright ray of light, one who guards and cares for people

erase (03, 62b): hold on, *rub out*, walked on, make sad

error (70c): command, lucky, signal, *mistake*

eruption (58a): June, shipper, *bursting*, girl

establishment (61d): loafer, *business*, nest, pond

even (39): eye, elect, *equal*, elm

evening (59c): machine for weaving cloth, not have any longer, *time between sunset and bedtime*, wife of a count

event (55a): gladly, frown, *happening*, broken

ever (43): joining, *any time*, grower, table

evergreen (78): jug, *plant*, goodness, meal

evermore (43): mob, *always*, reader, postage

every (UNCL): *each one*, prepare food, look after, noisy bird

everybody (UNCL): everyday, *every person*, copy letters, first stop

everyday (43): daybreak, dip, *daily*, drill

everyone (UNCL): eager people, eastern, *each one*, edge

everything (UNCL): *all things*, letter box, held true, nothing

everywhere (36): hotel worker, *in all places*, metal cup, be owned by

evil (28): ring, *bad*, steak, toast

examination (62b): swing, hobby, wooden, *test*

example (62b): taking, candle, hairy, *sample*

exchange (06): ear of corn, crowd around, *give and take*, important

excuse (70a): Wednesday, shake, *pardon*, view

exit (54): heavy stick, ill will, not fine, *way out*

expand (07): a color, three inches, horse shoe, *spread out*

expedition (55c): *journey*, zebra, season, clown

experience (62b): shot fired, white-faced, *knowledge gained*, leap on

expert (71b): narrow piece of metal, mark on a tree, *one with special skill*, ease the grief of

explanation (62b): a wish for happiness, cover the eyes, *clearing up a difficulty*, bunch of flowers

explore (55c): *travel through*, savage animal, lie down, red liquid

explorer (55c, 67e, 71e): *traveler*, manager, sheer, trainer

explosion (58a): zone, quilt, *blast*, old-fashioned

eye (67b): *part of the body*, piece of furniture, stir to action, in great amount

eyebrow (67b): ask for directions, give the evil eye, make a fist, *hair above the eye*

eyelash (67b): small car on a train, see eye to eye, science dealing with stars, *hair on the eyelid*

eyesight (65): *power to see*, not sleeping, eating house, front yard

face (67b): a large farm, light of a candle, *part of the head*, buy a ticket

fact (62b): spots on the skin, to be very hungry, days of the year, *thing known to be true*

faintness (65): business, greenness, *weakness*, happiness

fairy (60b): an inn, *tiny being*, set down, cross out

faith (66): *trust*, polish, laid, chin

fall (11): *drop*, skirt, receive, escape

false (28): *not true*, apart from, red beard, daytime

family (71c): to play on a seesaw, holder for a wax candle, guide an animal by a lead, *mother, father, and their children*

famous (34): *well known*, satisfactory, hopscotch, affectionate

fan (90a): *cause air to blow*, being in prison, where plays are shown, put back in place far (27): kind of candy, three times ten, *a long way*, hunt for facts

faraway (27): favor, farm, *far*, fast

farm (67a, 91): quart, nurse, *ranch*, lookout

farmer (67a, 71e): short point on a stem, take from one place to another, *man who raises crops or animals*, do harm in return for

farmhouse (67a, 89): monkey, *building*, newspaper, wildcat

farther (27): make merry, went far, even if, *more far*

fast (20): horn, *quick*, rack, peanut

fat (45): loose, net, post, *heavy*

father (71c): raisin, thought, *parent*, spread

fatherland (63, 91): written statement, *native country*, an opponent, present time

fatherly (71c): mother and father, chance of harm, measure of weight, *like a father*

fault (70c): bounce, comfort, *mistake*, acorn

favor (70a): loud noise, *kind act*, tumble down, make rough

favorite (28): act toward, share a room, *liked best*, foolish talk

fawn (51): hose, gone, *deer*, aunt

fear (72a): *be afraid of*, group of people, red powder, lower the value

fearful (72a): *frightened*, canyon, fourteen, defend

February (59d): girl, bite, clang, *month*

feed (82c): having no work, of a boat, ways of living, *give food to*

feel (18): hero, walnut, village, *touch*

feeling (72b): not the same, of a citizen, make a sound, *sense of touch*

female (71f): get the meaning, *woman or girl*, not good enough, hold things

fence (90c): *wall*, happen, took, vase

few (UNCL): to kiss, fat lady, *not many*, large farm

fiddler (60a, 71e): return, hurried, *musician*, weigh

field (67a, 91): moon, every, *land*, rode

fifteen (57): sit in an airplane, to a higher place, something paid for, *five more than ten*

fifth (57): brown fruit, set of directions, place of charm, *next after fourth*

fifty (57): one who receives, hills and mountains, to wind around, *five times ten*

fight (67e, 69): covered truck, knowing again, *war against*, written paper

fighter (69): triangle, *soldier*, hammer, prune

final (43): blank, goblin, *last*, heal

finally (43): plant life, *at the end*, part left over, way of acting

finger (67b): causing strong dislike, sense of sight, *part of the hand*, small flat cake

finish (16): officer in the army, make a loud noise, *bring to the end*, walk through water

finish (90b): *surface*, ribbon, address, eyeball

fire (58a): make right, love story, *something burning*, roll about firearm (69): friend, horse, sweep, *weapon*

fireproof (58b): where people wash, a male animal, *will not burn*, powder for cheeks

firewood (90e): foam, fifth, *fuel*, frown

fireworks (68d, 85): song sung by several persons, man who looks after cattle, *things that make a loud noise*, using or spending too much

firing (69): *shooting*, feather, honking, outward

first (37): on the lookout, *coming before others*, move against another, machine for lifting

fish (49, 67j): calendar, brain, *animal*, fake

fishery (67j, 91): *place for catching fish*, straight strip of wood, moving swell of water, eats fish on Friday

fit (80): edge of a pond, call back to mind, living person or animal, *be of the right size*

five (57): thing used to fight, have on the body, *one more than four*, men on a ship

flash (58c): wet sand, *sudden light*, bed cover, large building

flashlight (84): *electric light*, long strip, light a match, writing pad

flat (38): hang, give, tip, *level*

flatten (08): repay, *level*, stool, them

flavor (30): swan, *taste*, worst, church

flea (50): plane, *insect*, hello, kitchen

flier (71e, 88b): *pilot*, trade, winter, view

flirt (72a): take care of, more or less, *play at love*, make a record

float (67j, 68a): small round fruit, next after ninth, *stay on top*, the back of

flood (67h): *flow over*, not long ago, fine cloth, young hen

floor (90c): eighty, Indian, *ground*, hotel

florist (71e): from end to end, *person who sells flowers*, come back to health, floor of a tent

flour (82d): *ground wheat*, lame person, apple orchard, reach out

flower (75): angel, holiday, *blossom*, piggy

flowery (44): wife of a king, *covered with blossoms*, try to deal with, car on a train

fluid (67h): wayside, general, *liquid*, pickle

fly (11, 88b): have a strong taste, *move through the air*, a frame with bars, speak in a loud voice

foam (67j, 90f): steamboat, *bubbles*, thankful, everyone

fog (67h): steep, push, errand, *cloud*

foggy (67h): fully, kitty, party, *misty*

foil (90e): long strip of land, *metal in thin sheets*, point a gun, build a fire

food (82d): a tool to shave with, a small stream, *anything that people eat*, to understand clearly

fool (71d): *clown*, straw, whiskey, aloud

foolish (28): skin of cattle, cookie dough, freight train, *without sense*

foolishness (72b): tablecloth, sunflower, necklace, *stupidity*

foot (67b): *part of the leg*, group of three, spring back, house or barn

football (68c): schoolroom, grandma, rub down, *a game*

footlights (60a): take from one place to another, to bring back to good condition, matter for a law court to decide, *lights in the front of the stage*

footstool (90b): redbreast, milkman, *low stool*, stool pigeon

footwear (80): mouth, robber, closet, *shoes*

forbidden (64): soft wool, large building, *not allowed*, piano player

forehead (67b): not yet born, top of a room, *part of the face*, make fresh again

foreleg (67b): open wide, chair leg, *front leg*, make better

forenoon (59c): *time between early morning and noon*, brother of one's father and mother, place for burying the dead, a wedding held at high noon

forepaw (67b): feel sorry, *front paw*, special service, paw print

forest (67c): *woods*, often, quite, behind

forever (43): passage, *always*, harvest, theater

forget (14): *fail to remember*, slice of meat, not ever used, carry further on

forgiveness (72b): ladybug, hearing, potatoes, *pardon*

fork (92): monument, *crossroads*, policeman, English

forty (57): jacket of cloth, *four times ten*, making over, worth much money

forward (26): *ahead*, pound, exchange, beggar

four (57): *one more than three*, a house or home, belong to all, place to eat

fourteen (57): made with cake flour, that which happens, be a friend to, *four more than ten*

fourth (57): *next after third*, paid for work, go back over, small hard lump

fox (51): eraser, punish, *animal*, swore

freedom (63, 67e): *liberty*, whipped, tricycle, afterward

freeze (67h): go back to, apron strings, win a victory, *turn into ice*

freezer (90a): *refrigerator*, umbrella, speaker, necessary

French (62a, 67f): gladly, visitor, alley, *language*

fresh (43): *new*, after, waist, truth

freshman (71b): *student*, wring, ostrich, banana

freshness (43): money payment, *fresh condition*, wooden beam, college freshman

Friday (59a): sense of right and wrong, *day of the week*, how heavy a thing is, grain of a plant

friend (71d): *pal*, due, car, hot

friendless (32): *without friends*, from the west, make a connection, be friendly with

friendly (32): western, *loving*, tonight, adventure

fright (72a): foot, *fear*, flea, flock

frighten (01): *make afraid*, white flake, tramp down, left at home

frog (53): *animal*, wave, torn, clown

from (UNCL): dandy, be in, *out of*, buckle

front (37): flat, *first*, fence, father

frost (67h): flew, forty, *freeze*, floor

frosty (67h): *icy*, healthy, dry, baby

frozen (67h): just like another, *turned into ice*, at what time, chance of harm

fruit (82d): *part of a plant*, stream of water, air spinning around, bank of a river

fry (82b): *cook in fat*, winner of a game, make many holes, author of a book

fudge (82f): truck, blow, accept, *candy*

fuel (90d): make white and pure, persons who make laws, *anything that can be burned*, put up a fence

full (35): *can hold no more*, make a loud noise, part of a wheel, person who is afraid

fully (35): juice of grapes, *as a whole*, on a ship, open and close

fun (68c): house plant, *merry play*, over again, thick cord

fund (61a): *money*, wear, rest, spoon

funeral (55b): part of a plant, *ceremonies done at burial*, shaped like a ball, make a deep sound

fur (67b): and, *hair*, tag, very

furnish (06, 90d): writing, cookies, *supply*, unless

furnishings (90b): *furniture*, flower, forepaw, further

furry (44): further down the road, pack of cards, *covered with fur*, made of wood

future (59b): kings and queens, make dough rise, *time to come*, picture in words

fuzzy (23): beautiful day, finished work, done in, *not clear*

gallon (83): funny, hurried, shoulder, *a measure*

game (68c): bean, due, want, *sport*

gang (56b): settlement, *group*, village, began

gangster (64): borrow, attack, *criminal*, practice

garage (89): sum up to, make hard to understand, cause to laugh, *place for keeping automobiles*

garbage (90e): agree, *waste*, anyhow, fuzzy

garden (90c, 91): part left over, became shorter or smaller, as well as, *ground for growing flowers*

gardener (71e): *person hired to take care of a garden*, iron block on which metals are hammered, place where water is collected and stored, thing made to be just like another

gardenia (73): vacation, material, June, *flower*

gas (67h): *gasoline*, movies, gas motor, accept

gate (90c): move in time with, *door in a fence*, sit on a horse, get out of bed

gay (72a): *happy*, hickory, toss, bunch

gentle (32): gooseberry, ray, *kind*, arrived

gentleness (72b): baptize, equipment, *kindliness*, greenness

geography (62a): make many holes in, *study of the earth's surface*, cloth used on wound, moving in a circle giant (40): turkey, *great size*, known, in groups

gift (70b): moose, flow, January, *present*

gingerbread (82f): *cake*, awkward, fear, rascal

giraffe (51): clay, *animal*, mend, shore

girl (71f): flood, whose, *child*, easy

girlish (71f): an edge, put on, *like a girl*, boy or girl

give (06): *hand over*, fairy, round stone, harvest

glad (72a): fellow, *happy*, held, popped

gladness (72a): *joy*, bungalow, union, decent

globe (38): kind of grass, pretest a car, gathering of people, *anything round*

glory (70b): *praise*, anybody, goldfish, wicked

glove (80): make many holes in, with a folding top, *covering for the hand*, mark by burning

glue (90d): *paste*, wagon, likely, boast

go (11): found, boot, him, *move*

goat (51): fault, grow, *animal*, pretty

godlike (66): injury, *heavenly*, sunrise, wander

godmother (71c): talk about reasons for and against, *woman who takes vows for a child*, piece of lead from a gun, box in which food and drink are kept

golden (24): *yellow*, bitter, honeymoon, pitcher

goldfish (53): fish pond, stiff hat, *small fish*, hard to bear

goldsmith (67i, 71e): *man who makes articles of gold*, belong to the same family, finding out what disease a person has, breaking in to steal gold

golf (58c): bathing, *a game*, plum, wipe

good (28): *behaving well*, pay no attention, move quickly, other hand

goodness (72b): cream, neighborhood, business, *kindness*

goodwill (72b): pier, head servant, loosen up, *kindly feeling*

goose (47): comic, *bird*, railway, month

goose (71d): *silly person*, liquid, drug, good flavor

gorilla (51): faithful, memorial, *ape*, chair

government (62a): *ruling of a country*, help in trouble, top of a door, give up candy

governor (63, 67e): paper giving powers, near the north pole, *head of a state*, place to eat

grab (06): *take away*, schoolmaster, that happens, go to bed

gracious (32): housetop, *pleasant*, often, written

grade (62b): *class*, wonderful, riddle, pencil

graduate (62b): *finish school*, try out, lead others, mix up

grandchild (71c): join one thing to another, *child of one's son or daughter*, large mass of falling snow, close friend of a child

grandfather (71c): *father of one's father or mother*, sense of right and wrong, having no father at all, for a short time only grandpa (71c): grandmother, metal, *grandfather*, interested

grandparent (71c): ready to take in, *grandfather or grandmother*, repeat exactly, grand old flag

grape (74): captain, dozen, *fruit*, lost

grapefruit (74): lamp, fruit cake, *fruit*, sound noisy

grass (75): *plants*, law, length, shadow

grasshopper (50): shepherd, champion, *insect*, scarf

grassy (24): celebrate, *green*, spool, gift

grave (66, 91): time during which one is young, *hole where a dead body is buried*, part of a house or other building, three or more notes of music

gravel (67i): *stones*, adventure, sadness, neighbor

gravity (67h): call by sailors, the same kind, hooked nail, *a natural force*

gravy (82d): meow, *food*, sweat, glue

gray (24): begun, hose, *color*, went

grayheaded (71a): powerful, person who helps, *gray haired*, gray skies

graze (67a, 82c): sum up to, as well as, close tightly, *feed on grass*

great (40): sidewalk, *big*, wink, brick

greatness (30): nervousness, *bigness*, married, cocktail

green (24): knock, *color*, payment, worry

greenhouse (67a, 89): *building for growing plants*, come near or nearer to, loose outer coat, mass in the sky

greeting (70a): *welcome*, armor, because, roomy

greyhound (51): mineral, nobility, perfume, *dog*

grocer (71e, 82d): rubber with teeth, time to go to bed, *person who sells food*, covered with rust

grocery (82d, 89): further, *a store*, hillside, theatre

ground (67d): *earth*, protect, tiny, enter

group (56a): wife of a king, the same or different, *number of things together*, man who shoes horses

grow (07): *become bigger*, thing asked, arithmetic, blaze

guard (13, 64): *watch over*, snowflake, short hair, keep on

guardian (71d): automobile with a folding top, *person who takes care of another*, place where two lines meet, grain that grows on large ears

guess (10): butterfly, honor, *suppose*, trade

gulf (67d, 67j): *bay*, film, October, tinkle

gunner (69): withdraw, bent, *soldier*, number

gunpowder (67e, 69): *powder that goes off with noise*, something that keeps things cold, taking pleasure in the pain of another, powder used on the face

guy (71f): cabinet, hotel, *person*, ranch

gymnasium (62c): belief in God, say bad words, *room for sports*, brown metal

gymnastics (68c): broth, *sports*, emperor, unusual

hail (67h): friend in court, breaking in on, *frozen rain*, much the same

hailstone (67h): help one another, *frozen drop of rain*, make music with the voice, turn upside down

hair (67b): laws, grab, sweet, *fur*

hairdresser (71e): longer, white, five, *barber*

hairy (44): knitted cloth, without hair, *covered with hair*, being to blame

half (35): *partly*, note, dance, flew

halfway (36): *in the middle*, person who lies, shake up, mixed with rain

hallway (90c): lifting, enough, special, *passage*

ham (82e): tiger, rocket, lonesome, *meat*

hamburger (82e): six times, *ground beef*, not long, do something

hammer (84): beautiful, *tool*, walk, smooth

hand (67b): *part of the arm*, of a city, a climbing plant, box for mail

handbag (80, 86): music, title, *pocketbook*, door key

handkerchief (80): arithmetic, fork, *cloth*, hundred

handle (18): *to touch*, all people, the face, kitten

handsome (28): *good-looking*, reward, perform, happiness

hanging (64): a liquid or a gas, the following day, with sharp points, *death by a rope*

hangman (64): *one who hangs persons*, to hang clothes, out of danger, set of keys

happen (55a): ice chest, sailing ship, *take place*, jellyfish

happily (72a): *gladly*, slowly, major, cardboard

happiness (72a): godmother, yesterday, *joy*, drawer

happy (72a): *gay*, worm, sixty, fret

hard (31): *not soft*, because of, young cat, lower prices

hardy (41): *strong*, basket, dodge, yearly

harmful (25): beautiful, herself, snapshot, *hurtful*

hat (80): put into words, *covering for the head*, month of the year, not willing to work

hate (72a): twelve, share, moonlight, *dislike*

hateful (32): mirror, lung, pussycat, *nasty*

have (13): hair, creep, upper, *hold*

hawk (47): valley, screw, master, *bird*

hay (67a): make longer, cook eggs, *cut grass*, take out

hayfield (67a, 91): *pasture*, naughty, flashlight, butter

haystack (67a): *pile of hay*, picture book, sharp thing, cannot be erased

he (UNCL): *the male spoken about*, ocean going ship, part of the body, rise from the water

head (67b): *top part*, without end, ill, springtime

headache (65): head of cabbage, *pain in the head*, done in a house, grow in the sea

headdress (80): *covering*, steady, buttermilk, daisy

headlight (84): inner covering, portion of time, member of a senate, *light on car front*

headstrong (32): *stubborn,* flúte, chair, fume

headwater (67d): disease that can spread, hit with a bullet, *upper parts of a river,* not letting sound pass through

health (65): at once, all people, do nothing, *not sick*

healthy (65, 72d): machine, plug, noon, *well*

hear (72d): man who repairs locks, place where one thing crosses another, wood to hold a broken bone, *get sound through the ear*

hearer (72d): *listener,* sewer, attic, fence

hearing (72d): to be inside, *power to hear,* strong light, not to be heard

heart (67b): season after winter, waste time with, *part of the body,* turn

heartbroken (72a): put money to use, covering for the leg, misplace again, *crushed by sorrow*

heater (90a): finish, *stove,* egg, just

heaven (66): *sky,* fail, ham, playmate

heaviness (30): *great weight,* light meal, careful search, narrow channel

heavy (45): used in cleaning, person not known, small red fruit, *hard to carry*

heel (67b): living on an island, iron or steel sheets, sit with the legs apart, *back part of a foot*

height (30): noisy bird, put out, *how tall,* make stronger

hell (66): short piece of wood that makes a fire, tall plant having very large yellow flowers, *place where wicked persons are punished after death,* meeting of people for buying and selling

hello (UNCL): *a greeting,* set of clothes, very good, bring to mind

help (70a): *aid,* bag, mad, limp

hemisphere (38): face to face, without practice, *half a globe,* below average

hen (47): careful, govern, *bird,* deck

henhouse (67a, 89): not fresh, charge with, *chicken house,* tree house

her (UNCL): belong to a group, done in a house, *woman spoken about,* body of water

here (36): free from harm, of the mind, *in this place,* fat and large

hereabout (27): not here, at once, list of food, *near here*

hero (60b): large bird, full of fun, *brave man,* bad smell

hers (UNCL): *belonging to her,* in place of, a short time, not herself today

high (40): art, wire, *tall,* unless

highland (67d): small scale, *hilly country,* fly upward, short cry

highroad (67e, 92): *street,* minister, trash, cracker

highway (92): *road,* visit, beet, cone

hike (11): person who sells jewels, *take a long walk,* place where money is coined, sharp growth on plants

hill (67d): turn around, sixty seconds, *raised earth,* looking glass

hilly (67d): climb a hill, *having many hills,* a very short time, begin to grow

him (UNCL): *the male spoken about,* picture cut into pieces, behave very badly, not likely to move

hip (67b): win a race, not running or flowing, *part of the body*, something to gain

hippopotamus (51): *animal*, shook, gym, cosy

his (UNCL): *belonging to him*, place to walk, fall through a hole, woman who milks cows

historian (71b): *person who writes about history*, cover for the face, tub where dirty water collects, history of the Indian people

hive (48): smoke and fog, *house for bees*, funny story, care for the hands

hobby (68c): song to put a baby to bed by, *something a person likes to work at*, breathe during sleep with sound, foam made with soap and water

hockey (68c): womanhood, driver, *a game*, while

hog (51): colt, aid, quack, *pig*

hole (54): beech, *opening*, gingerbread, pasture

holiday (55b): *day when one does not work*, man who serves in the army, turning the heels over the head, ask the time of day

home (90c, 91): *place where a person lives*, in a short time, time of great joy, the hand or eye

homeless (72b): home for the night, let sound pass through, *without a home*, seventh month

homelike (28): thorn, ruby, stall, *friendly*

homemaker (71e): *housewife*, bobcat, mouse, homesick

homesick (72a): pancake, cotton, *unhappy*, lemonade

honest (28, 64): arose, *true*, seventeen, ground

honesty (72b): April, *truth*, wallet, dice

hook (90d): at rest, wind with rain, person who lies, *piece of metal*

hoopskirt (67e, 80): tulip, December, bookshop, *petticoat*

hop (68a): camp, instead, *jump*, tinkle

hope (70d): yonder, *wish*, blackberry, guide

hopeless (22): hope to do something, the first letter, light meal, *feeling no hope*

horror (72a): drank, Monday, begone, *terror*

horse (51, 67c): diamond, teaspoon, march, *animal*

horsehair (52): *fur*, reheat, arise, job

horseman (68b): *rider*, perform, advance, bore

horseshoe (67e, 68c): *plate nailed to a hoof*, put in the place of, barley used in making beer, use money to buy something

hose (90d): judge, enemy, bed, *pipe*

hospital (65, 89): draw into the mouth, putting in place of, shelf above the fireplace, *place for the sick*

hot (42): joke, queer, *warm*, expect

hotel (89): *inn*, supper, return, fable

hour (59b, 83): high tower, party mask, *fixed time*, very good

hourly (59c): half an hour, work of art, *every hour*, turn around

house (89): hoof, file, *home*, goat

household (71c): beyond, degree, extra, *family*

housekeeper (71e): *housewife*, henhouse, object, gallop

housekeeping (90e): bird house, tall pole, *housework*, firecracker

housetop (90c): explain, *roof*, journey, telephone

housewife (71e): feeling interest, raised floor, be allowed to, *family manager*

how (UNCL): *in what way*, wrapped up in, grassy land, with all people

hug (18): *hold close*, break in, motor driven, spread about

human (72b): in tune, solid liquid, country house, *of persons*

hummingbird (47): suffer hunger, *small bird*, bird house, tight spot

hundred (57): bars of a wheel, keep in the mind, turn around rapidly, *ten times ten*

hungry (72d): taste like lemon juice, serve in an army, hollow piece for holding, *feeling a desire for food*

hunter (71e): piece of snow, try to grab, *person who hunts*, went hunting yesterday

huntsman (68b): mailman, *sportsman*, tobacco, wax

hurricane (67h, 67j): *storm*, universe, mermaid, down

hurried (20): silver, rubbish, loved, *rushed*

hurriedly (20): lovely, spirit, covered, *quickly*

hurry (11): not drunk, *move quickly*, singing voice, nothing else

hurt (05): highway, flutter, juice, *harm*

husband (71c): sticky mud, *married man*, short time, not large

I (UNCL): birth, ring, *myself*, train

iceberg (67d, 67j): icebox for food, earth and sky, *large mass of ice*, figure out a problem

icebox (90a): toward the north, plate nailed to a hoof, ice skate, *ice chest*

iced (42): policeman, tin, *cooled*, walked

icy (42): vegetable, stop, candle, *freezing*

idea (17): holder, see, *thought*, place

if (UNCL): eastern, *supposing*, player, hear

ill (65, 72d): driver, baking, tree, *sick*

illness (65): greatness, extra, *sickness*, crush

illustrator (60c, 71e): *artist*, together, pig, flower

imaginable (22): march, burned, *possible*, automobile

imaginary (60b): *not real*, make powerless, gangster, traveling show

imaginative (32): enemy, *original*, borrow, clip

improve (03): *make better*, usually, roads, hurt

improvement (58a): *making better*, set of two, of the earth, like a cube

in (UNCL): sharp pain, a machine, *not outside*, going around

inch (83): *a measure*, route, snake, ear

incorrect (28, 70c): smell, kindly, much, *wrong*

independence (63, 67e): musical, patch, *freedom*, shell

index (62d): arm, land, *list*, people

indoor (36): paid in advance, round like a ball, destroy hopes, *done in a house*

indoors (90e): being with young, *in a house*, smooth and shiny, getting rid of

industrious (61d): *hard-working*, first choice, shore, small fish

industry (61d): *business*, special, now, left

infect (65): *cause disease*, hunted for food, son or daughter, pictures

infection (65): tin, *disease*, blaze, grandmother

inn (67e, 89): *hotel*, sale, gladly, citizen

insect (49): cozy, pride, later, *bug*

instructive (62b): do much, book of hymns, hallway, *giving information*

intelligent (32): owed, *smart*, gem, rot

interesting (28): braid of hair, *holding the attention*, end of journey, done wrong

into (UNCL): most people, huge snake, *to the inside*, not soft

invent (03): *make something new*, form of worship, give warmth, matter for a court

iodine (65): *medicine*, explore, clue, earth

iron (67i): *metal*, guide, wear, act

isle (67d): *island*, confusion, politics, is long

it (UNCL): full, *thing*, whole, race

ivory (24): meet, *white*, police, leaving

jacket (80): *coat*, member, what, railroad

jacks (68c): *a game*, amount, burning, rain

jail (64, 89): *prison*, close, mountains, honest

January (59d): surprise, built, yet, *month*

jar (81, 90e): wild, too, cake, *pot*

jaw (67b): *part of the face*, piece of iron, brief story or tale, set down in writing

jay (47): unknown, added, become, *bird*

jean (87): once again, perfect, *heavy cloth*, mirror

jelly (82f): *food*, remove, hammer, record

jellyfish (53): used, book, empty, *animal*

jet (88a): healthful, *plane*, physical, reduce

jeweler (67i, 71e): left by a wreck, a jewel of a child, come to a place, *person who sells jewels*

jigsaw (68c): lightly, *puzzle*, spring, pole

jittery (72a): health, tax, torn, *nervous*

job (61d): cup, box, *work*, different

jockey (68b, 71e): warm, *rider*, spoon, map

join (09): *bring together*, message, same family, field glass

joke (68c): cause to remember, large monkey, odd shoe, *funny story*

joker (71d): gossip, political, *clown*, loose

joking (72a): verb, *teasing,* living, party

journey (55c): idea, *trip,* daring, plenty

joy (72a): curl, pointed, bush, *happiness*

joyful (72a): deer, wheat, up, *glad*

joyless (72a): toss, barrier, insect, *sad*

joyous (72a): *glad,* rough, sore, bird

judge (10); finger, *decide,* spoiled, plant

judgment (64): waste, shopper, tiger, *decision*

juice (82a): dull, bathroom, *a drink,* one of

July (59d): *month,* also, stone, beam

jump (68a): receive, lowest, pain, *leap*

June (59d): path, kind, follow, *month*

junior (71a): hand over, payment, light wind, *younger person*

jury (56b, 64): do harm in return, flow in a small stream, *persons chosen to give judgment,* brush with a long handle

justify (17): *give a good reason for,* day of the week, bank of a river, lead from a gun

kangaroo (51): *animal,* dodge, office, neighbor

keep (13): *hold,* fife, ink, gum

keeper (64, 71e): *guard,* northerly, hill, fair

kerchief (80): *cloth worn over the head,* one who is dead, mark the skin of, raw green vegetables

key (86): often, lump, fall, *tool*

kid (71a): grateful, fig, both, *child*

kill (05, 64): deep, buggy, *murder,* hymn

killer (64): electricity, meaning, *murderer,* handwriting

kind (32): chase, darn, *friendly,* harp

kindly (32): quickly, *friendly,* ninety, ready

kindness (72b): lightness, *goodness,* fourth, grove

kiss (18): head of a state, part of the forehead, two slices of bread, *touch with the lips*

kitchen (82d, 90c): destroy, bright, *room,* grandpa

kite (68c): froze, broom, *toy,* cupboard

kitten (51): dried fruit, *young cat,* end part, blue stone

kitty (51): drop, *cat,* inch, joyride

knife (84): animal fat, book for study, *cutting tool,* good enough

knight (60b, 67e): puzzle, *soldier,* bleed, musician

knit (80): crack, bottle, *weave,* pipe

knock (08): grapefruit, *hit,* castle, dance

knot (09): *tie,* have, empty, brook

knothole (67c): money laid away, put into words, *hole in a board,* hard to get know (17): carload, always, *understand,* instead

knowledge (62b): gracious, hollow, *learning,* merchant

labor (61d): culture, throat, *work,* eagerness

ladder (90d): recess, hilltop, balloon, *steps*

lady (71f): ax, *woman,* general, radish

ladybug (50): glossy, freedom, *beetle,* science

lake (67d): marry a man, strong cloth, *body of water,* young sheep

lamb (51): eat fast, make known, giving birth, *young sheep*

lamp (90a): youth, reindeer, *light,* nearby

land (67d): picture, naughty, weather, *ground*

landing (55c): unit, spice, *arrival,* game

landowner (67e, 71e): study of rights, hold fast, book owner, *property owner*

lane (92): seven, teaspoon, honor, *path*

language (67f): *speech,* graveyard, plaything, lonesome

large (40): fur, *big,* horseback, beehive

last (43): praise, *end,* double, cherry

late (43): *tardy,* skater, rocket, elephant

laugh (72a): having a hurt leg, foot or arm, *sounds you make when you hear a joke,* a word at the end of prayer, an automobile with a folding top

laughter (72a): sport, prisoner, *joy,* total

laundress (71e, 90f): a crowd, stick of wax, messenger of God, *cleaning lady*

laundry (90c, 90f): look steadily, big gun, very mad, *wash house*

law (64): gobble, eighteen, ticket, *rule*

lazy (32): move away from, fight on horseback, plain to see, *not willing to work*

lead (69): *direct,* radio, morning, frost

leader (63, 67e, 71d): able, *boss,* lawyer, quilt

learn (17): something to eat, *find out,* large boat, open to

leather (52): a piece of candy, one hundred years, *skin of animals,* set to music

leave (11): *go away,* rainbow, forgotten, stream bed

lemon (74): careless, quarter, servant, *fruit*

lemonade (82a): throat, balloon, animal, *a drink*

length (30): juicy, *a measure,* pussycat, tablespoon

less (40): uniform, reward, *smaller,* library

lesson (62b): things or persons together, below the mouth, dealing with stars, *something to be learned*

let (70a): monkey, *allow,* gracious, thankful

letter (62d): *note,* junk, flop, cupboard

lettuce (79): *plant,* dart, attention, western

liar (71d): respect and love, *person who lies*, feed on grass, on the line

liberty (63, 67e): marble, *freedom*, sugar, tiptoe

library (90c): squirrel, throne, fast skater, *book room*

lice (50): *insects*, sleepy, dishes, tomato

license (64): citizens, *permission*, adrift, complain

lick (18): *pass the tongue over*, covered with clouds, in a bad temper, in back of

lid (90d): *cover*, rope, sentence, bought

lie (64): coloring matter, small stream, *false story*, large toy

life (63): ugly woman, stiff hat, even now, *being alive*

lifeless (20): annoy, remainder, amaze, *dead*

lifelike (20): one and two, pile up, lightening, *looking alive*

lifetime (59b): *period during which life lasts*, life of the party, easy slow walking pace, shelter for large ships

light (90b): *lamp*, anyway, crumble, log

lighten (15): strong dislike, eighth, so be it, *make bright*

lighthouse (67e, 67j, 89): memory, injury, honest, *tower*

lightning (67h): sum up to, *flash of electricity*, in tune, get away from

like (UNCL): has not, carry along, *much the same*, give a bath

lime (74): brave, *fruit*, dying, them

lime (67i): visited by ghosts, for a year, amount of being different, *substance to improve soil*

limestone (67i): starve, whistle, television, *rock*

limit (27): *furthest point*, cut and dry, rounded roof, sacred song

line (83): footprint, *row*, knit, nail

lion (51): *animal*, exchange, humble, rake

lip (67b): *one of the edges of the mouth*, at or near the North Pole, present reasons for or against a person, get sounds through the ear drum

lipstick (86): *make-up*, confusion, neighborhood, section

list (62d): *record*, army, drew, thumb

listen (72d): hard to carry, amount of medicine, *try to hear*, get up and go

little (40): group, rise up, *not big*, snapping

live (72d): put off, *have life*, lift up, foot part

liver (82e): *meat*, selfish, loan, grandma

lizard (51): poor, *animal*, fever, bind

lobster (53): dizzy, *animal*, except, become

locker (62c): plot, wedding, *closet*, petticoat

log (67c): silly, mask, *wood*, knob

lonely (32): *without company*, feed on grass, hard candy, throw down

lonesome (72a): *alone*, miller, large, lone rider

long (40): *tall*, joke, groan, blaze

longitude (67d, 67j): blow up by dynamite, for the first time, *distance on the earth's surface*, color between white and black

look (12): *see*, blow, defense, hump

lookout (12): *sharp watch*, gray haired, draw away, crowd around

loose (40): ill will, lower place, *not tight*, eat fast

lord (60b, 67e): barber, inside, behave, *master*

lose (13): railroad, song of joy, *not have*, old lady

loser (63, 71d): easily broken, loose tie, take to one place, *one who loses*

loss (61a): not losing money, with light winds, form of iron, *having lost something*

lot (35): *many*, rug, shut, magic

lotion (86): evening, *liquid*, listen, street

loud (33): of a room, gather in, *not quiet*, get by paying

love (72a): *strong liking*, of the face, great wait, move quickly

loveliness (30): *beauty*, singer, uncertain, material

lovely (28): figure, horseshoe, *beautiful*, kitten

lover (71d): flag, *sweetheart*, airplane, hasty

low (40): *not high*, steering gear, wild cat, thick piece

luggage (81, 86): appendix, *baggage*, conceited, garbage

lukewarm (42): joint between leg and foot, person who sells food, *neither hot nor cold*, care of horses

lumber (67c, 90d): lesson, paw, muddy, *logs*

lumberman (71e, 67c): *woodsman*, ice man, approaching, prison

lunch (82c): candle, dry, raise, *meal*

lung (67b): part of the arm, make hard to understand, *one of the breathing organs*, get in the way of

machine (84): save, *engine*, knocks, loaves

machinist (71e): stop up, good chance, *skilled worker*, make known

mad (72a): glove, *angry*, horse, pace

madman (71d): be against, tell about, *crazy person*, careful search

magazine (69): *place for cartridges*, kitchen of a ship, group of persons, part of the eye

magnet (84): movable bridge, easily made angry, *piece of iron*, a water animal

maid (71e): lake, *servant*, tickle, rose

mail (62d): *letters*, suffer, reason, father

mailbox (90c): *letter box*, more than, icebox, shake up

mailman (71e): manner, nobody, push, *postman*

make (03): hide, forgive, *build*, equal

maker (71e): doorway, collector, *builder*, brownie

male (71f): motion, memory, mug, *man*

mama (71c): May, *mother*, merry, miner

mammal (49): lick, rattle, forward, *animal*

man (71f): mice, mask, murder, *male*

manager (61d): *boss*, name, purse, snowflake

manly (41): *strong*, flag, grain, radio

many (UNCL): make dark, put in, *great number*, ladies day

map (67d): *chart*, person, begin, cloudy

maple (78): washtub, *tree*, read, behind

marble (67i): *rock*, film, peek, thank

march (11): bless, angry, *walk*, sorry

March (59d): *month*, aim, daughter, muddy

mark (38): under, *line*, eat, pepper

market (61c): yolk, uniform, nose, *sell*

marriage (55b): prune, overhear, *wedding*, airfield

marry (09, 55b): possible, nowhere, *wed*, burst

marshmallow (82f): October, confess, *candy*, price

marvelous (28): railroad, swimming, *wonderful*, princess

mask (86): banana, daytime, year, *cover*

material (87): *what a thing is made from*, loss of the power of motion, father of one's father or mother, break in on a meeting

mathematical (67g): *numerical*, physical, sunflower, running

mathematics (67g): father and mother, feed on grass, show the way, *study of numbers*

May (59d): *month*, meal, music, myself

maybe (22): lightning, housewife, rubber, *possibly*

mayor (63): *head of a city*, paper pasted together, living on an island, cloth sewed together

maypole (68c): *stick*, hate, mamma, shower

me (UNCL): so, on, *I*, at

meal (82c): *food*, plane, gang, carpet

meal (82d): enough, *grain*, wolf, trolley

mean (72a): *nasty*, gasoline, kitty, singer

means (70d): puffs, toilet, *intends*, crawl

measles (65): everything, *a disease*, churn, feel sorrow

measure (10): *find the size*, cotton candy, in most cases, blow up

meat (82d): garage, pave, through, *food*

medicine (65): boast, wonder, *drugs*, giant

meet (09): for a child, *come together*, fine powder, at once

melon (74): skunk, agree, *fruit*, puppy

member (71d): a loud noise, amount taken in, *one who belongs*, body of water

membership (56b): a store that sells food, having few nice things, goes off with noise, *persons belonging to a body* memory (14): member of a wedding, liked by most people, stop by to see, *ability to remember*

mend (13): *repair*, ladies, haircut, prince

menu (62d, 82c): *list of food*, keep safe, charge with, in a hurry

merry (72a): nickel, cheat, *joyful*, drew

mess (56a): being with young, *dirty group of things*, at a later time, to like better

messenger (71e): *person who goes on errands*, fit to be seen, a holiday from school, take into the house

meter (83): keep safe from, held by an enemy, *something that measures*, ask to do something

midday (59c): *noon*, liver, outfit, lifeboat

middle (36): proper, nothing, bicycle, *center*

mighty (41): hammer, pancake, *strong*, firearm

mildness (72b): *gentleness*, northeast, selfishness, pineapple

mile (83): moving in, *a measure*, meat, misspell

milk (82a): *a drink*, to look, finish, goal

milky (24): length, even, *white*, become

mill (89): lion, gone, raise, *factory*

miller (71e): more than one goose, end of a fork, *one who runs a mill*, get a million dollars

million (57): in many cases, *one thousand thousand*, a picture puzzle, show the truth to

mind (67b): time of being a girl, to make a person angry, make an offer of marriage, *part of a person that thinks*

miner (67i, 71e): *man who works in a mine*, stopping for a time, wanting to know about, a mine that blows up

mineral (67i): *substance in the earth*, person who plays a bagpipe, a lever on a bicycle, airplane without a motor

minute (59b, 83): *space of time*, stick together, drip through, thread a needle

mirror (90e): *looking glass*, bite at, is paid, to find out

mischief (70c): *trouble*, building, windmill, tonight

misfortune (70c): take a bow, on a fence, *bad luck*, painted wagon

Miss (71f): easy to do, sour berry, *young woman*, pitch a ball

mistake (70c): weigh, round, *fault*, plaything

mistaken (28, 70c): putting, nation, dwarf, *wrong*

misunderstand (70c): inhabitant of a country, musical instrument, *make a mistake*, in the open air

mitten (80): lettuce, *glove*, weed, trunk

mix (09): *put together*, landing strip, skin swelling, be sorry

moist (46): flown, *damp*, satisfactory, talk

moisture (67h): palace, greeting, *humidity*, saloon

mole (51): *animal*, direction, classroom, hickory

mommy (71c): *mother*, main, minister, musician

Monday (59a): *day of the week*, to keep from happening, picture puzzle cut in pieces, things joined together

money (61b): *coin*, drank, bodies, insect

monkey (51): place, *animal*, never, drink

monster (60b): *imaginary animal*, sharp points, elementary education, advance in rank

month (59b, 83): makes sounds, *four weeks*, pool of water, kindly feeling

moose (51): income, fail, biscuit, *animal*

more (35): swamp, rubbed, *greater*, faraway

morning (59c): on the other side, *part of the day*, man to be married, to show the way

mosquito (50): service, gift, *insect*, hundred

moss (75): limb, enter, Friday, *plants*

mossy (44): ivory, skill, *grassy*, here

most (UNCL): *greatest*, jaw, potato, stocking

moth (50): hood, street, politeness, *insect*

mother (71c): room, late, haystack, *parent*

motherless (71d): fence, *orphan*, gravel, shove

motherly (71f): an organ player, *like a mother*, kind of writing, father or mother

motor (88b): eastern countries, do with pleasure, not quite enough, *travel by automobile*

motor (84): *engine*, comfort, bracelet, ranch

motorcar (88a): coward, *automobile*, kitten, sardine

motorist (71d, 88b): child whose parents are dead, musical notes in a chord, *person who travels by automobile*, a covering for the shoulders

mountain (67d): *high hill*, last longer, chicken house, brave man

mouse (51): *animal*, homesick, wheel, truly

mouth (67b): towel, weave, sense, *opening*

mouthpiece (86): run faster than, *part of a pipe*, very hilly country, joint on a door

move (11): *go*, store, yesterday, led

movie (60a): *picture*, settlement, laid, huge

much (UNCL): comb hair, a building, *great amount*, heavy coat

mud (67i): grow big, *wet earth*, in what way, funny story

muddy (67d): jacks, really, *dirty*, them

mulberry (78): violin, witch, *tree*, scream

mule (51): safety, phono, *animal*, himself

multiply (67g): walk a mile, *make more*, move around, crooked stick

mummy (65): light umbrella, to be done, *dead body*, period of time

murderous (25, 64): *deadly*, varnish, wander, leather

muscular (41): *strong*, food, warning, besides

museum (68d, 89): the act of cutting the hair, *building in which a collection is kept*, be made of paper pasted together, work to be done in housekeeping

music (60a): kill germs, *pleasing sounds*, an invention, passage of time

muskrat (51): noisy, leak, *animal*, pupil

must (70d): pair, overcoat, flop, *should*

mustache (67b): glasses, *whiskers*, waterfall, player

mustard (82d): *flavoring*, people, nineteen, widow

my (UNCL): gather in, *belonging to me*, to visit someone, without any money

mystery (34): *secret*, juice, woodchuck, four

nail (90d): small bag, mark the skin, *piece of metal*, keep off

name (72c): clothing, bran, message, *title*

nameless (34): name of the month, look at closely, part of the forehead, *having no name*

nap (72d): place for learning, causing fear, fit to eat, *short sleep*

napkin (90e): *piece of cloth*, having to do with, take out, book for study

narrow (40): of electricity, *not wide*, pictures, to them

nation (63, 91): jewel, careless, leg, *country*

natural (28): go into, bookshelf, wood for building, *true to life*

naturalist (71e): the prepared leaves of certain plants, person who writes letters for a company, *person who makes a study of nature*, long for what someone else possesses

naughty (32): rabbit, cannon, speed, *bad*

near (27): *close*, important, face, block

nearby (27): *close*, hard, foolish, punch

nearly (22): busy, *almost*, creep, jolly

neat (28): *in order*, last, drive out, cage

neck (67b): a blowing up, hit with a bullet, *part of the body*, unpleasant to look at

necklace (86): traveler, buyer, repeat, *jewelry*

need (70d): see to, few people, know the way, *in want of*

needle (84): refuse, late, past, *tool*

needless (22): *unnecessary*, picture, sneak, loyal

needlework (90e): trousers, *sewing*, plaster, true

Negro (67e, 71d): toothpick, *colored person*, farm house, upset

neighbor (71d): *someone who lives nearby*, snow mixed with rain, one that sleeps, like a father

neighboring (27): whistle, *near*, rising, nobody

neighborly (72a): mostly, fern, celebration, *friendly*

neither (UNCL): praise, *not either*, offer, go and get

nephew (71c): *son of one's brother or sister*, land with few or no trees, cloth to support a hurt arm, one of two born at the same time

nervous (72a): soft sticky mud, strong thread, *easily excited*, five times ten

nervousness (72a): small fruit, containing oil, sew a fold, *being easily upset* nest (48): having a taste like lemon juice, place built to hold a fire, *place in which birds lay their eggs*, piece of flesh in the mouth

net (48, 81): *web*, lice, blast, tool

network (56a): one more than four, *system of lines*, female pig, little child

never (43): bit of fire, *at no time*, too much, part of a country

nevermore (43): never said, run away, *never again*, fall in drops

new (43): flying, small scarf, *not used*, ink

newborn (71a): *just born*, used up, not ever born, flow over

news (62d): fake, headache, bathtub, *message*

newsreel (60c): ill will, sell flowers, *motion picture*, pull hard

next (27): *nearest*, lightning, nickel, patter

nice (28): maybe, loop, *pleasing*, office

nickel (61b): warm, orchard, *coin*, mess

nickname (72c): liquid, footwear, a tooth's name, *pet name*

niece (71c): pipe for carrying off water, shirt worn next to the skin, anything that plants or animals eat, *daughter of one's brother or sister*

night (59c): *dark hours*, without sense, stretch out, send over

nightcap (67e, 80): full of life, cap for cold, easily seen through, *cap worn in bed*

nightfall (59c): caution, firm, *evening*, vehicle

nightmare (60b): cold frost, chirping, not aware, *bad dream*

nine (57): long pointed tooth, *one more than eight*, find out about, covering for the leg

nineteen (57): of that kind, *nine more than ten*, man who raises crops, nine small children

ninety (57): press together, *nine times ten*, rich meal, have nine dogs

no (UNCL): feel pain, *not any*, small trees, something made

nobody (UNCL): no tables, another country, *no one*, strong line

noise (58d): *sound*, grave, file, prison

noiseless (33): armor, single, one, *silent*

noisy (33): *loud*, arrange, overturn, magazine

nomination (63): dance and skip, *naming as a candidate*, person who sells, roll of paper

noon (59c): *twelve o'clock*, very strong, sea animal, male parent

nor (UNCL): not large, half a circle, highest, *neither*

normal (28): fuel, exit, tools, *usual*

north (36): mirror, pound, lazy, *a direction*

northerly (26): north star, play at love, group of words, *toward the north*

nose (67b): wave back and forth, partly dark place, wash the hair, *part of the face*

not (22): time between morning and noon, *a word that says no*, figure of a man, the teeth of whales

note (62d): level, pine, *letter*, moon

notebook (62f): stop sleeping, book of matches, write carelessly, *record book* notice (12): rag, lace, *see*, bite

November (59d): kindness, *month*, English, hardship

now (43): being male, day of the week, *at this time*, because of

nowhere (36): loss of a ship, not all things, a wild animal, *in no place*

number (67g): excuse, hang, govern, *figure*

nurse (65, 71e): *person who takes care of the sick*, brother of one's father or mother, bubbles made with soap and water, the yard connected with farm buildings

nursery (90c): sense of touch, *room for children*, by some means, go and get

nut (82d): tooth, engine, insult, *fruit*

oak (78): aunt, cure, poke, *tree*

oaken (44, 77): *made of oak*, not quite, an oarsman, testing place

oatmeal (82d): uncle, sister, *cereal*, real

oats (76): poor, spinach, *grain*, wore

obey (70d): owing money to someone, *do what one is told*, make the winning point, something that is good fun

object (85): underwear, *thing*, rather, mine

obliging (32): brownie, noon, popcorn, *helpful*

ocean (67d, 67j): can be spread, find out, *body of water*, group of soldiers

October (59d): shine, *month*, lawn, gentle

octopus (53): misconduct, *animal*, shining, grandmother

odd (39): mane, clock, bobwhite, *strange*

of (UNCL): Saturday night, make angry, ill feeling, *belonging to*

offering (70a): sleeper, driven, grounded, *contribution*

office (61d, 90c): raise or move a house, make free from fear, *rooms in which to work*, pass the tongue over

officer (67e, 69): hairpin, childhood, *policeman*, intend

often (35): freight train, *many times*, evil deed, carry out

oftentimes (43): offer, *often*, onward, officer

old (43): kindness, steamboat, carve out, *not young*

on (UNCL): *upon*, cone, pony, song

once (35): on top of, *one time*, wise man, hair cut

one (57): found, *single*, horn, chief

onion (79): *vegetable*, forgot, curtain, bright

only (35): playhouse, go slow, November, *by itself*

open (54): *not shut*, mailbox, fool around, wood peg

opening (54): rake, cough, *hole*, sensible

operation (55a): good-for-nothing, seven times ten, *way a thing works*, small clothes closet

operation (65): *surgery*, caterpillar, autumn, need not

opposite (39): hilly, *different*, apartment, count

orange (74): patter, *fruit*, soup, high

order (69): *command*, daddy, sill, ground

order (19): plane, cream, thrown, *arrange*

ordinarily (22): multiply, fully, *usually*, chilly

organization (56b): *group of persons*, skin of a sheep, oil or grease, a picture puzzle

oriole (47): *bird*, graze, arrow, poem

other (39): fog, *else*, idea, pill

ought (70d): silver, *should*, every, bathe

ounce (83): *weight*, rear, knob, notice

our (UNCL): loss of a ship, woman servant, stick of ice, *belonging to us*

ourselves (UNCL): saw, rib, *us*, mad

out (27): seat, moss, *away*, lace

outer (36): let be seen, put together, be imagined, *on the outside*

outermost (27): *farthest*, sixteen, least, crown

outlaw (64): tardy, *robber*, smoke, decide

outnumber (07): lunch or supper, glide over, *be more than*, stomach condition

outrun (68a): *run faster than*, run a bank, use power on, come face to face

oven (90a): goods for sale, a hurt arm, *space for baking*, sea spirit

over (UNCL): *above*, twig, fuel, mother

overboard (26): full of fun, cause to slip, under or over, *over the side*

overcoat (80): weaken, near, parent, *jacket*

overeat (82c): melt ore, *eat too much*, climbing plant, eat hard candy

overflow (67h): tower, limp, *flood*, glide

overhead (36): *above*, small, china, hint

overjoy (01): on a small scale, *make very joyful*, tall chimney, enjoy a party

overland (67d): a game, take secretly, *on shore*, minister

overlook (12): flavor with, tight spot, try to hold, *fail to see*

overpower (69): unmarried woman, *be stronger than*, baseball glove, soft white

overshoe (80): partner, hayfield, August, *boot*

overspread (03): island, *cover*, beach, grove

overtime (61d): fishing net, daytime, grandfather, *extra time*

overturn (67e, 69): icy, pants, *defeat*, squirrel

overweight (45): the weight of a truck, of the present time, ball made of snow, *having too much weight*

overwork (61d): making fun, *too much work*, up to date, arrive at work

owe (61c): *have to pay*, a hollow shape, in that way, through the nose

owl (47): lane, pass, *bird*, due

own (13): *have*, peck, cork, bind

owner (61a, 71d): *holder*, cover, leather, flower

ox (51): purple, *animal*, bookcase, cocoon

oxygen (67h): suit, uptown, *a gas*, go out

oyster (53): rider, American, *shellfish*, nervous

page (62f): young frog, shake the ground, bed cover, *sheet of paper*

pail (81, 90e): liberty, elephant, *bucket*, another

pain (65, 72d): knives, birthday, *hurt*, ski

painful (65, 72d): anybody, dusty, runner, *hurting*

paint (90d): *coloring*, ribbon, large, bunny

painting (60c): terrible, Saturday, elbow, *picture*

pair (67g): ladder, froze, snowflake, *two*

pajamas (80): get hold of, a worm, floating platform, *nightclothes*

pal (71d): rubber, nine, *friend*, fortune

palm (78): *tree*, sash, flavor, rainfall

pan (81, 90e): turtle, *pot*, room, part

pancake (82d): hymn, quilt, *food*, tiptoe

papa (71c): *father*, servant, meadow, goldfish

papoose (71a): *Indian baby*, get the meaning, grace and richness, male voice

parade (11): *march*, envelope, butcher, switch

paragraph (67f): fit to be chosen, kind of dog, *group of sentences*, machine that cuts grain

paralyzed (65, 72d): coming back, go around, *made powerless*, close together

parent (71c): land and buildings, end to end, *father or mother*, make pure

park (68d, 91): foggy, beehive, joyous, *garden*

parrot (47): *bird*, delay, belong, time

part (54): smack, yellow, *piece*, rosebud

particularly (22): *especially*, duty, beyond, small

party (56b, 68d): stretch of land, bird's skin, be carried along, *meeting of friends*

pass (11): an edge, give food, the mind, *go by*

past (43): around a yard, *gone by*, of a rose, big box

paste (62f): rainbow, *glue*, kettle, chatter

path (92): *route*, crazy, airship, shower

patrolman (64, 71e): the part left over, *member of a police force*, land which a person uses, a card to a sweetheart

paw (67b): *foot*, bulb, kingdom, reading

pay (61c): not correct, easy to eat, above the eye, *give money*

payment (61a): go back over, *that which is paid*, cover of skin, not wanted

pea (79): *vegetable*, shadow, lane, fig

peace (63): go to bed, *freedom from war*, lose color, upward climb peach (74): *fruit*, misty, empty, row

peanut (76): *seed used for food*, part of the eye, show people their seats, bone of the body

pear (74): baseball, July, *fruit*, tablespoon

pecan (76): rear, *nut*, dimple, cone

pencil (62f): on the upper side, *tool to write with*, house on a farm, make a horse go

penny (61b): tickle, angel, *cent*, chipmunk

people (56b, 63): *persons*, candlestick, pepper, swift

perfect (28): leave empty, food basket, *having no faults*, stream of water

perfection (30): parrot, joker, puppy, *faultless*

perfume (86): Wednesday, *sweet smell*, rich meal, greeting card

perhaps (22): wagon, schoolboy, plenty, *possibly*

period (59b, 83): hills or mountains, the second month, *portion of time*, pit of a fruit

permit (64): *written order*, great deed, covered wagon, an insect

person (71a): *man, woman or child*, a kind of plant, blood vessel, a chair

pet (49): *animal*, radish, loud, knock

phone (04): machinery, *call up*, lamp, blossom

phonograph (90a): cross again, *record player*, not thin, make unhappy

photo (60c): truly, plant, owl, *picture*

photograph (60c): idea, response, *picture*, pleasant

photographer (60c, 71e): get the meaning of, coming back to health, *person who takes pictures*, showing good taste

physical (58b): *of the body*, vacation place, lose color, give warning

pick (10): lettuce, extra, harness, *choose*

pickle (82d): whisper, *vegetable*, schoolboy, fort

picnic (68d, 82c): record, sew, length, *meal*

picture (60c): *drawing*, laundry, million, enough

piece (54): excuse, prayer, *part*, mitten

pig (51): lover, feet, *animal*, glow

pigeon (47): fiddle, elm, house, *bird*

pigtail (67b): polite, unsteady, sign, *braid*

pile (56a): food, mail, *heap*, known

pill (65): *medicine*, lake, faith, helmet

pillow (90e): field, eyebrow, candle, *cushion*

pin (90e): *piece of wire*, come back, little child, person who works

pine (78): fact, *tree*, eldest, bird

pineapple (74): belt, connect, *fruit*, autumn

pink (24): goal, budge, honey, *color*

pint (83): hood, glory, *a measure*, face

pioneer (67e, 71d): happening, *leader*, menu, ability

pitch (68a): minute, *throw*, letter, rate

plain (23): rocky, far away, *clear*, bluejay

plain (67d): promise to marry, member of tribe, *flat land*, rave about

plan (17): get caught again, standing up straight, *way of doing something*, very, very large

plane (88a): *airplane*, plant, cart, war

plant (75): *a living thing*, part of a house, without any mistake, small case for money

plantation (67a, 91): *farm*, brag, dock, wicked

planter (67a, 71e): surrender, teacup, damp, *farmer*

plastic (31): not finished, leaving out, stir up, *easily molded*

plate (90e): aboard, *dish*, linen, ram

plate (67i): bird's nest, not lucky, increase in size, *cover with metal*

play (68c): *fun*, cattle, maypole, tomato

playful (32): on a farm, full of wonder, *full of fun*, doing things

playground (68c, 68d, 91): *place for play*, play with stones, kings and queens, kind act

playhouse (60a): *theater*, beautiful, am, guest

playmate (68c, 71d): green, fight, blank, *friend*

plaything (68c): *toy*, bonnet, across, china

pleasant (28): week, *nice*, church, hem

please (01): go far, *make happy*, little wave, a river

pleasurable (72b): woolly, *agreeable*, substitute, ticket

pleasure (72a): furniture, electric, improve, *joy*

pledge (70d): maker, falsely, proper, *promise*

plowman (67a, 71e): stupidity, *farmer*, image, automobile

plum (74): bother, clang, *fruit*, eagle

plumber (71e): the acting together of a number of people, something to make a fire in, person who belongs to the same family, *man whose work is putting in pipes*

plural (35): long band, *more than one*, coming before others, part left over

plus (UNCL): container, *added to*, begin again, making over

pocket (80): stand for, one tooth, water rising, *small bag*

pocketbook (80, 86): polish, liver, barber, *purse*

poetry (62a, 62d): pooch, voice, sermon, *poems*

point (38): being full, make known, red flower, *sharp end*

poisonous (25): examination, assemble, *harmful*, burst

polar, (67d, 67j): *near the North Pole*, one more than three, do harm in return, say that one is popular

police (64): something that keeps things very cold, *person whose duty is to keep order*, write that something has been paid for, metal cap worn on the finger

policeman (64, 71e): fresh, *officer*, habit, knife

polish (90e): exciting feeling, *make smooth*, without sense, fill again

political (63): *having to do with government*, from end to end, tell what is coming, time between morning and noon

politician (63, 71e): political fund raising, *person in politics*, short thick finger, known beforehand

pond (67d): large animal, *body of water*, to the time of, sudden fear

pony (51): glow, king, either, *horse*

poodle (51): *dog*, tipsy, apply, trainer

pool (67d): never tired, one who reads, *body of water*, write again

pool (68c): mushroom, crash, itch, *game*

poor (32): *having few things*, in the direction of, cook in fat, think over

poorhouse (89): a poor little boy, measure of weight, bring back again, *home for the poor*

popcorn (82d): ears of corn, full of anger, day after today, *a kind of corn*

popular (34): no matter what, give an angry look, piece of iron, *liked by most people*

pork (82e): service, *meat*, secret, through

port (67j, 91): *harbor*, invest, weak, act

possible (22): *can be*, small plant, unfair play, love story

postage (62f): *amount paid on mail*, cold enough for frost, bank of a river, small case used for money

postcard (62d): a bad report card, fight against a leader, *card for sending a message*, a train, truck, ship or plane

postman (71e): bird's nest, *mailman*, account, vegetable man

postmaster (71e): *person in charge of a post office*, water rising into the air in a spray, one of the front legs of an animal, bang a nail into a post

postscript (62d): against the law, *addition to a letter*, cross a river, hunting for facts

pot (81, 90e): view, *dish*, guide, awhile

potato (79): rubber, song, fast, *vegetable*

pound (83): any bird, *a measure*, become red, not done

pour (82b): *cause to flow*, not a slave, without beauty, one who records

powerful (41): cellar, year, *strong*, now

powerless (41): question, *weak*, shampoo, repeat

practice (62b): having a poor memory, saved from danger, *action done many times*, have faith in

pray (66): begin again, *ask God*, making over, a light

preacher (66): compose, discover, *minister*, extend

preserve (13): pretty, *protect*, mother, lamb

presidency (63): where a president lives, part of the face, *office of president*, of the voice

president (63, 67e): *chief*, trash, grim, buddy

press (62d): amount, grocer, *newspapers*, bathrobe

pressure (30): snack, *weight*, eyelash, defrost

prevent (16): cross a river, line of mountains, side of a building, *keep from happening*

priest (66): habit, liquid, wolves, *minister*

prince (60b, 67e): place where water is stored, sound made through the mouth, acting of one's own choice, *son of a king or queen*

princely (32, 60b, 67e): *royal*, sharpen, days, cake

princess (60b, 67e): person in charge of a forest, move from side to side, *daughter of a king or queen*, lights in the front of a stage

principal (37): *most important*, thick woods, stop sleeping, make known

print (62d): *words on paper*, ship used in fighting, metal in thin sheets, lump on the skin

printer (71e): *person whose work is setting type*, bowl for holding water to wash in, payment for the use of property, something to help one remember

prison (64, 89): roast, catsup, *jail*, upstairs

prisoner (64): *criminal*, notice, onward, lash

prize (70b): camp, shore, day, *reward*

problem (62b): classic, fuel, *question*, knife

process (55a): low stool, *course of action*, make many holes, like winter

productive (61d): guitar, *profitable*, honest, panel

progress (58a): kneel, *development*, wade, swap

progressive (58a): fare, slot, *advancing*, detour

proper (28): *correct*, breathing, law, folks

protection (13): *being kept from harm*, draw a line, person who gathers news, of the face

proud (72a): *feeling pleasure*, take out, water rising, making over

prove (10): not to be depended upon, wood at rear of boat, *show that a thing is right*, goods that a train carries

prune (74): get the meaning of, thing fastened in place, caring for others, *plum that is dried*

public (63): *of the people*, without any mistake, make pure, open to question

publisher (71e): unfasten the button or buttons of, a journey for a special purpose, *company whose business is to produce books*, one of two born at the same time

pump (67j, 84): *machine*, net, flower, buffalo

pumpkin (74): bullet, highway, outfit, *fruit*

punishable (64): animal injured, fine meal, *deserving punishment*, did not punish

puppy (51): a game, *young dog*, factory, move

purple (24): found, tired, shame, *color*

purse (80, 86): fortune, *bag*, roar, making

push (08): dance and skip, *move against*, thing asked, case for money

pussy (51): *cat*, form, why, receive

put (19): *place*, pistol, come, bed

quart (83): finally, kettle, *a measure*, lend

quarter (67g): suppose, every person, post, *one fourth*

quarterback (68b): collapse, *sportsman*, diary, over

queen (60b, 67e): send out of one country, being away from others, hot or cold, *wife of a king*

queer (28): *strange*, rumble, tablespoon, faraway

question (62b): gasoline, *thing asked*, raisin, showing

quick (20): read, hawk, *fast*, batch

quickly (20): airfield, *fast*, swept, rich

quickness (30): *speed*, admirer, chubby, satin

quicksand (67i): in the sand, price, *wet sand*, evil

quiet (33): war against, many times, *no sound*, piece of iron

quit (16): *stop*, fix, pocketbook, mailbox

rabbit (51): poke, *animal*, lie, tricycle

raccoon (51): stick, *animal*, place, worry

race (68a): rent, excited, *run*, vase

racer (68b): medicine, receiver, *runner*, clay

rag (87): not trained, *piece of cloth*, the same way, watch over

railroad (88a): happiness, *train*, gift, bee

railway (88a): rain, look at, measure, *railroad*

rain (67h): large fork, short dress, *water falling*, fire away

rainbow (67h): hair bow, *bow of colors*, way of doing, wild cat

rainfall (67h): naughty, street, raised, *shower*

rainy (67h): firecracker, length, *wet*, fashioned

raise (19): *lift*, guy, hall, middle

raisin (74): *dried grape*, secret plan, room to sleep, farther away

ranch (67a, 91): holy, *farm*, person, moonlight

rancher (67a, 71e): *farmer*, split, luster, tree

rapid (20): pipes, earth, medal, *swift*

rapidly (20): *quickly*, dance, language, partly

raspberry (74): *fruit*, whistle, tempt, covering

rat (51): ticket, milkman, sweep, *animal*

ray (58c): *beam of light*, buildings for soldiers, toward the west, naming for office

read (62b): having no name, walk with short steps, free from fault, *get the meaning of*

real (28): alligator, *true*, knives, platform

realize (17): *understand*, metal, flannel, tablespoon

really (22): waken, *truly*, aching, skater

receive (06): *take*, climb, break, eastern

red (24): unfinished, *color*, sandwich, message

refresh (03): *make fresh again*, piece of music, lowest woman's voice, a fresh boy

refuse (70d): get again, not important, small house, *say "no"*

regret (72a): not young, wild cat, *feel sorry*, thin cake

regular (43): foolishness, *normal*, purple, dog

reheat (82b): collect, *warm over*, time of war, harmful

rejoin (09): dull yellow, cozy corner, *unite again*, sharp blow

relationship (71d): *connection*, moonbeam, jigsaw, smoke

relative (71c): a greeting card to a sweetheart, *person who belongs to the same family*, from one side to the other, every part and piece in place

remember (14): doctor who treats animals, book for holding things, *call back to mind*, freedom from war

remind (14): the same road, freedom from school, *cause to remember*, large water bird

reminder (14): *something that helps one remember*, remove the clothes from, view of the surface, limited share set aside

remove (06): full value, open air, *take away*, shows time

rent (61a): laugh, envelope, *payment*, beginning

repair (13): *fix*, laundry, everywhere, Bible

repeat (19): *do again*, plant seeds, which way, grow up

replacement (39): drink, eighth, *substitute*, courtesy

report (62b): after second, *an account*, fine powder, wide street

reporter (71e): give a prize, *person who gathers news*, desire for something to drink, meat of a pig

reprint (62d): boating, *copy*, meet, strange

Republican (63): *one of the political parties*, something to do with mail, throw water out of, against the current of a stream

respecting (UNCL): home, *concerning*, steamship, floating

rest (72d): *sleep*, tape, language, plaything

restaurant (82c, 89): not ever failing, *place to eat*, around the earth, on the sea

restless (72a): plane, nearby, *disturbed*, criminal

restlessness (72a): father, lightness, display, *nervousness*

retire (61d): between hills or mountains, number of different kinds, *give up one's business*, far above the earth

return (11): *come back*, noise to warn, snowflake, plant life

review (17): northern, *study again*, large porch, public sale

rheumatism (65); clay, shore, *disease*, fuel

rib (67b): next, stamp, *bone*, anyone

rice (76): *food*, class, behave, prince

rich (32): stack of words, easy slow pace, jump up suddenly, *having much money*

ride (88b): *be carried along*, walk through water, part of a tree, of great value

rider (68b): ask about, side of river, riding to town, *person who rides*

right (28): prayer, batch, *true*, loaves

ring (38): history, prison, *circle*, little

rise (11): lamp, elbow, *get up*, bathtub

risk (25): set to music, foot passenger, science of government, *chance of harm*

river (67d): factory, before, *stream*, airport

road (92): *street*, tailor, language, finger

roadway (92): noodle, *street*, tomorrow, lack

roar (58d): plainly not true, *make a loud noise*, group of sentences, happening by chance

robbery (64): poison, theater, became, *stealing*

robin (47): ant, *bird*, dip, strawberry

robot (84): telling in detail, brother or sister, make familiar to, *machine made person*

rocky (44): redbreast, rooster, road, *rough*

rodeo (60a): *show*, week, land, apartment

romance (62d): very little, a law, *love story*, do battle

roof (90c): mattress on a bed, *covering of a building*, blossom of a flower, the wrong answer

roofing (90d): where mail is sent, paper pasted together, *part of a house*, is next to .

roommate (71d): break up or off, up to the time of, love of one's country, *person who shares a room*

rooster (47): *animal*, tulip, maypole, banana

root (75): officer in the Navy, one who makes peace, *part of a plant*, change to another language

rope (90d): your own, mountain top, should be done, *thick cord*

rose (73): *flower*, August, screen, bob

rough (44): grasshopper, the other side, one cent, *not smooth*

round (38): think alike, small pocket knife, *shaped like a ball*, in a tree

route (92): *way to go*, kind of dog, it may be, flying machine

row (56a): see a view, false name, every one of, *line of things*

rower (68b): playmate, *oarsman*, goodness, speedy

rub (18): make some change in, choice between two things, *move one thing against another*, person who takes pictures

rug (90b): *floor covering*, United States, open air, laugh or smile

rule (63, 67e): *direct*, tiger, apart, plum

run (68a): *move quickly*, wild car, school house, in any way

rush (11): call for aid, *go with speed*, large fork, end the book

rye (76): sunflower, asleep, peanut, *grain*

sack (81): *bag*, fool, hour, possible

sad (72a): because of, *not happy*, young sheep, to blame

sadden (01): *make sad*, frozen rain, sad child, help another

saddle (52, 67a): stuck, housewife, about, *seat*

sadness (72a): silver, tight, driver, *sorrow*

safeguard (13): *protect*, baggage, varnish, postmark

safety (13): *freedom from harm*, ugly woman, wild animal, to learn

sail (67j, 87): *cloth to make a ship move*, get in the way of, goods that a truck carries, quickly pass the tongue over

sailboat (67j, 88a): grandmother, *ship*, everyone, beginning

sailor (67j, 71e): *person who works on a ship*, cloth for wiping the nose, time between early morning and noon, bar for raising or moving

saint (66): take place, sign falsely, bright light, *holy person*

salad (82d): babe, drove, thought, *vegetables*

sale (61c): large pile of hay, *selling at lower prices*, the sound of steps, rings of a chain

salesman (61c, 71e): *person whose work is selling*, a pain in the head, tell what is coming, bread baked as one piece

salesmanship (61c): sandpaper, *selling*, neck, pumpkin

saleswoman (61c, 71e): *woman whose work is selling*, light at front of automobile, woman who drives a boat, place where one is living

salmon (53): notice, chance, drawer, *fish*

salty (29): salt free, gives warmth, *containing salt*, long points

same (39): allow, donkey, *like*, connect

sample (10): crown, unborn, goes, *test*

sand (67i): how tall a person is, great deal of money, neither hot nor cold, *tiny grains of rocks*

sandwich (82d): hark, frost, brain, *a food*

Saturday (59a): a time of day, *a day of the week*, lowest part of a ship, covered with fur

saucepan (81, 90e): without a home, busy with trifles, hard limestone, *cooking utensil*

sausage (82e): *meat*, paid, flash, which

save (13): unless, *keep*, write, leather

saver (67j, 85): *preserver*, camper, me, ground

savings (61a): ill with longing, time to come, *money laid away*, person who shoots

savior (66): *rescuer*, bullfrog, cocktail, boiler

saw (84): *tool for cutting*, makes honey, repairs wiring, dark red ink

sawdust (67c): *particles of wood*, keep from talking, showing good taste, soft wet land

sawmill (67c, 89): *building where machines saw timber*, learn how to saw well, ride at full speed, run away to get married

say (04): sofa, rim, matter, *speak*

scale (83): keeping automobiles, give work, *weighing machine*, party masks

scare (01): map, *frighten*, bluejay, copper

scholar (71b): eat fast, rub out, *learned person*, use machines

schoolboy (71b): cheese, fur, *pupil*, mast

schoolhouse (62c, 89): peel, *building*, harp, Wednesday

schoolmaster (71b): *man who teaches in a school*, without beginning or ending, form a picture in the mind, time to go to school

schoolroom (62c): piece of candy or cake, without any mistakes at all, with room enough to move, *room in which pupils are taught*

science (62a): mower, somewhere, learned, *a subject*

scientist (71e): in the middle of, science of rocks, *person trained in science*, head of a state

scissors (84): odd, lump, pork, *tool*

scold (04): quarter of a dollar, small short gun, major in the army, *blame with angry words*

score (68a): *make a point*, front of a car, in these times, piece of metal

scrapbook (62d): ruby, light, potato, *album*

scratch (08): a trip to do something, person who shoots well, back part of a house, *cut with something sharp*

scream (58d): *shout*, face, joke, soda

screw (90d): *kind of nail*, soft and light, from this time, one who belongs

sea (67d, 67j): payment, *ocean*, hardware, comfort

seal (53): drowsy, champion, *animal*, gooseberry

seaman (67j, 71e): sunshine, likely, *sailor*, imagine

seaplane (88a): place where planes are kept, *airplane that can rise from water*, person who takes care of another, something that is not true

searchlight (84): *powerful light*, inner covering, light air, well known

seashore (67d, 67j): *beach*, around, nearness, railway

seasick (65, 72d): public, main, fellow, *ill*

seaside (67d): season, proud, *seashore*, rain

season (59e): *time*, purple, neighborhood, goat

seat (90b): fuzzy, guard, tinkle, *chair*

seaweed (67j, 75): *plant*, outer, together, were

second (57): thing that protects, put a baby to sleep, in a hurried way, *next after the first*

secrecy (34): few or no trees, iron or steel, *being kept secret*, tell a secret

secret (34): part of a fish's body, *known only to a few*, box from which animals eat, airplane without a motor

see (12): pine, *look*, napkin, than

seed (67a): place built to hold a fire, living together as husband and wife, person with a hump on his back, *thing from which a flower grows*

seedling (67a): loud noise, tall pole, *young plant*, male animal

seek (10): shaking, time, *search*, eldest

seesaw (68a): *move up and down*, frozen drops of rain, animal in the water, bundle of things

self (72c): rocky, *person*, bit, chorus

selfish (32): *caring too little for others*, upper parts of a river, wool that covers a sheep, in the time between

sell (61c): part of a room, in the middle, *offer for sale*, by means of

seller (61c, 71e): pencil, traveler, *trader*, lash

semicircle (38): *half a circle*, circle with a picture, legends of people, ride at full speed

send (19): *cause to go*, person in a forest, one thousand thousand, in most cases

senior (71a): loud, trumpet, *older*, whisker

sense (72d): nine, elf, *feeling*, grease

sentence (67f): take a long walk, a looking glass, *group of words*, making fun of

separate (03): lime, faith, blame, *divide*

September (59d): *month*, catbird, alarm, interesting

seriousness (30): *importance*, flour, plank, trash

service (70a): more than seven, *helpful act*, touch with the lips, being to blame

set (56a): bomb, key, *collection*, hail

settler (67e, 71d): nurse, bolt, *colonist*, ablaze

seven (57): having done wrong, steps for use in climbing, large four-footed animal, *one more than six*

seventh (57): sudden rush of wind, *next after the sixth*, in some other place, having a hurt leg

seventy (57): a racetrack, seven young dogs, need for action, *seven times ten*

sew (09, 80): *join by a thread*, put in an envelope, foam made from soap, art of cutting hair

sewing (62a): a time during the dark hours, a person who helps make the laws, bring forth young from an egg, *work done with a needle and thread*

sex (30): *being male or female*, person in a contest, a case in court, dislike very much

shade (58c): *partly dark place*, willing to work, cut dry grass, to do something

shadow (58c): help another, spoken about, without ending, *dark figure*

shake (11): *move from side to side*, upper parts of a river, many persons making laws, different from the rule

shameful (72b): containing books, *bringing disgrace*, money belt, gives warmth

shampoo (02): gained by doing, all one's life, *wash the hair*, the back part

shark (53): hum, welcome, okay, *fish*

sharp (38): *pointed*, vine, rice, language

shave (02): very lovely, improve soil, the future, *cut hair*

she (UNCL): bits of thread, spend the winter, covering the skin, *the girl*

sheep (51): multiply, everyday, *animal*, oven

sheet (87): fine, herself, *covering*, tune

shellac (90d): lady, pepper, fireplace, *varnish*

shellfish (53): librarian, *animal*, ending, outline

shepherd (67a, 71e): machine, joint on a door, *man who takes care of sheep*, cause air to blow

sheriff (64, 71e): inclose, *officer*, baggage, nothing

shine (15): getting free, *be bright*, not quiet, kind act

shiny (21): devil, *bright*, jerk, field

ship (67j, 88a): fife, kick, *boat*, hurry

shipyard (67j, 91): flour paste used for food, ship goods to another country, *place where ships are built*, able to bear fruit or young

shoe (80): *covering for a foot*, piece of iron, plain and simple, land with trees shoemaker (71e): *person who mends shoes,* hair on horse's neck, shoe for a woman, light from a fire

shoot (69): *hit with a bullet,* bee that makes honey, care for the hands, coming before all others

shop (61c, 89): brake, clay, *store,* soon

shopkeeper (61c, 71e): puppet moved by strings, *person in a store,* the holiday spent together, animal that lives in water

shopper (61c): compare, glance, hunger, *buyer*

shopping (61c): erase, flock, *buying,* kidding

shoreline (67d, 67j): *seacoast,* sheepskin, host, fly

short (40): *not long,* meeting people, without leave, close hand

shoulder (67b): touch with the lips, ditch to carry water, *part of the body,* the direction of the sunrise

shout (04): *call,* there, moss, bunny

shovel (84): dark, anything, yesterday, *tool*

show (19): *let be seen,* young cat, swallow food, the middle

shower (67h): *rain,* bud, wish, lane

shower (02): apart, kit, *bathe,* web

showman (60a, 71e): airy, *director,* jerk, morn

shrimp (53): *shellfish,* hood, spike, wove

shut (16): tow, let, forth, *close*

shyness (72a): deafness, trespass, rudeness, *bashfulness*

sick (65, 72d): four-footed animal, case for a pistol, north or south, *in poor health*

sicken (65): cleaning lady, get married, stiff material, *fall ill*

sickly (65, 72d): very expressive, hot rock, engine power, *not healthy*

sickness (65): *illness,* business, happiness, hopeless

side (36): send, *surface,* sea, several

signal (85): *sign,* silly, single, sore

signature (72c): without beginning or ending, *person's name written by himself,* a plant used for salad, story of Christ's life

silence (58d): sunlight, socks, stopping, *stillness*

silk (87): noise, *cloth,* firecracker, here

silkworm (51): tickle, distant, rib, *caterpillar*

silly (28): title, *foolish,* windy, belt

silver (67i): crush, *metal,* butcher, knew

silverware (90e): little by little, try to find out, leg, arm or wing, *knives, forks and spoons*

silvery (21, 24): checker, hint, *bright,* rate

simply (28): capital, dusty, quite, *easily*

sin (66): front part, gray haired, *evil deed,* animal fat

since (59b): feed on grass, showing no favor, *from then till now,* length of wood

sing (04): *make music with the voice,* cause air to blow upon, make neat and tidy, store that sells food

singer (60a, 71e): machine for weaving, act of kindness, *person who sings,* man to be married

sink (90d): rid, *tub,* left, pear

sister (71c): box from which animals eat, *daughter of the same parents,* five more than ten, sudden rush of wind

sit (11): one of the parts of the hand, *rest on the lower part of the body,* meeting of people for buying and selling, get in the way of by moving

six (57): soft white candy, *one more than five,* praise too much, to touch or hold

sixpence (61b): *British coin,* Merry Christmas, United States, Monday morning

sixteen (57): book of directions, cover for the face, a man of sixty, *six more than ten*

sixth (57): kind of writing, act of flying, *next after the fifth,* work of art

sixty (57): join in a pair, covered with blossoms, *six times ten,* sixteen years old

size (30): head of a city, death by a rope, *space a thing takes up,* a rush of water

skate (68a): little, fire, *glide,* robber

skeleton (67b): instead, delivery, *bones,* feather

ski (68a): fasten from above, *glide over snow,* lunch or supper, holder for paper

skillful (32): flea, kite, today, *trained*

skin (67b): shed for airplanes, *covering of the body,* lights on the stage, way of finding size

skinny (38): runner, lip, flake, *thin*

skip (68a): grandpa, huge, *jump,* rat

skirt (80): having sore feet, *part of a dress,* the art of medicine, going well together

skunk (51): tone, *animal,* geography, flesh

sky (67h): fail to remember, *the heavens,* list of food, bring forth young

skyscraper (89): too proud, nothing else, *tall building,* brown spot

slacks (80): food, moth, pastures, *trousers*

slap (08): tack, *hit,* rule, grand

slave (67e, 71d): hairpin, indoors, blueberry, *worker*

sleep (72d): earth, *rest,* cottage, breath

sleeper (71d): unable to sleep, miles traveled, *one that sleeps,* day of the week

sleepless (72d): bluebird, transport, forepaw, *wakeful*

sleepwalker (71d): baby's walker, own a mill, great weight, *night walker*

sleepy (72d): dumb, *tired,* cone, robin

sleeveless (80): dress with sleeves, close tie, minister's duties, *without sleeves*

sleigh (88a): *sled,* slit, sly, slept

slip (11): slave, sixty, slowly, *slide*

slipper (80): *shoe,* eager, scorch, chocolate

slop (90f): *spill,* necklace, tomorrow, sour

sloppy (28): *careless,* pump, led, gentleman

slow (20): human being, worry about, *not fast*, spell wrongly

small (40): *not large*, get in return, the second day, care for

smallpox (65): *a disease*, nevertheless, rifle, clover

smart (32): *clever*, diamond, hiss, bread

smell (18): take place, *breathe in*, state of mind, fit to eat

smile (72d): *look pleased*, not quite, following day, long fish

smog (67h): *smoke and fog*, study of the earth, like a dog, round body

smoke (58d): get on a horse, a quick look, *give off steam*, one more than seven

smoker (71d): *person who smokes*, bend of the arm, without a motor, smoke and fog

smokestack (90c): buttonhole, *chimney*, praise, dove

smooth (44): *level*, careless, knee, gentleman

snail (51): *animal*, that, without, hot

sniff (18): the Navy, *breathe in*, fight against, show how

snow (67h): help remember, *white flakes*, the forehead, no one

snowbank (67d): meaning much, cozy corner, *drift of snow*, throw a snowball

snowflake (67h): begin again, *piece of snow*, cannot be, play in the snow

snowy (24): ripe, leg, *white*, pear

soak (90f): this time, not outside, *make wet*, feeling thanks

soapsuds (90f): *bubbles*, toot, muffin, youngster

society (56b, 63): *all people*, sell directly, burn trash, without water

society (56b): *community*, mean, farmer, unheard

soft (31): end to end, hot cereal, make more, *not hard*

soften (03): carried along, owing money, body of water, *make tender*

soil (67i): tardy, *earth*, bench, clothes

soldier (67e, 69): getting no help from others, bar on which birds rest, fifth day of the week, *man who serves in an army*

some (UNCL): pale color, grandchild, *a few*, kite

someday (59b): some small child, person who keeps an inn, a short opera, *at some future time*

someone (UNCL): brown bread, look over, some books, *some person*

sometimes (59b): put into order, *now and then*, juicy fruit, of a book

somewhere (36): somehow or other, *in some place*, a water animal, night of this day

son (71c): move quickly, at bat, *male child*, buttermilk

song (60a): pain in a tooth, do more than, shaking motion, *something to sing*

songster (60a, 71e): slender, *singer*, skyscraper, shower

sonny (71f): with, *boy*, timber, aspirin

soon (43): tumble down from, *in a short time*, mixed-up mess, in the open air

sore (72d): *painful*, made, chest, along

soreness (65): hike, *pain*, bathe, rather

sorrow (72a): *sadness*, lot, season, granddaughter

sorrowful (72a): *sad*, car, ball, hair

sorry (72a): *sad*, smooth, six, squeak

sound (58d): live longer than, asking many questions, *what can be heard*, put the hand on

soup (82a): *food*, carpenter, proper, dash

south (36): *direction*, throw, gas, house

southern (26): to drive south, like an egg, rise high up, *toward the south*

souvenir (14): that cannot be erased, *something for remembrance*, extend above, eat too much

spaghetti (82d): grateful, then, *food*, jaw

spank (08): *hit*, think, jelly, frog

sparrow (47): put, *bird*, check, driven

speak (04): feast, bookcase, kindly, *talk*

speaker (63): charm, dwelt, *talker*, hammer

special (39): *different*, pretend, rainy, hut

speech (04): burn, cobbler, graze, *talk*

speechless (72a): set down in writing, use power on, *not able to speak*, one more than eleven

speedily (20): reader, merrily, *quickly*, jacket

spell (62b): *write or say the letters of a word*, person that lives in a certain place, clothes worn under a suit or dress, place where one thing crosses another

spend (61c): draw a line, *pay out money*, like a nut, breaking in on

spendthrift (61a, 71d): a fur bearing animal, beginning of a book, *person who wastes money*, take the clothes off

spider (50): holy, for, *animal*, brass

spin (11): quit, *turn*, itself, tell

spinach (79): hung, ought, *plant*, bone

splash (90f): chew, *wet*, room, fried

spoil (05): carriage, drug, ivy, *damage*

spokesman (63): person who shares a room, disease that can be spread, *person who speaks for another*, liquid that gives a glossy appearance

spoon (90e): *bowl at the end of a handle*, a trip in the open air, cut wood with a sharp knife, person who comes into a country

sport (68c): tail, *game*, children, desk

sportsman (68b): sports award of the year, the juice of purple grapes, *person who takes part in sports*, cushion to stick pins in

spot (38): clown, fox, *mark*, height

spotless (21): *clean*, gate, bird, tea

spotlight (84): *strong light*, desire to drink, set of two, light meal

spray (90f): study, skull, soul, *splash*

spring (11): pity, blot, *jump*, cranky

springtime (59e): sound, stole, sailboat, *season*

sprinkle (90f): *spray*, sting, cab, dress

spy (64): *person who keeps secret watch*, inside of the hand, glittering copper in thin sheets, lacking of some part

spyglass (83): feed, *telescope*, plow, handwriting

square (38): pillow, went to, *a figure*, cliff

squeeze (18): father, haircut, bus, *crowd*

squirrel (51): popcorn, *animal*, heart, toilet

stair (90c): store, soft, spinach, *step*

stamp (62f): *make a mark*, bone of the body, open to question, worked by the foot

start (16): tie, male, night, *begin*

starve (72d): sweet candy, not neat, *suffer hunger*, make holes

statesman (63, 67e): *person skilled in public affairs*, form of the verb, pay no attention to, lift up the head

station (91): *place*, built, drink, low

stay (16): orange, mend, tail, *remain*

steak (82e): cloth with checks, making better, *slice of meat*, all that time

steal (64): rag, middle, *rob*, pole

steamship (67j, 88a): coaster, aged, polite, *boat*

steer (88b): *guide*, April, duck, cherry

stem (75): way of doing something, from then on, many and close together, *part of a plant*

step (11): arm, *walk*, pipe, bakery

stepfather (71c): shell in which plants grow, having to do with workers, what a person thinks about, *man who has married one's mother*

stepmother (71c): having to do with government, chair in which a king sits, being liked by most people, *woman who has married one's father*

stew (82b): incorrect, mighty, *cook*, angel

steward (71e): snuff, ponies, *servant*, ouch

stick (67c): on one's toes, *piece of wood*, jump suddenly, turn upside down

stiff (31): ten, *hard*, born, circus

stilts (68c): swim, *supports*, seventy, sometimes

stink (18): *bad smell*, with child, mushroom, out of order

stockholder (61a): moving, *stockowner*, hidden, stock yards

stocking (80): *covering for the leg*, a small floating island, thing that toasts, brought to public notice

stomach (67b): movable piece of wood, *part of the body*, subject to a penalty, land surrounded by water

stone (67i): cuff, *rock*, blue, myself

stop (16): men, thin, won, *halt*

store (61c, 89): *shop*, scratch, should, snug

storekeeper (61c, 71e): hasten, party, grassy, *merchant*

storm (67h): brush for cleaning the teeth, make offer of marriage, pointed end of a fork, *strong wind with rain*

stormy (20, 67h): *windy*, thirsty, case, manager

story (62d): chop, *tale*, open, hill

stove (90a): divide, having, *oven*, cheek

strangeness (72a): darkness, punish, low, *queerness*

straw (67a): people, tan, mew, *grain*

strawberry (74): heel, *fruit*, map, coast

stream (67d): *body of water*, fur bearing animal, wild dog, climbing plant

street (92): owe, hers, chill, *road*

strike (08): *hit*, mow, twin, ugly

stroke (65): at dusk, *sudden attack*, brother or sister, picture puzzle

strong (41): more than one, lively dance, *having much power*, a new kind

student (71b): against, unburned, *pupil*, drank

studio (60c, 90c): deal, back, popcorn, *workroom*

study (17): bow the head, *try to learn*, that cannot be, not yet born

style (61c): envelope, *fashion*, teaspoon, homesick

submarine (67j, 88a): *boat*, handful, reach, tomato

subtract (67g): cookie crumb, *take away*, do no harm, angel wings

subtraction (67g): rate as too low, *taking one number from another*, draw a line under, try to be like

subway (88a): *underground railroad*, card for sending, red poppy, blueberry cake

such (39): make a picture, *of that kind*, green vegetable, having no work

sudden (20): needle, foggy, *quick*, biting

suffer (72d): redwood, *feel pain*, thereto, church

suffix (67f): freedom from work and school, person who knows how to teach, *addition to the end of a word*, show someone the way to go home

suit (80): holder for pencils, ask many questions, *set of clothes*, flop on the floor

suitcase (55c, 81, 86): guard, protect from, fancy clothes, *traveling bag*

sum (67g): suppose so, *the whole*, pleasant, mousetrap

summer (59e): school, someone, slave, *season*

sun (67h): *heavenly body*, song bird, work together, strawberry pie

Sunday (59a): cheer a person up, having yellow flowers, *day of the week*, in line with

sundown (59c): *sunset*, graveyard, fiddle, sunflower

sunflower (73): *plant*, letting, ticket, overhead

sunless (21): *dark*, crocodile, golden, elsewhere

sunlight (58c): friendship, joyous, thimble, *daytime*

sunny (21, 67h): temper, young, *bright*, electric

sunset (59c, 67h): a day with no sun, to walk with short steps, *the going down of the sun*, small island in the ocean

sunshine (67h): master, oatmeal, rabbit, *light*

sunshiny (21, 67h): harvest, factory, *bright*, number

superintendent (61d): lantern, *manager*, churchyard, package

supermarket (82d, 89): translation, learned, sprinkle, *store*

supervisor (61d): *manager*, lovely, repent, color

supper (82c): excited, honor, paste, *meal*

support (70a): wickedness, moonlight ride, *provide for*, naughty child

sure (22): *certain*, lawyer, blood, hiss

surely (22): book, kindly, *certainly*, whirl

surprise (01): lump on the skin, hold wash water, *come upon suddenly*, watch over

swamp (67d): freeze in, capital letter, *wet land*, train conductor

sweater (80): cardboard box, tired feet, *knitted jacket*, downstairs

sweep (90e): wood used for fire, *clean with a broom*, form thread into a thing, chief officer in charge

sweeper (90a): hotel, *cleaner*, footprint, boiler

sweeten (82b, 82f): stuck together, sing a song, *add sugar*, go to sleep

sweetheart (71d): meadow, brick, *lover*, ant

swim (68a): *move in the water*, white ball for tennis, flower in the garden, give a valentine

swing (68a): *move back and forth*, daughter of a king, absent from school, go on a horse

sword (67e, 69): elbow, cliff, *weapon*, theater

syllable (67f): ridge on the skin, *part of a word*, tax on a house, from the west

syrup (82f): without mercy, living thing, stop smoking, *sweet liquid*

table (90b): ship, head, like, *furniture*

tablecloth (90e): *covering*, key, cheat, foot

tablespoon (90e): vegetable, *large spoon*, goodness, with no spoon

tablet (62f): aimed at, *writing pad*, school, because

tableware (90e): having little ability, *knives, forks and spoons*, sign of welcome, carried on the back

tack (90d): window, *nail*, wrong, handle

tag (62f): *ticket*, insect, smell, thin

take (06): not seen, *get hold of*, north or south, teach school

talk (04): careless, join, smallest, *speak*

talker (71d): member, rub, go away, *speaker*

tall (40): airplane, shelf, who, *high*

tan (24): mistake, *brown*, aid, lamp

tang (29): only a few, the same, comes in, *strong taste*

tape (90d): first letter, very many, young plant, *long strip*

tasteless (29): shameless, helper, *flavorless*, original

tasty (29): put in play, waste time, no more taste, *tasting good*

tax (63, 67e): angel, *charge*, ink, surface

taxation (63, 67e): change from one place to another, title used in addressing a lord, person to take care of a building, *amount people pay for support of government*

taxi (88a): not quiet, *automobile for hire*, shake with cold, make something new

tea (82a): coat, poison, hunk, *a drink*

teach (62b): person who sells, telling a lie, where things are, *show how to do*

teacher (71b): happiness, engine, *schoolmaster*, player

team (56b, 68b): loudly, *group*, steel, gay

teamwork (70a): enlarge, bather, smart, *cooperation*

tease (01): unfinished, hair, drag, *bother*

teaspoon (90e): spoon bread, for the hands, in a book, *a spoon*

teens (71a): *years of life*, in poor health, large house, hold ink

telegram (62d): breathe, *message*, farthest, chart

telegraph (04): *wire*, blind, rather, shoot

telephone (04): *call*, learn, still, candy

telescope (83): canal boat, thread, *field glass*, surprise

tell (04): beach, *say*, card, junior

temperature (30): porch, sleigh, tennis, *heat*

temptation (66): cork, favorite, *attraction*, poison

ten (57): month of the year, glide over snow, *one more than nine*, done in a house

tender (41): roadside, *soft*, ugly, win

tennis (68c): remove, schoolhouse, bleed, *a game*

tent (87): not real, seasoning, friend, *a cover*

terrible (28): class, *awful*, sprinkle, liberty

test (10): *try*, body, enter, helpful

testament (66): rock, easily, *the Bible*, hut

testimony (64): *statement used for evidence*, edge of the mouth, care of sheep, keeper of a jail

textbook (62b, 62d): female lion, shelf for books, to protect, *book for study*

thank (72a): *be grateful*, being alive, full of juice, give a score

thankful (32): *grateful*, waste, animal, wonderful

thankfulness (72b): busy, *thanks*, find, Thanksgiving

thankless (72b): squash, closet, *ungrateful*, rejoice

theater (60a): man who makes locks, *place where plays are shown*, money that comes in, on the earth's surface

their (UNCL): jockey, heaven, rob, *of them*

there (36): not high, *in that place,* can spread, cutting grass

thereby (UNCL): from the coast, wood across the bottom, solid mass, *in that way*

thermometer (67h, 83): *instrument for measuring temperature,* one in a hundred numbers, ability to learn facts, caught in a thunderstorm

thief (64): *person who steals,* living on an island, next after the fifth, done by magic

thieve (64): honk, godmother, *steal,* magazine

thin (38): elephant, housework, everybody, *not thick*

think (17): male person, partly melted snow, full of smoke, *use the mind*

thinker (71b): *man of learning,* very big, sniff again, human race

third (57): shelf above fireplace, *next after second,* owing money, hollow piece

thirst (72d): walk in step, hard-working, in an army, *desire to drink*

thirsty (72d): cowboy, March, hoof, *without water*

thirty (57): of the sea, letter of a word, *three times ten,* at some time

thought (17): enjoy, howl, *idea,* keep

thoughtful (32): eighteen, officer, *considerate,* behind

thoughtfulness (72b): brook, salad, *care,* airship

thousand (57): *ten hundred,* put in, medicine, of summer

three (57): able to learn, where money is coined, *one more than two,* bit of fire

thrill (72b): *exciting feeling,* do something, lose, canyon

throat (67b): *front of the neck,* out of order, land with water, fail to catch

throw (68a): fifteen, harness, mama, *toss*

thumb (67b): grand, hospital, package, *finger*

thunder (67h): *loud noise,* locomotive, swimming, put out

thunderbolt (67h): state of mind, separate thing, *lightning and thunder,* thunder all day

thundercloud (67h): cloud the eyes, blossom, *dark cloud,* umbrella

thunderous (33): alike, *booming,* dollar, scrub

Thursday (59a): climbing ivy plant, in the wind, travel by automobile, *day of the week*

thy (UNCL): *your,* beneath, haystack, princess

ticket (60a): yonder, savings, eyebrow, *card*

tiger (51): root, *animal,* lift, eleven

tight (40): forgotten, rainbow, looking alive, *not loose*

time (59b): a meeting of people for buying and selling, *all the days there have been or will be,* having to do with the art of medicine, move from one place to settle in another

timepiece (59b, 83): *clock,* redbreast, stoop, lip

tiny (40): fence, henhouse, willow, *small*

tissue (86): person who takes, factory, *thin paper,* the winner

title (72c): *name,* rosebud, furniture, workman

title (63): *recognized right,* filling for pies, not capable of, make very wet

toast (82d): *bread,* daily, wreck, excuse

toaster (90a): *thing that toasts,* duties of a minister, soft sticky mud, drink a toast

tobacco (77): having some fault, *leaves of certain plants,* cloth around the neck, a suit or dress

today (59b): giving a sweet smell, stick to shoot pebbles, wrong direction, *the present time*

toe (67b): a measure of length, move in a sly way, *end part of the foot,* put in the wrong place

toilet (90c): mayor, battleship, youngster, *bathroom*

tomato (74): pound, *fruit,* candlestick, towel

tomorrow (59b): *day after today,* something new, not drunk, form into shape

ton (83): would, beech, to comb, *a measure*

tongue (67b): second day of the week, *piece of flesh in the mouth,* man who gives up everything, thin flat piece of wood

tonight (59b): a ray of moonlight, *night of this day,* cannot be done, morning noon and night

too (35): *also,* having, green, theater

toothache (65): lacking some part, *pain in a tooth,* person with limited mentality, tooth of an elephant

toothpick (86): in poor health, *pointed piece of wood,* that cannot be erased, like a mother

tornado (67h): steady effort, charge, jellyfish, *violent wind*

touch (18): write, reason, *feel,* bedbug

tourist (55c, 71d): place where hay is stored, glide over snow, chance to play, *person traveling for pleasure*

towel (90e): break in on, of the sea, *piece of cloth,* rest body and mind

town (63, 91): *place with many people living in it,* piece that has broken off, bend forward at the head and shoulders, things for use or for sale

township (63, 91): partly melted snow, *part of a county,* rock used for building, prize fighter or boxer

toy (68c): chicken, toadstool, *plaything,* background

track (92): banana, woodpecker, *rails,* goody

tractor (67a): *engine for pulling,* friend in court, cannot be, take a nap

trade (61c): *buy and sell,* north or south, again and again, full of snow

trader (61c, 67e, 71e): hosiery, *merchant,* joint, boy

trail (11): *follow behind,* gliding down, containing mistakes, in the future

trailer (88a): front part of a coat, *wagon pulled by an automobile,* pay no attention to, something that is good

train (88a): knowing nothing, halfway between, *railroad cars,* sounds you make

trainer (71b, 71e): beauty, enemy, hunter, *teacher*

training (62b): special, *education,* belief, criminal

trash (90e): *rubbish,* sandwich, marry, bridge

traveler (55c, 67e, 71d): jigsaw, clerk, drum, *voyager*

treasure (60b): *valuable things,* September, foot and leg, horn treasurer (61a): *person in charge of money,* seat without back or arms, ability to remember or keep, where one thing crosses another

tree (67c): dim, tonight, railroad, *plant*

triangle (38): remains alive, of the moon, with a bang, *a figure*

trip (55c): aid, *journey,* doctor, inn

troop (56b, 69): sheath, up, *group,* told

trophy (70b): meal, *prize,* gay, responsible

trouble (72a): rocket, carry, above, *worry*

truck (88a): who a person is, *strongly built automobile,* walking stick, find the size

true (28): *real,* needle, shoot, bedspread

truly (22): bookkeeper, misty, *really,* birth

truthful (28): original, model, *honest,* yellow

try (10): sort, letter, *test,* flash

tub (81, 90d): elder, angel, weed, *bucket*

Tuesday (59a): *day of the week,* because of hunger, from one to another, cannot be done

tuna (53): *fish,* skilled, instrument, distance

turkey (47): valley, remind, *bird,* ate

turn (11): *move around,* baseball, thunder, married man

turtle (53): stretch, *animal,* dinner, beard

twelve (57): lose one's way, *one more than eleven,* unhappy state of mind, money that comes in

twenty (57): flowing thing, causing mistakes, *two times ten,* make more

twice (35): schoolroom, long and thin, postman, *two times*

twin (71c): a plant whose green leaves are eaten, *one of two born at the same time,* part of a pipe placed in a person's mouth, lines and spaces on which music is written

twinkle (15): *shine,* repay, forenoon, panel

twirl (11): beautify, death, *spin,* jump

two (57): *one more than one,* in the smoke, go up a hill, put in a class

type (62f): king or queen, *write with a typewriter,* type of glass, mutter low sounds

typewriter (84): small bit of fire, *machine for making letters,* killing a human being, special line of work

typist (71e): a collection of type, animal with eight legs, *person operating a typewriter,* large mass of ice

ugly (28): *unpleasant to look at,* put into the hands of, as it should be, person who is away

umbrella (86): thing known to be true, ready to take in, *folding frame covered with cloth,* the kitchen of a ship

unashamed (32): hearing, *shameless,* shampoo, temperature

unbecoming (28): thin layer, plant container, wooden frame, *not appropriate*

unborn (71a): born too late, something burning, *not yet born,* what is given

uncle (71c): *brother of one's father or mother,* spirit of one who is dead, plan or action carried out, time of being a girl

unclean (28): tune, wren, solid, *dirty*

uncover (54): vision, pitch, *open*, neck

under (UNCL): pink, lady, fare, *below*

underground (34): forest, *secret*, hasty, winning

underline (62f): volcano, different, cutting, *mark*

undersell (61c): idle talk, *sell cheaply*, imaginary, sell vegetables

understand (17): *get the meaning of*, building for growing, dance & skip, some sticky tape

undone (54): make heat, sulky person, *not finished*, just right

undress (80): *take the clothes off*, number of things together, in a bad temper, a feeling of delight

unemployed (61d): in the middle, ring of light, divide into, *having no work*

unequal (39): fasten from above, exciting deed, part of grammar, *not the same*

unfailing (28): to be done, *never failing*, failing grades, small tree

unfair (28): far away, chicken house, say firmly, *not just*

unfit (28): one who inherits, house or room, *not good enough*, second thought

unfold (07): shiny metal, make well, cut grass, *open out*

unfriendly (32): a good friend, *not friendly*, above the earth, an added part

ungrateful (32): a spoonful, strong wind, *not thankful*, formal notice

unguarded (25, 64): *not protected*, hammered and shaped, movable bridge, waste food

unhappiness (72a): pathless, undress, greenness, *sadness*

unhappy (72a): rot, *sad*, tip, law

unharmed (72b): unheard of, *unhurt*, unwashed, unwritten

unhealthful (65): be in good health, ground for growing, bow and arrow, *bad for the health*

unhealthy (65, 72d): sneak out, white flower, deep cut, *not well*

unheard (33): catch the breath, give reasons for, wheel having teeth, *not listened to*

unhurt (72d): run, *safe*, tan, wipe

uniform (67e, 80): *clothes*, worth, top, getting

unimportant (28): *lesser*, stopped, hand-made, root

unkind (32): *cruel*, hem, fan, easy

unkindness (72b): *cruelty*, snowstorm, professor, ding-dong

unlawful (64): a law officer, large meeting hall, *against the law*, beautiful in form

unlearned (62b): learn by heart, give a prize, seize suddenly, *not learned*

unlike (39): *different*, watermelon, soundproof, schoolboy

unlikely (22): animal fat, natural force, *not probable*, spool of thread

unlock (54): *open*, refresh, airy, bath

unlovely (28): *without beauty*, in the Navy, having education, take a risk

unlucky (32): lucky charm, should be done, more than seven, *not lucky*

unnamed (34): following in back of, *without a name*, name a child, choose by voting unnatural (28): most cases, *not normal*, nibble food, in advance

unopened (54): prepared, however, smudge, *closed*

unpack (55c): *take out*, relieve, get caught, great size

unpaid (61a): fan, *due*, hit, ivy

unpleasant (28): pleasant day, different kinds, *not pleasant*, cotton cloth

unreal (60b): savings, *imaginary*, tennis, playful

unsatisfactory (28): account book, put into words, shine in the dark, *not good enough*

unsuccessful (32): meet with success, reddish brown, farm building, *without success*

unsuspected (22): ruler of the world, male parent, *not thought of*, articles of gold

unsuspecting (72b): universe, fifteen, *unaware*, help

untaught (62b): union, happily, electric, *unlearned*

until (UNCL): something good to eat, *up to the time of*, thing to sleep on, land with few trees

unto (UNCL): ten, the, tow, *to*

untrained (62b): on a train, ahead of time, *not trained*, very happy

untroubled (72a): shield, either, *calm*, indeed

untrue (28): jump, enjoy, *false*, refill

unwelcome (28): *not wanted*, by order of, hard rock, splendid day

unwilling (32): deep valley, willingly, dearly loved, *not willing*

up (UNCL): story of Christ's life, break one's promise, *to a higher place*, light from a fire

upholster (90b): head of a state, liquid for drinking, beautiful in form, *provide with covering*

upland (67d): under a spell, *high land*, give praise, land safely

upon (UNCL): or, blot, egg, *on*

upper (36): *higher*, gather, bump, damage

uppermost (36): borrow, *highest*, gravel, harvest

uproar (58d): grandfather, *loud noise*, sharp pencil, because of

upside (36): *top*, bet, dam, key

upstairs (36): *on an upper floor*, in small pieces, wish for happiness, up to date

upward (26): this piece of wood, *toward a higher place*, handle with points, warm the hands

us (UNCL): to, *we*, at, ox

use (19): *put into service*, large spot, the first year, high steep cliff

useful (28): becoming, crowded, beautiful, *helpful*

useless (28): hostess, robbery, *worthless*, basement

vacation (55c, 61d, 62b, 68d): containing silver, *freedom from duties*, sports equipment, federal court

valentine (62d): true to life, *greeting card*, large store, a little wave

vegetable (82d): seat without a back, someone who lives nearby, having much money, *plant used for food*

verb (67f): *part of speech*, nine times ten, high singing voice, spring back

very (35): leaf, *much*, pour, fort

victorious (37): waiter, choice, daily, *successful*

village (63, 91): blackbird, cousin, soldier, *town*

vinegar (82d): beard, *acid*, coach, within

violet (73): *plant*, twice, stitch, coat

violinist (60a, 71e): the season after winter, control by home rule, *person who plays the violin*, violin, harp, or guitar

visit (11): *go to see*, do more than, summer sun, begin to grow

visitor (71c): hair, *guest*, shelf, cocoa

vitamin (65): keep secret watch, over the side, *substance for the body*, crouch down low

vocabulary (67f): teakettle, connect, *words*, silk

voice (58d): four sides of a figure, be much stronger than, the part left over, *sound made through the mouth*

voiceless (33): customer, berry, robbery, *silent*

volt (83): *unit for measuring electric energy*, bundle of things wrapped together, to call back to mind, line on which music is written

vote (63): bean, owl, *choice*, snug

voter (63): stem of a plant, *person who votes*, approved model, cast a vote

voyage (55c): sudden, rescue, *travel*, police

wagon (88a): lemonade, ponies, engineer, *cart*

waist (67b): each one hundred years, *middle of a person's body*, in the same way, man who teaches in a school

wait (16): pansy, *stay*, grandson, knife

waitress (71e, 82c): not able to wait for someone, *woman who waits on tables*, the bed of a stream, cut with something sharp

wake (72d): pulled by horses, far above the earth, thin piece of ice, *stop sleeping*

wakeful (72d): familiar talk, *without sleep*, distance upwards, seacoast port

waken (72d): costing little, *stop sleeping*, part of milk, being kept secret

walk (11): *go on foot*, sum up to, a sweet nut, appear to be

walker (55c, 71d): piece of iron, caring too little, *foot passenger*, giving birth

wall (90c): feeling very lonely, *side of a building*, front of the jaw, to offer for sale

wallet (86): give formal notice of, the act of choosing, *small case for money*, having good sense

walnut (76): friend, nut cake, nine, *nut*

want (70d): *wish*, winter, wrote, wedding

warehouse (89): necessary, doctor, *storeroom*, alarm

warfare (67e, 69): nonsense, *fighting*, automobile, hurried

warm (42): *more hot than cold*, servant on a ship, choose between two things, fish without scales

warmth (30): oats, *heat*, gobble, present

warn (04): face powder, lose money, *give notice*, at rest

warning (04): pocketbook, toadstool, *notice*, seventy

wash (02): newspaper, *clean*, family, almost

washbowl (90d): *sink*, trumpet, arithmetic, dull

washer (02, 71d, 90f): *person who washes*, wash the floor, cause to laugh, play a game

washing (90f): angry manner, make rough, *clothes washed*, window washer

washroom (90c): downtown, suffocation, bedroom, *bathroom*

wasp (50): stagecoach, charge, *insect*, unfriendly

waste (19): *throw away*, twin sisters, very pleasing, bend forward

wasteful (35): *using too much*, horn of a deer, drive an automobile, wind with rain

watch (12): *look*, flood, judge, allowed

watchdog (49): *guard*, awhile, discover, goldfish

watchman (64, 71e): bury, *guard*, however, voice

watchtower (67c, 67e, 89): *lookout*, suitcase, umbrella, remember

waterfall (67d): shepherd, medicine, *falls*, stop falling

waterway (67d): *river*, gooseberry, sidewalk, between

waterworks (90d): champion, *pipes*, sweeper, blanket

watery (46, 67j): shipwreck, cottage, another, *liquid*

wave (67d, 67j): *a moving swell of water*, shooting with bow and arrow, a large slice of meat, part of a rope

way (92): mitten, able, *road*, yarn

wayside (92): the art of numbers, *edge of a road*, a house of prayer, bed for carrying the sick

we (UNCL): *the persons speaking*, covered with fur, tobacco for smoking, move the hand

web (48): rub, lay, *net*, elf

weak (41): a visitor, burned wood, *not strong*, study hard

weaken (05): mounted guns, of a citizen, *make weak*, a weak attack

wear (80): on the lookout, *have on the body*, close very tightly, taking one from another

wed (09, 55b): submarine, treasure, review, *marry*

Wednesday (59a): burn with a blue flame, man who has not married, band around the neck, *day of the week*

weed (67a): *plant*, business, measure, walnut

weedy (67a): in the rear, *full of weeds*, like ice cream, weed the garden

week (59b, 83): a theatre, without hair, *seven days*, loud noise

weekend (59b): *Saturday and Sunday*, large body of water, a stupid person, burned up wood

weekly (43): *every week*, free from danger, make certain, weekend trip

weep (72d): sandwich, *cry*, level, facing

weigh (10): caring little for others, *find out how heavy*, very great surprise, lump of earth

weight (30): science dealing with the stars, cause to go away, work for another person, *how heavy a thing is*

weighty (45): sleepy, match, *heavy*, preacher

west (36): grocery, engineer, slipped, *direction*

western (26): partly dark place, cover for bed, from northwest to southwest, *from the west*

wet (46, 67j): an egg, *not dry*, go away, cut hair

whale (53): jump, *animal*, fir, narrow

whalebone (52, 67j): *teeth of whales*, covered with clouds, care of children, school of whales

whaler (67e, 67j, 71e): friendly, *hunter*, bookkeeper, minute

wheat (76): frighten, canary, aboard, *grain*

wheel (38): free from dirt, *something round*, law officer, in the rear

when (UNCL): call to mind, front part, *what time*, of a citizen

whenever (UNCL): larger than, piece of wood, ways of living, *at any time*

where (UNCL): *in what place*, a cereal box, notes of music, shake with cold

whereabouts (UNCL): sudden crash, *near what place*, stop the breath, animal with wings

wherever (UNCL): third base, *whatever place*, every week, loud sound

which (UNCL): mix together, *the one that*, become smaller, shining metal

while (59b): wild cat, part of a dress, *space of time*, light rowboat

whirlpool (67d): make weary, unable to get, a short time, *water spinning round*

whirlwind (67h): *air spinning*, male child, supreme ruler, chain of beads

white (24): excuse, touch, runner, *color*

who (UNCL): *any person*, know much, fairy tale, blew out

whoever (UNCL): out of money, high tower, get caught, *any person*

whole (35): become, goat, *all*, wiggle

whom (UNCL): very hard, *what person*, the air, soft leather

whose (UNCL): wagon, red wool, *of whom*, willow

why (UNCL): by the sun, *for what reason*, male animal, connected rooms

wide (40): powerful light, being clean, *filling much space*, kind of flower

wildcat (51): team, marry, engine, *animal*

wildfire (58a): throat, *blaze*, spoonful, artist

will (70d): bunch of flowers, person who carves, not often, *is going to*

willing (32): maypole, fifth, *ready*, surface

wind (67h): servant, nearly, forehead, *air* .

windmill (84): take what is given, *machine worked by the wind*, light of a candle, come to the window

window (90c): *opening for air or light*, a tool to write with, part of a flower, person who takes moving pictures

windowpane (90c): help out, *piece of glass*, car on a train, give up one thing

windy (67h): mew, rusty, *stormy*, lizard

wine (82a): *juice of grapes*, young cow, rather quickly, pay for work

wing (67b): more than one calf, *part of a bird*, part of the throat, kind of shoe wink (72d): machine for taking pictures, card with one spot, *close and open an eye*, juice of a plant

winner (63, 71d): group of tents, one winter day, *person who wins*, small bag

winter (59e): *season*, roadside, blush, deed

wipe (90f): sea, major, *rub*, cherry

wire (90d): *metal thread*, ripe fruit, fold in two, square

wireless (90a): grown, bench, tablecloth, *radio*

wish (70d): whip, written, worm, *want*

witch (60b): big gun, chopped meat, measure of land, *ugly old woman*

witchcraft (60b): small container, *magic power*, store up, exactly right

within (36): gown, bonnet, tomahawk, *inside*

without (UNCL): song of joy, known to you, look at closely, *not having any*

wizard (60b): tenth, *magician*, asleep, housetop

wolf (51): glory, visitor, lunch, *animal*

woman (71f): *lady*, truth, bitter, cuff

womanhood (71f): either man or woman, from one side to the other, statement of a program, *time of being a woman*

womanly (71f): songbird, not imaginary, man and woman, *like a woman*

wonderful (28): schoolhouse, *surprising*, mountain, peppermint

wood (67c): stretch, owe, eraser, *lumber*

woodchuck (51): sterling, enjoy, *animal*, inside

woodcraft (62a): soldier on horseback, respect and love, *knowledge about the woods*, heavily wooded ground

woodcutter (67c, 71e): top of a room, *man who cuts down trees*, give a suggestion, piece of cut glass

wooded (67c): art of navigating, a special day, *covered with trees*, program of action

wooden (44, 77): *made of wood*, copper coin, far away, cut some wood

woodland (67c): statement of fact, *land covered with trees*, have the means, facts and laws

woodpecker (47): held, *bird*, block, admire

woodsman (67c, 71e): bed of a stream, *man skilled in hunting*, some other time, man of the hour

woodwork (90b): linked tightly together, *things made of wood*, look down upon, on the woodpile

woody (67c): *having many trees*, central part, time of life, rub hard

wool (52): *fur*, swan, plum, busy

woolen (44, 52): *made of wool*, invite to a game, wind the wool, on fire

woolly (44, 52): indoors, juicy, *fleecy*, telegraph

workman (61d, 71e): hard work, *worker*, interested, hail storm

workmanship (61d): as if by magic, on the shore, lots of work, *skill in working*

workroom (61d, 90c): *shop*, teapot, grease, hunger

workshop (61d, 90c): *studio*, hawk, rainbow, television

world (56a, 67d): stop suddenly, cry of pain, fight hard, *all things*

worm (51): oven, rapidly, *animal*, time

worry (72a): low tone, prison wall, *be afraid*, walk around

worth (30): *value*, correct, anyone, slide

worthless (28): seesaw, signature, sleeveless, *useless*

wrap (03): *cover*, skate, maid, promise

wrapper (85): tombstone, alligator, fortune, *covering*

wreck (05): service, county, *destroy*, mouth

wrestle (68a): *struggle*, pebble, breath, come

wrestler (68b): slightly open, near the sea, wrestling match, *person who wrestles*

write (62f): not in a whisper, *make letters or words*, burned up wood, at the side of

writer (60a, 71e): *author*, unhappy, jeweler, guess

wrong (28, 70c): male turkey, oil painting, *not true*, motor mount

yard (90c, 91): office, daily, railroad, *garden*

yarn (90e): *thread*, flesh, life, spots

year (59b, 83): *twelve months*, raises crops, spring back, being in prison

yearly (43): rich meal, good condition, *once a year*, yearn for

yell (58d): *cry out*, right size, song of joy, warm over

yellow (24): wave, load, barrel, *color*

yesterday (59b): front of the stage, safe from danger, *day before today*, day with no sun

yolk (82d): *part of an egg*, one more than three, that which happens, person in charge

you (UNCL): sausage, turn, driver, *anybody*

young (71a): delight, *not old*, speaking, tear

youngster (71a): crush, story, merry, *child*

youth (71a): set of bells, very great, *young people*, part of you

zebra (51): candy, clear, full, *animal*

zero (57): skill, *nothing*, tobacco, dress

zoo (68d, 91): *place where animals are kept*, rights of a citizen, mother, father and their children, move one thing against another

References

Dale, E., & Chall, Jeanne S. A formula for predicting readability. *Educational Research Bulletin*, 1948, 27, 11-20, 37-44.

Dale, E., & Eichholz, G. *Children's knowledge of words.* Columbus, Ohio: Bureau of Educational Research, Ohio State University, 1960.

Furth, H.G. A comparison of reading test norms of deaf and hearing children. *American Annals of the Deaf*, 1966, 3, 461-462.

McCarthy, D. Language development in children. In L. Carmichael (Ed.), *Manual of child psychology.* New York: John Wiley & Sons, 1946.

Rodale, J.I. *The synonym finder.* Emmaus, Penn.: Rodale Books, 1961.

Roget's international thesaurus. (3rd ed.) New York: Thos. Crowell, 1962.

Seashore, R.T., & Eckerson, L.D. The measurement of individual differences in general English vocabularies. *Journal of Educational Psychology*, 1940, 31, 14-38.

Smith, M.K. Measurement of the size of general English vocabulary through the elementary grades and high school. *Genetic Psychological Monographs*, 1941, 24, 311-345.

Thorndike, E.L., & Barnhart, C.L. *Thorndike Barnhart beginning dictionary.* (5th ed.) New York: Thomas Crowell, 1962.

Thorndike, E.L., & Lorge, I. *The teacher's word book of 30,000 words.* New York: Teachers College Press, 1949.

Webster's seventh new collegiate dictionary. (7th ed.) Springfield, Mass.: G. & C. Merriam, 1964.

Index